KAUTILYA

on Moral Hazard, Poverty & Systemic Risk

Balbir Singh Sihag, Ph D (MIT)

Vitasta

LET KNOWLEDGE SPREAD

www.vitastapublishing.com

Published by
Renu Kaul Verma
Vitasta Publishing Pvt Ltd
2/15, Ansari Road, Daryaganj
New Delhi - 110 002
info@vitastapublishing.com

ISBN 978-93-86473-54-7
Balbir Singh Sihag
First Edition 2019
MRP 795

Cover and layout by Vitasta Publishing Pvt Ltd
Printed by Chaman Enterprises

Dedicated

To all my Gurus

At Massachusetts Institute of Technology: Anthony Atkinson, Jagdish Bhagwati, R L Bishop, Cary Brown, Richard Eckaus, Robert Engle, Stanley Fischer, Robert Hall, Harold Freeman, Jerry Hausman, Charles Kindleberger, Anne Kruger, Paul Samuelson, Robert Solow, Lance Taylor, Hal Varian, Martin Weitzman.

At Punjab University Chandigarh: Sheela Bhalla, D R Handa, Vinod Gupta, S B Rangnekar, Manmohan Singh, B B Tandon.

At Dayanand College, Hisar: Vijay Chander, S K Kandhari, JC Menon, S Pal, D N Sharma, R M Talwani,

At Government High School, Sisai: Kabul Chand, Lachman Das, C L Dilbagi, Chiranchi Lal, R C Jain, Nand Lal, Nagar Mal, Raghu Nath, Hem Raj, Dhandi Ram, Mangat Ram, Ram Sarup, BL Sharma, O P Singal, Birbal Singh, Rishal Singh, Gulab Singh.

गुरुर ब्रह्मा गुरुर विष्णु , गुरुर देवो महेश्वरः ,
गुरुर साक्षात परम ब्रह्म, तस्मै श्री गुरुवे नमः

Gurur Brahmaa, Gurur Vishnuh, Gurur Devo
Maheshvara, Gurur Saakshaat Parambrahmaa
Tasmai Shree Gurave Namah!

Guru is the embodiment of Brahma (the creator),
Vishnu (the preserver) and
Shiva (the destroyer).

Guru creates and preserves knowledge and destroys the darkness of ignorance.

I bow to my Gurus

Contents

PART ONE
Kautilya's Ageless Insights for Solving some Unsolvable Problems

PART TWO
Exposing Chauvinism in Euro-Centric History of Economic Thoughts

Preface

Modern economics may not be a dismal science but it has definitely become an amoral science. Every consumer, investor, producer, bureaucrat or a politician is assumed to be a utility maximiser, serving his/her own interest. Transaction cost economics has taken it too far, since its sole reliance on contracts has crowded-out conscience-based committments. It has fostered trust deficit and a 'culture of suspecion' . Legalistic approach has replaced the ethics-based approach and fiduciary duty has replaced the moral duty. Instead of *alleviating* the *moral hazard problem*, it has made the problem more serious and widespread. It may be noted that the moral hazard problem is neither new nor confined only to the modern corporations. In fact, Kautilya understood and dealt with this problem during the fourth century BCE. What is new? An urge for instant-gratification and acceptance of the principle: greed is good. Then, why should people get surprised when they learn about insider-trading, cooking of books or resorting to bribery to get contracts? According to Kautilya, a moral hazard problem can never be alleviated by rules and regulations. He put heavy emphasis on ethical anchoring of children. The first part of the book brings out Kautilya's ageless insight: *an ounce of ethics is better than a ton of laws*. Unfortunately, both Machiavelli and Adam Smith undermined the role of ethics and there is no realisation on the part of economists or policy-makers that the moral hazard problem is unsolvable by rules, regulations or contracts.

Kautilya suggested that the creation of an ethical society was the only way to eliminate the moral hazard problem altogether. Board of Directors is a relic of the past industrial economy and has lost its usefulness to the knowledge-based economy. More importantly, it can never ameliorate the problem of moral hazard. Kautilya's organisational structure is more efficient for corporate governance and management. Adam Smith inappropriately compared an economic system to a machine. His *mechanistic definition of a system ignores people*. Parts of a machine do not negotiate terms of engagement with each other or display any moral hazard problem, but people do. Kautilya's ideas are ageless since even after 2,300 years, they are still relevant to solving many of today's unsolvable problems, such as systemic risk and corruption. Now think: will anyone remember Adam Smith in 4076 CE, that is after a passage of 2,300 years from the writing of *the Wealth of Nations* in 1776?

Sihag (2014, Chap 3) challenges the currently accepted history of economic thought that economics originated during the eighteenth century and Adam Smith is the founder of economics. For the first time, strong arguments are provided why Kautilya should be considered as the founder of economics. Adam Smith came to be accepted as the founder of economics based on the arguments that (i) he was the first one to write a treatise on economics, and (ii) he synthesised brilliantly the existing ideas. It is shown in my work that Kautilya was the first economist who accomplished all these feats and more, and two thousand years earlier than Adam Smith. Kautilya, not Smith, carved out economics as a separate discipline. Additionally, Kautilya's *Arthashastra* is much more sophisticated, both in method and content than Adam Smith's *Wealth of Nations*.

This chapter (Sihag 2014, Chap 3) contains the following paragraph: In summary, Kautilya's *Arthashastra* does contain what Schumpeter (p 248) called a 'theoretical skeleton' and thus it cannot be labeled pre-scientific. The above analysis establishes that Kautilya's *Arthashastra* declares economics as a distinct discipline and thus satisfies the first requirement to declare it as the first origin of economics.

I had sent a preliminary draft of this chapter to Prof Anthony Waterman. He commented, 'It can't be the "origin of economics" since there was no transmission to present-day economic discourse (which is what we mean by "economics"). It is, rather, an early example of the way good thinkers conceptualise economic problems. There's no reason to suppose the human mind has changed very much in the last three millennia. We might find other, similar examples in other civilisations, if we looked hard enough'.

This response aroused my curiosity and I started exploring it as soon as my book was published. Kautilya wrote his *Arthashastra* during the fourth century BCE and it is hard to believe that, despite a passage of two thousand years, Kautilya's ideas would not have gotten transmitted to Europe, since there have been extensive contacts between India and Europe for thousands of years. Additionally, there has been a consensus that Adam Smith's *Wealth of Nations* does not contain a single original idea. An important question would be: where did he lift those ideas from? Ferguson exposed Adam Smith for making a false claim related to the pin-factory example. He pointed out that the French *Encyclopédie* was a recognisable source of the concept of division of labour used in *The Wealth of Nations*.

Adam Smith burnt his papers to conceal his sources believing that no one could ever know that he had access to French *Encyclopédie* and Kautilya's *Arthashastra*. There is an irrefutable textual evidence that Kautilya's *Arthashastra* was a recognisable source for *Wealth of Nations* relating to canons of taxation, sources of economic growth and undesirability of monopoly. In that case, it is not necessary to explore Adam Smith's 'modus operandi' as to how he managed to have access to Kautilya's *Arthashastra*. That is, the transmission of Kautilya's ideas had occurred and how that happened is not that crucial. In fact, Kautilya's ideas were getting transmitted to other countries also. For example, Kautilya's ideas were transmitted to Sri Lanka and Indonesia.

For several for hundred years many writers have been inappropriately comparing Kautilya's *Arthashastra* to Machiavelli's *Prince*. Not long ago, Henry Kissinger not only blindly followed the same path, but added some new misrepresentations. An in-depth analysis is presented to correct such gross misrepresentations and distortions. Fibonacci is claimed as a'financial engineer'. Such outlandish claims are also exposed.

Balbir Singh Sihag, Patron

Kautilya International Foundation

February 2019

Acknowledgements

I am grateful to Dr Lallan Prasad, Dr Chandra Kant Raju and late Bhoopendra Sinha for suggestions, comments and advice on the earlier drafts. The generosity of L N Rangarajan and Penguin Books is greatly appreciated for giving me the permission to use the translation of *The Arthashastra* for interpretations. I owe my thanks to Ajit Tiwary of Kautilya International Foundation, for arranging numerous seminars on Kautilya's various contributions. I am grateful to Dr Sudhir for his helpful suggestions. Invaluable contributions from my publisher Renu Kaul Verma, my editor Papri Sri Raman and her production team and the markeing team are appreciated.

My wife, Neelam has been a senior partner in this enterprise. She not only provided moral and material support, but also provided insightful suggestions to improve the presentation.

I am grateful to several unknown referees for dissemination of Kautilya's ideas. I acknowledge with a sense of gratitude the various publishers for allowing me to use the following articles:

Kautilya's Arthashastra: A Recognizable Source of the Wealth of Nations; Theoretical Economics Letters, 2016, 6, 1-9.

Kautilya and Machiavelli on Justice, Prosperity and National Security; Theoretical Economics Letters, 2017, Vol. 7, 381-397

Kautilya, Fibonacci and Samuelson on Discounting, Advances in Management & Applied Economics, 2017, Vol. 7, No. 2, 45-57.

Exploring the Origin of Mathematical Economics; Theoretical Economics Letters, 2016, 6, 87-96.

Kautilya's *Arthashastra*: The Origin of Statistical Economics during 4CE; JRSA, 2013, Vol. 2: 1-14.

Kautilya on Engineering Shared Prosperity; in Eds. Burjor Avari and George Gheverghese Joseph, Interwoven world: Ideas and Encounters in History, February 2016, Common Ground Publishing, Champaign, Illinois, USA.

Kautilya on Foresight, Oversight, Regulations, Ethics and Systemic Risk; Theoretical Economics Letters, 2017, Vol. 7, 352-364.

Relevance of Kautilya's Insights to Corporate Governance and Management; Theoretical Economics Letters, 2017, Vol. 7, 1121-1133.

Confucius and Kautilya on Establishing Moral Order for Prevention of Government and Market Failures; Theoretical Economics Letters, 2016, 6, 20-27.

Kautilya's Ideas on Interests, Institutions, Incentives and Yogakshema; Journal of Systems Science and Engineering, 2015, Vol. 23 & 24.

Kautilya on Far-sight, Foresight and Freedom; 2014, Institute of Defense Studies and Analyses, New Delhi.

Prologue

Overview of Kautilya's Contributions to Economics

Kautilya was a learned, experienced, ethical, wise, secular, progressive, independent and original thinker. He understood that every individual aspires to enjoy prosperity, security, safety and the brightest possible future for his/her children and grandchildren. Kautilya's *Arthashastra* is a manual on fulfilling all the aspirations of all the people by attempting to eliminate the moral hazard problem, poverty and systemic risk. In fact, a stakeholders-model in which the businessmen, workers and consumers share prosperity, is discernible in his *Arthashastra*. Perhaps, based on his own experience, Kautilya believed that poverty was death while living. It is shown that his approach is suitable to both developed and developing economies. Kautilya stressed that unless each decision-maker (ruler or a CEO) is a 'rajarishi', that is ethical and wise like a sage, the moral hazard problem cannot be eliminated. Presentation of Kautilya's seminal contributions to economics also helps in dispeling some long-standing myths.

Kautilya (p 142) wrote, 'Government by Rule of Law, which alone can guarantee security of life and welfare of the people, is, in turn, dependent on the self-discipline of the king (1.5)'. He argued that law and order (i.e., institutions) is essential to bringing prosperity, which depends on the self-discipline of the ruler, which in turn depends on his ethical mooring. In other words, quality of institutions and governance depends on the character of those who formulate and implement laws and policies. That is, according to Kautilya, *dharma* (ethics) not institutions, is the deep determinant of growth and systemic risk. Kautilya understood the economic system as an organic whole with interdependent parts. He undertook an in-depth and detailed analysis of each part at the micro level without losing sight of the macro goal of engineering peaceful enjoyment of shared prosperity. He believed in the power of persuasion, moral and material incentives and not in coercion or force to elicit effort. He designed material incentives in such a way that no crowding-out occurred, that is without weakening the moral incentives. He advanced a holistic yet logical and comprehensive approach to achieve the objectives. He relied both on the invisible hand (the market) and the direct hand (principles, policies and procedures) to make life of every individual richer and fuller.

PART ONE

Kautilya's Ageless Insights for Solving some Unsolvable Problems

Kautilya's contributions to economics may be classified into two categories. The first category may be described as practical, offering suggestions for efficiently and effectively (i) removing poverty, (ii) reducing systemic risk, (iii) improving corporate governance and management and (iv) curbing corruption. Most importantly, Kautilya emphasised the relevance of ethics-intensive concept of trust and not the statistical concept of confidence to the creation and sharing of knowledge. That is, genuine trust eliminates risk whereas 'calculated risk' approach treats trust as a risk and unwittingly promotes 'the culture of suspicion'. An overview is presented below.

An Ounce of Ethics is Better than a Ton of Laws

Kautilya and other ancient thinkers believed that destructive deeds, such as rape (like the Nirbhaya tragedy), murder, discrimination, bullying, oppression, exploitation, subjugation, sexual harassment, injustice, corruption, cooking the books are motivated by greed, anger, lust, jealousy, hate, arrogance and addiction. Kautilya believed that no amount of laws can ever prevent such destructive deeds because these vices (anger, greed, lust etc.) cloud the mind and as a result the individual loses logical abilities to foresee the consequences of his actions.

Engineering Shared Prosperity

Kautilya's predecessors believed that ethical conduct paved the way to bliss. Kautilya added that ethical conduct also paved the way to shared prosperity. He believed that dharma is the 'deep determinant', not institutions, of economic growth and stability. He made a distinction between economic growth guided by dharma (ethics) and by self-interest. He preferred the former whereas Adam Smith emphatically advocated the latter. According to Kautilya, the ethics-based approach is inclusive and allows a maximal possible growth whereas the approach guided by self-interest is neither inclusive nor optimal.

Foresight, Oversight, Regulations, Ethics Systemic Risk

The current legalistic approach is not equipped to reduce systemic risk and inefficiency related to corporate governance. Relevance of Kautilya's insights to eliminate systemic risk and agents' conflict costs are brought out. For over two hundred years, an economic system has been compared to a machine. Such comparison is inappropriate since parts of a machine do not negotiate with each other the terms and conditions of engagement and similarly, no part of a machine ever displays moral hazard or strategic behaviour but people, who are the primary constituents of an economic system, do. Anyhow, such comparison is harmless, although inappropriate, to treat the baker, the barber and the butcher as parts of a machine but now it can be be disastrous since it diverts attention away from the real source of systemic risk. Kautilya believed that a kingdom or a system consists of people (policy-makers and others) and things.

Relevance of Kautilya's five insights for preventing financial crisis is presented: (i) A mechanistic definition of an economic system is inappropriate since it ignores the source of systemic risk and pays attention only to the propagation mechanism. (ii) Moral hazard due to ethical failure and not 'too big to fail' is the real source of systemic risk. (iii) Kautilya's ideas on the critical role of foresight in identifying and devising both preventive and remedial measures to deal with threats to prosperity. (iv) A mix of oversight and regulations is more effective than regulations alone but still inadequate for preventing financial crisis. (v) Ethical grounding is the only solution to the moral hazard problem and if combined with oversight and regulations, would provide a guarantee to prevent financial crisis.

Relevance of Kautilya's Insights to Corporate Governance and Management

There is a separation between owners and managers in a corporation. Managers, being utility maximisers, are likely to shirk and enjoy expensive perks. In literature, these are termed as agency costs, conflicts of interest or moral hazard problems. Current approaches suggest legalistic measures to mitigate this problem. Kautilya's conceptual framework does not just mitigates but eliminates this problem altogether. Secondly, it is shown that the current organisational structure for corporate-governance and management is sub-optimal, a relic of the past industrial economy. Thirdly, in this work is highlighted Kautilya's suggestion to hire three or four full-time experts to enhance efficiency and creativity, which are essential to the survival and growth of a business in today's increasingly knowledge-based economy.

Williamson (1985, p 47) characterises the potential behaviour of the other firm as: 'calculated efforts to mislead, disguise, obfuscate, or otherwise confuse' and 'seeking self-interest, but they do so with guile'. He does not explain that such behaviour has created trust deficit within the firm also. Legal contracts, to a large extent, have crowded-out the conscience-based commitments. Precious resources are being wasted in devising precautionary measures to protect against perceived (often imaginary) cheating/reneging. This cost-saving may be called Kautilya's ethical surplus. Precise measurement of the ethical surplus is beyond the scope of this work. World's GDP in 2015 was around $74 trillion. Roughly speaking, if corporate profits were 10 per cent of the GDP and ethical surplus 10 per cent of the profits, the magnitude of ethical surplus would have been $740 billion. It would be a major contribution if future research can devise a creative methodology to measure Kautilya's ethical surplus. Kautilya believed that a Fiduciary duty could never replace the Moral duty.

Confucius and Kautilya on Establishing Moral Order for Prevention of Government and Market Failures

The main objectives of this chapter are of two kinds: first one may be described as historical in the sense of correcting more than two thousand years of misinterpretations of the ideas of Confucius and Kautilya on establishing a moral order and the nature of its relationship to the legalistic approach. Secondly, to highlight the relevance of moral order not only to creating peace and harmony but also to enhancing the creation and sharing of knowledge and lowering of transaction costs. Since both creation and sharing of knowledge depend on genuine trust, which flourishes only in an ethical environment, and not in a 'culture of suspicion'. It is indicated that their insights or pearls of wisdom are more relevant to today's knowledge-based economies than they were to economies during their own times. They would have emphasised the warming of hearts to solve the problem of global warming.

Ideas on Curbing Corruption

Ancient people believed that (i) *adharma* (corruption, cruelty and other maladies) once started would spread like cancer and (ii) even if it was removed once, its reoccurrence was inevitable. They also believed that whenever *adharma* peaked to such proportions as to destroy the system itself and beyond the human prowess to come out of it, a saviour (*avatar*, viz., a being / superhuman with Godly qualities) would appear to eradicate evil (*adharma*). Kautilya's *Arthashastra* made a paradigm shift on the issue. Being an empiricist, he did not believe in fate and asserted that a person's destiny was quite in his own hands. He counted on human ingenuity to devise an organisational structure and a legal structure to complement the ethical norms to reduce scope for corruption and to impose punishment for digressions. His insights, such as an ounce of ethics was better than a ton of laws and market failure was bad, government failure was worse, but the moral failure was the worst, are as relevant today as they were in his time.

PART TWO

Exposing Chauvinism in Euro-Centric History of Economic Thought

The second category may be described as seminal: (i) being a source of other works, such as Adam Smith's *Wealth of Nations* and Machiavelli's *Prince*, and (ii) introduction of mathematical tools, such as combinatorial rules and discrete marginal analysis and statistical tools, such as expected return and risk to explain economic behaviour indicating that Kautilya's *Arthashastra* may be recognised as the origin of both mathematical and statistical Economics. (iii) Euro-centric economists have been making exaggerated claims regarding the founder of economics, origins of statistical and mathematical economics and contribution of Fibonacci. Part two exposes the chauvinism in the Euro-centric history of economic thought. An overview of this part is provided below.

Arthashastra: A Recognisable Source of Adam Smith's *Wealth of Nations*

It is almost unanimously accepted that *The Wealth of Nations* does not contain a single original idea establishing the fact that Adam Smith borrowed all key ideas from various sources. He believed that he could claim originality for all the important ideas if he concealed their sources. Ferguson exposed Adam Smith for making a false claim related to the pin-factory example. It is intended to continue the process initiated by Ferguson by identifying paragraphs on sources of economic growth, canons of taxation and undesirability of monopolies, the core of *The Wealth of Nations*, which are textually similar to those in *The Arthashastra*. Adam Smith lifted those ideas from *The Arthashastra*. It is indicated in Appendix that more than two hundred years before Adam Smith, Machiavelli also seems to have access to *The Arthashastra*. Hopefully this process continues until all of Adam Smith's sources are identified and duly acknowledged.

Kautilya and Machiavelli on Justice, Prosperity and National Security

As soon as Kautilya's *Arthashastra* was translated into English in 1915, its comparison with Machiavelli's *Prince*, particularly by the western Indologists, started in earnest. Their main goal has been to show that Machiavelli's *Prince* was pale in comparison to the ruthless realism in Kautilya's *Arthashastra*. It is intended to correct such distortions and misrepresentations of Kautilya's ideas. It is shown that Kautilya's approach was people-centric whereas Machiavelli's approach was king-centric. Kautilya's objective was to promote *Yogakshema* - peaceful enjoyment of prosperity-for all the citizens whereas Machiavelli did not entertain such lofty ideals. It is claimed that Kautilya's *Arthashastra* shifted the knowledge frontier outward whereas Machiavelli's *Prince* did not even come close to incorporating the existing knowledge. In sum, a strong case is made to end for good such grossly inappropriate comparisons of these works.

Kautilya, Fibonacci and Samuelson on Discounting

The concept of discounting plays an important role in allowing efficient inter-temporal choices. William Goetzmann (2004) claims that Fibonacci (1202/2002) introduced discounting. (i) It is shown that Fibonacci did not understand the concept of discounting or its relevance and his *Liber Abaci* is a book only of calculations and not of concepts. (ii) It is claimed that Kautilya (4th century BCE) originated the concept of discounting and inter-temporal analysis. (iii) More importantly, relevance of his insight to today's world is brought out. According to Kautilya, it is possible to reduce the risk premium by making rare disasters rarer. Samuelson (1964) made the same point but Jensen and Bailey (1972) completely missed it.

Kautilya as the Originator of Statistical Economics

Peter Bernstein (1996, p 77) claims that both Graunt and Petty may be considered as the co-fathers of statistics. He limits his search only to western contributors and does not see the need to look beyond Europe. Inferential statistics was introduced in India by Vishalaksha, a predecessor of Kautilya, that is, before 4th century BCE. In fact, Vishalaksha not only emphasised the critical role of inferential statistics to sound decision-making but also of pooling information and knowledge. However, Kautilya was the first economist, who introduced statistics to economics and may be considered as the founder of statistical economics.

The existing studies on the origin and history of mathematical economics are Euro-centric and cover only the past two centuries. It is intended to show that (a) mathematical economics has an ancient origin. Kautilya wrote *The Arthashastra* during the fourth century BCE and used discrete marginal analysis and combinatory rules to sharpen economic analysis. (b) It is indicated that in the west, image of mathematics has changed directly and that of economics indirectly as the theology/philosophy of the church changed. (c) It is claimed that in India the developments in both economics and mathematics have always been kept simple, secular and user-friendly to solve problems related to agriculture, construction, navigation and trade .

Kautilya as Originator of Mathematical Economics

In recent years, [1] Ingrao and Israel (1990), [2, 3] Mirowski (1989, 1991) and [4] Weintraub (2002) have explored the why and how of the emergence of mathematical economics in the western world during the last two centuries. These works have been reviewed extensively and have generated both heat and light. Unsurprisingly, all of them are Euro-centric. Weintraub argues that the image of economics changed as the image of mathematics changed but without realising that the image of mathematics in the west might have changed with the change in the theology/philosophy of the church.

Mathematics and economics neither originated in the western world, nor during the 17th or 18th century, implying that the scope of current studies on the emergence of mathematical economics is very limited. According to [5] Seidenberg (1962), mathematics originated in India earlier than Babylonia, Egypt or Greece.1 Similarly, Kautilya was the first economist, who established economics as a separate discipline, developed a score of economic concepts and understood economy as a system with its inter-linked elements (see [6] Sihag (2014)).2 [7] Kautilya's *Arthashastra* contains two parts: the exchange theory and the conflict theory but both use mathematics to enhance clarity of expression and statistical analysis for arriving at the best possible policy-decisions under risky situations and evaluations afterwards.

PART ONE

Kautilya's Ageless Insights for Solving some Unsolvable Problems

KAUTILYA'S TWO insights are quite unique and the world could benefit from them. First, ethical conduct and not institutions are the 'deep determinant' of economic growth. Secondly, he was concerned about the systemic risk and believed that an ounce of ethics was better than a ton of rules and regulations to reduce it. The current approach to tackling economic issues assumes amoral utility maximising individuals' and advocates' reliance on contracts in which there is no room for conscience or compassion. Consequently, the transaction costs are significantly high. It tries to tackle the wide-spread moral hazard problem through legal means and it fails miserably. Trust is the first casualty in such a contract-based system. Instead, we could adopt Kautilya's people-centric, proactive, progressive and ethics-based approach for a fairer and faster economic growth.

Complex contracts are written to safeguard against potential harm that might be caused by the partners' opportunism. It seems that propensity for opportunism is the dominant phenomenon everywhere. Economists and organisational scholars believe that it is not possible before hand to differentiate a trustworthy person from an untrustworthy one, so it is prudent to adopt a 'calculative' approach to trust, that is, *treat trust as a risk* and suggest taking necessary protective measures.

Critical Role of Trust in a Knowledge-based Economy: Trust may be an intangible asset/good but has the most tangible role in creating and sustaining the social, economic, cultural and political structures. It is the brick and mortar to building of inter-personal relationships. In a knowledge-based economy, trust (a) reduces transaction costs by reducing opportunism, enhances a feeling of wellness by reducing anxiety and (b) also might increase GDP by reducing the demand for lawyers and turning them into engineers.

Both creation and sharing of ideas depend on trust. The distinguishing characteristic of a knowledge-based economy is a frequent sharing of tacit knowledge and exchange of information among the knowledge workers. As soon as a person codifies his/her tacit knowledge, everyone has access to it. Knowing this fact, a person will share tacit knowledge only if s/he is sure of not getting fired. Creating ethical-based trust is the key to realising all the potential gains from creating and sharing of knowledge.

An Ounce of Ethics is Better than a Ton of Laws

> He who hoards provisions in vain and does not feed his elders and companions, is inhuman, unkind and stingy, verily he brings his own destruction. He who eats alone is a great sinner.
>
> **Rig Veda** (10-117-6)

KAUTILYA WAS ethical but not religious. He put heavy emphasis on preservation and promotion of dharma (ethics) since he believed *dharma* paved the way both to bliss and to artha (material well-being). He was against state promotion of any religion. If he were alive during Emperor Ashoka's reign, he would have strongly objected to Emperor Ashoka's promotion of Buddhism.

However, according to him, there is absolutely no conflict between state and teaching secular virtues such as non-violence, compassion, truthfulness, malice against no one, tolerance and cleanliness, and self-discipline to control destructive vices such as greed, anger, lust, jealousy, hatred and arrogance to young children.

He firmly believed that rape, murder, discrimination, bullying, oppression, exploitation, subjugation, sexual harassment, injustice, corruption, cooking the books, insider trading, backdating stock options could never be prevented by laws and regulations alone. Laws could not prevent Ivan Boesky, Charles Keating, Michael Milken, Jack Grubman, Kenneth Lay, Bernard Ebers and countless others from resorting to fraudulent practices. Laws deal with symptoms of egregious conduct and not with the underlying character disorder.

Kautilya, being an empiricist, did not believe in fate and asserted that a *person's destiny was quite in his own hands*. He counted on human ingenuity to devise an organisational structure and a legal structure to complement the ethical norms to reduce scope for corruption and to impose punishment for digressions. Sage Ved Vyas, composer of *The Bhagwadgita*, provided the concept of *Yogakshema* but did not offer any guidelines for its attainment. Kautilya filled the concept with detailed contents (see Chapter 2 below and Sihag 2014). Kautilya made a paradigm shift in the role of the government in promoting the private sector. This is discussed in Section 1.1.

According to Kautilya, both the formulation and implementation of rules, regulations, and policies depend on the character of the public servants (legislators and bureaucrats) implying ethics, not institutions, is the deep determinant of economic growth and stability. Section 1.2 presents Kautilya's conceptual framework to bring out the role of ethics. Kautilya presents historical evidence to support his claims that anger, greed, lust and other undesirable personality traits were destructive to some mighty kings. Section 1.3 contains this discussion.

1.1 Kautilya suggests Paradigm Shift in the Role of Rulers

Sages in ancient India had vision of a harmonious, healthy and peaceful society. They developed the dharmic values of non-violence, compassion, truthfulness, honesty, tolerance and cleanliness to realise their vision. They evolved a consistent model emphasising internal restraint (of ego, desire and attachment) through self-disciplining of senses, which resulted in a life style that helped one in getting rid of the cycle of birth-death-rebirth and attaining *moksha* – a state of eternal bliss. For the less enlightened, they created the concepts of heaven and hell and evolved moral codes for living a productive and good life here on earth and enjoying residence in heaven after death.

Their sole weapon for spreading such knowledge was persuasion. They were aware of the possibility that some individuals might not be convinced enough to adhere to the moral codes. Sure enough, some individuals breached the ethical norms and resorted to evil means. People in ancient times believed that (i) *adharma* (corruption, cruelty and other maladies) once started would spread and (ii) even if it was removed, its reoccurrence was inevitable. (iii) They also believed that whenever adharma peaked to such proportions as to destroy the system itself and beyond the human prowess to come out of it, a saviour (avatar, viz. a being / superhuman with Godly qualities) would appear to eradicate evil (adharma). For example, Lord Krishna in *The Bhagwadgita* assures Arjuna of His two responsibilities: (a) He would manifest Himself whenever needed to destroy evil. He states:

यदा यदा हिधर्मस्य ग्लानिर्भवतिभारत ।
अभ्युत्थानमधर्मस्य तदात्मानं सृजाम्यहम ॥ भगवद्गीता (4/7)

परित्राणाय साधूनां विनाशाय च दुष्कृताम् ।
धर्मसंस्थापनार्थाय संभवामि युगे युगे ॥ भगवद्गीता (4/8)

[Whenever righteousness is on the wane and there is ascendency of unrighteousness, then I give to Myself suitable forms of manifestation.]

Bhagwadgita (4/7)

[For the protection of the pious and for rooting out the evil and, also for re-establishing righteousness, I manifest myself in every age.]

Bhagwadgita (4/8)

(b) Lord Krishna continues his dialogue with Arjuna. He conveys to Arjuna that He takes full responsibility for the provision of Yogakshema to his faithful devotees. Lord Krishna states:

अनन्याश्चिन्तयन्तो मां ये जना: पर्युपासते।
तेषां नित्याभियुक्तानां योगक्षेमं वहाम्यहम् ॥

भगवद्गीता (9/22)

> [Lord Krishna says that He takes care of His faithful devotees by supplying them with what they do not have and preserving what they already have.]
>
> *Bhagwadgita (9/22)*[1]

An Avatar presumably provided *Yogakshema* for the people and destroyed prevailing adharma. The problem was that He stayed on earth only for a short time and did not leave behind someone who could prevent evil from taking roots again. That is, there were no satisfactory succession rules. Moreover, the Avatar removed the evil doers but not the causes of evil. More importantly, sage Ved Vyas did not provide any guidelines on how to attain *Yogakshema*. to achieve it. Understandably, Lord Krishna-Arjuna dialogue took place in a war setting and sage Ved Vyas thought that was not the time or place to elaborate on how to provide *Yogakshema*.

Kautilya's challenges were of two kinds: his first challenge was to prevent evil from taking root, that is, preventing moral decay and, thus, saving the public and the Lord from suffering unnecessarily. Kautilya was secular and a psychologist.

He (p 205) advises a courtier: 'He shall watch carefully the King's gestures and expressions; a wise man will know the mind of another who is trying to reach a decision by looking at the following: liking and hatred, joy and distress, resoluteness and fear.' Perhaps, Kautilya was aware that people, in general, would accept new ideas if these complement their current beliefs. It is fine with Kautilya if people are ethical because they want to go to heaven and to be provided with *Yogakshema* on earth by the Lord. He does not interfere with peoples' religious beliefs.

Kautilya made a paradigm shift in the prevailing thought at the time.

For the first time in human history, he assigned the responsibility of providing *Yogakshema* for the people to the king.

He is way ahead of his times. For example, US Congress took such a responsibility as late as the twentieth century.[2] In Kautilya's time, rulers used to waste tax revenue in enjoying a lavish life style or waging wars for pseudo glory.

Kautilya explains that a king has three options: (i) to be a *rajarishi* (ethical and wise like a sage) and enrich his subjects, (ii) an enlightened one (amoral) serving the public to the extent it served him/her or (iii) an immoral and short-sighted one.

As discussed in Section 1.3 below, Kautilya draws attention to the fact that an immoral ruler will not last for too long. Kautilya provides historical evidence to support his claim. He says, the choice is essentially between (i) and (ii). He points out that if the king follows his self-interest, he might retain his kingdom. On the other hand, if he is a rajarishi, he will be fulfilling his moral duty, will go to heaven and can rule for a long time. He is also concerned about succession. He (p 169) writes: Unless there are dangers in it, succession of the eldest son is praiseworthy. An only son, if he is wicked, shall not [under any circumstances] be installed on the throne. A king with many sons acts in the best interests [of the kingdom] only if he removes a wicked one from succession (1.17).

Note, the meaning of *Yogakshema* in *Bhagwadgita* and *The Arthashastra* is the same: yoga means acquisition and kshema means preservation.[3] Only difference is, in Bhagwadgita, Lord Krishna takes care of His devotees whereas Kautilya wants a rajarishi to take care of his subjects. He wrote:

तस्माद् दण्ड.मूलास् तिस्रो विद्याः ॥ (1.5.1)
विनय.मूलो दण्डः प्राणभृतां योग.क्षेम.आवहः ॥ (1.5.2)

> [The three sciences [philosophy, the three Vedas and economics] are dependent [for their development] on the science of government. [For, without a just administration, no pursuit of learning or avocation is possible.] [(Government by) Rule of Law, which alone can guarantee security of life and the welfare of the people, is, in turn, dependent on ([the) self-discipline (of the king).][4]

This is one of Kautilya's most important insights. Kautilya argues that Rule of Law (now-a-days called institution) is a prerequisite to 'security of life and welfare of the public'. He adds that Rule of Law depends on the ethics of the ruler. That is, if the ruler is amoral or immoral, rule of law will be compromised and consequently the wellbeing of the people will be suboptimal. It may be noted that Kautilya was strictly following the Indian thought and the use of the concept of *Yogakshema* by Kautilya was not accidental. His second task was to develop a manual on providing *Yogakshema* for all see the next chapter for details).

1.2 Kautilya's Conceptual Framework

Ancient sages realised that genuine trust was an ethics-intensive concept since non-violence, truthfulness, honesty and benevolence were the foundation for trust.

Kautilya accepts that insight wholeheartedly. That is, trust flourishes only in an ethical environment. How to make sure that children grow-up to be ethical adults? Kautilya suggests teaching ethical values at an early age. Kautilya believes that *dharmic* (ethical) conduct paves the way to bliss and, also to prosperity. That is, according to Kautilya, a society based on contracts alone is less productive and more anxiety prone than the one based on conscience and compassion. If the social environment is predominantly ethical, there is less of a need to take defensive measures to protect against opportunism. He emphasises ethical anchoring of children for replacing the 'culture of suspicion' with a harmonious and trusting one.

Kautilya (p 100) makes the following claim: 'By following [the principles set out in] this treatise one can not only create and preserve dharma [spiritual good], artha [material well-being] and kama [aesthetic pleasures] but also destroy [their opposites, i.e] unrighteousness, material loss and hatred. It is a guide not only for the acquisition of this world but also the next (15.1).' Kautilya's *Arthashastra* is comprehensive, coherent, consistent and clear. Following Table 1.1 may capture its scope.

Table 1.1: Kautilya on Public and Private Interests

	Public Interest	**Against Public Interest**
Private Interest	Agriculture, Cattle-rearing and trade Promote infrastructure: construction of roads, water works, creation of markets to engineer prosperity (see next chapter) Case I (no conflict, ideal)	Monopolisation, lobbying, financial manipulation, regulatory arbitrage, shirking etc. Case III (conflicts of interest)
Against Private Interest	Charitable activities, serving the motherland etc. Case II (conflicts of interest)	Destructive actions (rape, murder, discrimination, bullying, oppression, exploitation, subjugation, sextual harassment, injustice, corruption, cooking the books, insider trading, backdating options) are motivated by greed, anger, lust, jealousy, hate, arrogance and addiction etc). Case IV (worst case)

Incidentally, Adam Smith focused primarily on Case I in which there is no conflict between the private interest and the public interest whereas Kautilya deals with all the four cases. In fact, Kautilya's predecessors were also concerned, at least, about cases III and IV. Ancient sages identified the system-building virtues, such as non-violence, compassion, truthfulness, malice against none, tolerance and cleanliness for creating a healthy, harmonious and peaceful society. Non-violence meant not to harm anyone physically, financially or emotionally – implying case III would not arise in such an ethical society.

Pre-Kautilya thinkers also identified the system-destroying forces, such as anger, lust, greed and jealousy. Lord Krishna (in *Bhagwadgita*) says: 'Desire, anger and greed – this triple gate of hell brings about the ruination of the soul. Therefore, one should avoid all these three (16.21). Freed from these three gates of hell, man works his own salvation and thereby attains supreme goal i.e. God (16.22).' Similarly, Sage Apastamba (Olivelle, 1999, p 34) wrote:'Refraining from anger, excitement, rage, greed, perplexity, hypocrisy and malice, speaking the truth; refraining from overeating, calumny and envy; sharing, liberality, rectitude, gentleness, self-control, amity with all creatures, Yoga, Arya-like conduct, benevolence and contentment–there is agreement that these applies to all orders of life. By practicing them according to the rules, a man attains the All.

According to the ancient thinkers, if someone wanted to go to heaven, s/he must practice the virtues, do charitable deeds and control the destructive vices. They implicitly conveyed the message that unless heaven was created on the earth one could not go to heaven after death (see Sihag 2014, Chap 6). Kautilya's predecessors considered any deed resulting from greed, lust or anger as a sin and a gateway to hell. Kautilya believes that dharma paves the way both to bliss and prosperity and similarly, the destructive vices paves the way to hell and, also to the destruction of one's life and property right here on earth (see the next Section for historical evidence).

Kautilya was concerned about the *likelihood of cooking the books* by a greedy official.

He (p 286) writes: 'Greed which prompts him to use false balances, weights and measures or to make false assessments and calculations (2.7.10).' Had there been a stock market at that time,

Kautilya would have been equally concerned about insider trading or backdating the stock options by a greedy person. Logically speaking, case IV should not happen since it is against both private and public interests. However, Kautilya argues that 'greed clouds the intellect', that is, a greedy person loses the logical ability to process information properly and fails to foresee the consequences of his – actions implying rules and regulations. No matter how numerous these are, these cannot ever prevent him from such activities. As a result, a greedy person not only ignores the public interest, is also unlikely to follow his own interest. Therefore, personality traits, such as being greedy, prone to anger and lust, are very destructive not only for the greedy person but also for the society at large.

Kautilya was aware of the existing beliefs that adharma once started, would spread and impact the rule of law adversely. That means activities in Case I will be affected adversely.
He firmly believes if the destructive vices and unproductive activities are not controlled, economic growth will be hampered. Note, Kautilya is not against the legalistic approach, he considers it not a substitute to but as a complement to ethical approach.

Table 1.2 Kautilya on Destructive Vices

Cause of Demise	Names of the Ancient Kings
Lust	Dandakya, a Bhoja king and Karala, a Videha King
Anger	Janamejaya and Taljangha
Greed	The son Ila and Ajabindu of the Suviras
Conceit	Ravana and Duryodhana
Arrogance	Dambodhbava and Arjuna of Haihayas
Foolhardiness	Vatapi and Vrishni

1.3 Empirical Evidence on Harmful Effects of Vices

Kautilya was a man of letters but very humble. He had an open mind and was willing to learn even from a child. He was knowledgeable about ancient history. Being an empiricist, he (p 144) provides a list of some of the mightiest kings destroyed by lust, anger, greed, conceit, arrogance and foolhardiness.[5]

Kautilya (p 144) concludes: All these, and many others, lacking self-control and falling prey to the six enemies [lust, anger, greed, conceit, arrogance and foolhardiness] perished with their kinsmen and kingdoms. On the other hand, kings like Jamadagnya and Ambarisha, who had conquered their senses, long enjoyed their kingship on earth (1.6).

Kautilya's goal is to internalise preventive and positive measures for imbuing governance with *dharma,* for doing which he adopts a multi-disciplinary approach. There has been no known thinker like Kautilya, who made seminal contributions to economics, law and national security in an integrated manner.

1.4 Concluding Observations

Reliance on legalistic approach has created a 'culture of suspicion' and that has created trust deficit. People, in general, have become anxiety-prone, amoral and guiltless. One needs a lawyer to sue a lawyer, who did not represent the client in the expected way. The moral hazard problem has become serious and is widespread. Consequently, the transaction costs have been rising. It has lowered the rate of return and increased the risk. Kautilya points out that laws are only as good as the people who formulate and implement them. Laws are passed to fix the loopholes in the existing laws and very quickly some individuals discover loopholes in the new laws. That is, there are tons of laws and still ineffective in serving the intended objective. So, it is time to pay attention to Kautilya's insight and introduce ethical education in schools.

Engineering Shared Prosperity

VISHNUGUPTA CHANAKYA (son of Chanaka), Kautilya, was a man of letters. He was addressed as an Acharya (professor) and a statesman. He was secular, logical, far-sighted and foresighted. He was very ethical but not religious. He was an empiricist and did not believe in fate. He was a great organiser but was not a bureaucrat like Adam Smith. He has been credited with the destruction of the oppressive and corrupt Nanda Dynasty and installing Chandragupta Maurya (321-297 BCE) on the Magadha throne. Everyone knows that he was a king-maker but very few know or acknowledge that he was *a maker of his age. He was a revolutionary for his times*.[1] Chandragupta Maurya considered him as his mentor and sought his advice on both political and economic matters.

Kautilya wrote the *Arthashastra*, the science of wealth and welfare, during the fourth century BCE.[2] It contains 150 chapters that are distributed subject-wise in fifteen books. Arthashastra, economics as a sciece and study stream, and literature around the subject originated sometimes between 650 BCE to 600 BCE, but it was Kautilya, who provided consistent and coherent interpretations of concepts prevailing at the time and innovated a score of key concepts in economics. Kautilya's contributions compared to those of his predecessors or to Adam Smith's are much deeper and more comprehensive.

Bentley MacLeod (2013) provides an insightful review of *Why Nations Fail* by Acemoglu and Robinson (2012) and *Pillars of Prosperity* by Besley and Persson (2011). The conclusion of these works is that one cannot 'engineer prosperity'. MacLeod wonders – if prosperity cannot be engineered, then what is the purpose of such analysis? These works reach this pessimistic conclusion because they fail to identify all the relevant factors of economic growth.

Kautilya knew why nations failed. He wrote his Arthashastra to offer concrete measures to avoid such failures and a complete manual on how to promote Yogakshema (peaceful enjoyment of prosperity) of all the people, that is, (i) *engineer prosperity* and (ii) for all the people.

He believes that the establishment of rule of law, an impartial judicial system, protection of private property rights, good governance and ethical grounding of decision-makers, are the key ingredients for the creation of a prosperous economy. Kautilya's people-centric and proactive approach to shared prosperity is presented in Section 2.1.

Kautilya believes that if the farmers receive lower prices because of monopsony, consumers pay higher prices because of monopoly, the workers cannot negotiate their wages and the weak do not get help and protection, *then what is the purpose of high economic growth?* Keeping this in view, Kautilya advances progressive principles and policies that are relevant even for our times.[3] He proposes laws (i) against sexual harassment and child labour whereas Aristotle, a near contemporary of Kautilya, ignores his own views on justice to keep slavery intact[4] (ii) against fraud, monopoly and monopsony (iii) respects workers' right to unionise and negotiate for better working conditions and (iv) he suggests helping the helpless, such as the old, the sick, widows and minors. Also, he does not believe in just declaring certain principles and then not suggest laws and policies to implement them. Some of his progressive principles and policies are collected in Section 2.2. Concluding observations are provided in the final section.

2.1 Kautilya's Ethics-based Approach to Engineer Prosperity

> In the happiness of his subjects lies his happiness; in their welfare his welfare. He shall not consider as good only that which pleases him but treat as beneficial to him whatever pleases his subjects (1.19).
>
> —**Kautilya**

Conditions at the Time: Most of the poeople lived in the countryside but a few semi-urban towns were getting established. According to Chandler's (1987) calculations, Pataliputra, the capital of Chandragupta Maurya's kingdom, was the largest city in the world with a population of little over 200,000 in 300 BCE (about Alexander's time in the western world). Agriculture, cattle-rearing and trade were the main economic activities. Mining, metallurgy and manufacturing industries were getting established. The metals mined were gold, copper, lead, tin and iron. Making weapons and salt, brewing liquor, weaving textiles and manufacturing jewellery were the main industries. Gambling and betting were well-established but with urbanisation, laundry services were also sprouting. The process of monetisation had started. The king issued silver and copper coins. The highest value coin, called *pana*, was rectangular-shaped and served as the medium of exchange and the unit of accounts. The Indian-subcontinent was divided into small kingdoms. Corruption was rampant. Kautilya and Chandragupta Maurya inherited an economy in shambles.

Achieving both Material Wellbeing and Spiritual Wellbeing: Kautilya's predecessors had focused primarily on spiritual well-being. Kautilya believed, just like his predecessors, that if there was no *dharma* there would be no society.

His goal is to complement spiritual well-being with material well-being so that every individual cand enjoy a fuller and richer life. The scope of the *Arthashastra* is much broader than that of *The Wealth of Nations*. The *Arthashastra* is not only an inquiry into the sources of economic growth but also a manual on engineering shared prosperity, whereas the scope of *The Wealth of Nations* is limited simply to an inquiry. Kautilya understands the concept of backward induction and applies it very effectively to engineer shared prosperity. He developes a causal chain of five inter-linked steps identifying from obvious and direct sources to increasingly deeper/important sources of economic growth and suggests measures to strengthen each link.

Causal Link 1: He identifies increases in capital (K), labour (L) and land (T) as the most obvious sources of economic growth. He argues that capital increases labour productivity by manifolds. Similarly, he considers increase in manpower and expansion, particularly in irrigated areas under cultivation as important sources of economic growth. Some technical progress had started but it was insignificant at that time. Algebraically we may express causal link 1 as:

$$Y \text{ (output)} = F(K, L, T) \qquad (2.1)$$

Causal Link 2: After determining capital, labour and land as sources of economic growth, he proceeds to identify the factors that increase their supplies. He believes that (i) lowering the risk (σ) and (ii) raising the expected return (μ) will lead to higher investment in land, labour and capital (see Sihag 2014a, Chapter 8). Causal link 2 may be written as:

$$K = G(\sigma, \mu) \qquad (2.2)$$

Similar expressions could be written for land and labour.

Causal Link 3: After identifying risk and return as the important determinants of supplies of inputs, Kautilya turns to exploring the factors relevant to reducing the risk and increasing the rate of return. He understands the inverse relationship between the degree of riskiness and the quality of institutions, that is, as the quality of institutions deteriorate the degree of riskiness increases.

Thus, he believes that existence of good institutions (GI), fairness in administration of justice and some provision of insurance against theft are essential to the reduction in risk. Incidentally, he (p 377) defines fairness as a practice that holds the three cardinal principles of justice: that punishment must be (i) certain, (ii) proportional to the crime and (iii) above all must be administered impartially.

He also advocates establishment and protection of private property rights. He proposes a genuine labour theory of property almost two thousand years earlier than John Locke (see Sihag 2014a, Chapter 16). He is against expropriation of private property. He (p 121) writese: 'The wealth of the state shall be one acquired lawfully either by inheritance or by the king's efforts (6.10).'

Provision of Insurance: No market insurance was available at that time and Kautilya suggested, that gap be filled. He (p 235) writes: 'Trade routes shall be kept free of harassment by courtiers, state officials, thieves and frontier guards and from being damaged by herds of cattle (2.1.38). Frontier officers shall be responsible for the safety of the merchandise passing on the roads and shall make good what is lost (2.21.25).' There is no deductible and no insurance premium to be paid to government in Kautilya's sceme of transaction.

Good Governance (GG): Kautilya understands that good governance is required to increase the rate of return on investment. He suggests several policies to expand the opportunity set and to increase the rate of return to investment in the private sector. Incidentally, Adam Smith's inquiry into the causes of prosperity was limited only to good institutions since he assigned a minimal role to governance.

(a) *Pro-growth Policies for increasing supply of inputs*: Kautilya suggests policies to increase supplies of land, labour and capital. He (p 231) recommends (i) tax holidays for bringing land under cultivation for a period of two years. Similarly, 'for building or improving irrigation facilities' exemption from water rates are to be granted (3.9). (ii) Concessionary Loans (p 179): '[On new settlements] the cultivators shall be granted grains, cattle and money which they can repay at their convenience (2.1).' (iii) No Excessive Burden: He is against putting any excessive tax burden on the people. For example, he (p 181) suggests to the king: '(He) shall protect agriculture from being harassed by [onerous] fines, taxes and demands of labour (2.1.37).'

(b) *He suggests building of roads to link different regions.* He (p 235) suggests: 'He (the king) shall promote trade and commerce by setting up trade routes by land and by water and market towns/ports (2.1.19).'

(c) *Emphasis on Productive Activities*: At that time, kings were responsible only for maintaining law and order and protecting the public against foreign aggression. They used the residual tax revenue to maintain a luxurious lifestyle and build luxurious palaces and did not spend much on building infrastructure to expand the productive capacity of the economy. Kautilya was against squandering away the tax revenue on their personal consumption.

He expands the role of state from protection to prosperity. He (p 149) suggests: Hence the king shall be ever active in the management of the economy. The root of wealth is economic activity and lack of it brings material distress. In the absence of fruitful economic activity, both current prosperity and future growth are in danger of destruction. A king can achieve the desired objectives and abundance of riches by undertaking productive economic activity (1.19).

Pooling of Information and Knowledge: More importantly, he suggests pooling of information, knowledge and wisdom of the team of highly qualified advisers to arrive at the most efficient choice, thus benefiting from cognitive division of labour. He (p 198) writes: Vishalaksha says, 'never can a single person arrive at the right decision'. The work of government is dependent on [complete] knowledge – that which the king personally knows, that which is reported to him and that which he has to infer. To find out what is not known, to clarify doubts when there are alternatives, to obtain more information when only a part is known – all these can be done only with the help of advisers. Hence a king shall conduct his deliberations with advisers of mature intelligence. (As the saying goes:) 'Despise no one, [but] listen to all views; for, wise man pays heed to all sensible advice, even those of a child (1.15)'.

Kautilya made sure that for every proposal he advances, he suggests specific measures to accomplish it. He understands the concepts of value added, constrained maximisation and *develops accounting methods* to accomplish this task of selecting the most productive projects. Sihag (2014b) presents Kautilya's ideas on selection, implementation and evaluation of a project. According to Kautilya, Good Institutions (GI) reduce risk (σ) and Good Governance (GG) raises the rate of return (μ). Causal Link 3 may be expressed as follows:

$$\sigma = H\ (GI, Insurance) \quad (2.3a)$$

$$\mu = U\ (GG) \quad (2.3b)$$

Causal Link 4: Kautilya had a deeper understanding of the growth process.

He believes that knowledge of economic principles and political science is necessary but not sufficient to serve the common good. He argues that good institutions, administration of justice and good governance depended on the ethical conduct of the decision-makers. He (p 142) writes: 'Government by Rule of Law, which alone can guarantee security of life and welfare of the people, is, in turn, dependent on the self-discipline of the king (1.5).' Thus, according to him, ethics (E) of the decision-makers is the 'deep determinant' and not institutions. He believs that without dharma, maximal economic growth is neither feasible nor desirable. If the decision-makers are not ethical, institutions, justice and governance is of sub-optimal quality.[5] According to Kautilya, good governance (GG) and quality of institutions (GI) depend on the ethical conduct (E) of decision-makers. Causal Link 4 may be written as follows:

$$GG = S\ (E) \quad (2.4a)$$

$$GI = R\ (E) \quad (2.4b)$$

Reduction of Systemic Risk: Kautilya argued not only for creation of wealth but also in its preservation. He emphasises the role of foresightedness (see Chapter 7)) in identifying sources of systemic risk arising from natural and man-made calamities.

He suggests both preventive and remedial measures to make sure that progress made over several years, is not destroyed by a calamity. He (p 116) writes: 'In the interests of the prosperity of the country, a king should be diligent in foreseeing the possibility of calamities, try to avert them before they arise, overcome those which happen, remove all obstructions to economic activity and prevent loss of revenue to the state (8.4).' Kautilya did not use current jargons but his phrase 'try to avert them before they arise' is called self-protection by Ehrlich and Becker (1972) and similarly, his phrase 'overcome those which happen' is termed as self-insurance by them. These concepts have been found useful in many contexts and almost a small cottage industry has sprung around them. Most importantly, he believs that an ounce of ethics is more effective than a ton of laws in reducing systemic risk (see Chapter 3).

Causal Link 5: Kautilya's predecessors emphasised the role of dharma (ethics) in creating a peaceful and harmonious society (see Sihag (2014a, Ch. 6)). Kautilya wholeheartedly accepted and promoted their ideas on the role of ethics.

He asserts: 'For the world, when maintained in accordance with the Vedas, will ever prosper and not perish. Therefore, the king shall never allow the people to swerve from their dharma.'[6] He believs that if the king is ethical, his advisers and public also will be ethical. He (p 121) writes: 'A king endowed with the ideal personal qualities enriches the other elements when they are less than perfect (6.1).' He (p 123) adds, 'Whatever character the king has, the other elements also come to have the same (8.1)'.

Kautilya's challenge was to persuade the ruling king to be a rajarishi and make sure that the future king (prince) is ethical too.

He (p 145) defines it as: A rajarishi [a king, wise like a sage] is one who: has self-control, having conquered the [inimical temptations] of the senses, cultivates the intellect by association with elders, is ever active in promoting the security and welfare of the people, endears himself to his people by enriching them and doing good to them and avoids daydreaming, capriciousness, falsehood and extravagance (1.7).

In Kaytilya's time, the king was supreme and there was no constitution to require him to be ethical. Incidentally, democratic constitutions put constraints on the abuse of power by a President/ Prime Minister but contain no clause that requires him/her to be ethical, wise or intelligent. Kautilya approaches it very logically. He explains to the king that he has three choices: (he) can be corrupt, utility maximiser or ethical. Kautilya's first goal is to convince the king not to be unethical. He (p 141) writes: 'A king who flouts the teachings of the *Dharamshastras* and the *Arthashastra*, ruins the kingdom by his own injustice (8.2.12).' If a king wants to stay in power, he cannot afford to be unethical. So, a king has a choice only between being a utility maximiser and ethical.

Utility Maximiser (guided only by self-interest/a for-profit entity): According to Kautilya, a king whose objective is to stay in power, can achieve it only by removing poverty, that is, it is in the king's own interest to provide, at least some minimum standard of living to his subjects. He (p 159) explains: When a people are impoverished, they become greedy; when they are greedy, they become disaffected; when disaffected, they either go to the enemy or kill their ruler themselves (7.5). In the modern context, they vote the ruler out of power.

Moral Incentive: Kautilya suggests moral incentives to persuade a king to behave like a rajarishi. He repeatedly reminds the king of his dharma (moral duty) to enrich his people.[7] He (p 128) also writes:'It is the duty of the king to protect the people from all calamities (4.3).' Additionally, if the king follows his duty, he will go to heaven. On the other hand, if the king follows only his self-interest, he will fail in his moral duty and will be denied entrance to heaven.

Ethical Anchoring of the Future Ruler: Kautilya explained the role of education in developing restraint over senses.

He (p 137) believes: 'Vices are due to ignorance and indiscipline; an unlearned man does not perceive the injurious consequences of his vices (8.3).' He (p 144) states: 'The sole aim of all branches of knowledge is to inculcate restraint over the senses (1.6.3).' He emphasises the teaching of ethical values, such as non-violence, compassion, tolerance, truthfulness, honesty to children. Accordingly, he (pp. 155-156) observes: 'Just as a clean object is stained with whatever is smeared on it, so a prince, with a fresh mind, understands as the truth whatever is taught to him. Therefore, a prince should be taught what is *dharma* and *artha*, not what is unrighteous and materially harmful (1.17).'

This observation is as relevant today as it was then and applies to every child and not just to a prince. Kautilya is ethical and secular but not religious. It is significant to note that teaching of these ethical values in schools does not violate the separation of the church and state. Kautilya suggests moral incentives to persuade a ruling king to be ethical and ethical anchoring for a future king to be ethical. Causal Link 5 may be expressed as follows:

$$E (R) = M (MI) \quad (2.5a)$$

$$E (F) = D (EA) \quad (2.5b)$$

Where E (R) Ethical conduct of the ruling king, MI= moral incentives, EA= ethical anchoring,

E (F) =Ethics of a future king.

Kautilya's approach to engineering prosperity has three advantages over that of Adam Smith's approach.[8]

First, Kautilya allocates a higher percentage of tax revenue to the building of infrastructure leading to a higher productivity in the private sector. Secondly, Kautilya suggests adoption of cognitive division of labour, leading to more efficient policies to promote the growth in the private sector. Most importantly, Kautilya's ethics-based approach will generate an ethical surplus. An ethical king is likely to help in the creation of an ethical environment and that will promote ethics-intensive trust and that will lower transaction costs. Thus, *dharmic* (Ethical) Surplus may be defined as = Economic growth guided by *dharma* (or ethics-based trust) - economic growth based on self-interest (or based on calculative trust).

2.2 Kautilya's Progressive Principles and Policies

Kautilya emphasised the development of internal restraints through ethical education. But he knew some individuals might not acquire self-discipline and needed to be constrained by law.

He suggests laws that are efficient and strengthens the ethical fabric of society, that is, have no crowding-out effect. Essentially, in Kautilya's approach to shared prosperity, there is no Sinclair's (1906) Jurgis Rudkus (the poor and exploited worker).

(i) *Protecting those who could not Protect themselves*: Kautilya is aware of the possibility that weaker sections of the society can easily be exploited and harassed and need protection. He suggests passing laws against child labour and sexual harassment.[9]

Laws against Sexual Harassment: Kautilya (p 333) recommends: '[The Chief Commissioner shall not misbehave with women with whom he has to deal officially]. For looking at the face of a woman or talking about anything other than work, he shall be punished with the lowest level of fine (2.23).' Women are getting paid for doing the work and the officer is not doing any favour to them, Kautilya points out.

Laws against Child Labour: He (p 449) adds: 'A minor, below eight years of age and no relatives, shall not be made to work against his will, in menial jobs or in a foreign country (3.13).' Some of his ideas such as, enacting laws against child labour and sexual harassment truly belong to the later part of 20th century.

(ii) *Consumer Protection*: Consumers expect fair and honest dealings from suppliers of products and services. Kautilya discusses consumer protection at length. He (p 250) recommends: 'Cartelisation by artisans and craftsmen with the aim of lowering quality, increasing the profits or obstructing the sale or purchase and by merchants conspiring to hoard with the aim of selling at a higher price (4.2)' be dealt with stiff punishments of 1000 panas for such offenses. Such a high penalty indicates the perceived seriousness (pp 249-250) of the offense. He recommends punishment for 'adulteration', 'fraud', 'false description in selling', 'showing one product and selling another', and 'stealing precious metal in making new objects', etc. (4.2). According to him, all such practices are unethical and illegal; he equates charging high prices through the formation of cartels to theft.

Regulation of Monopoly and Monopsony: Both monopoly and monopsony were perhaps serious problems during the ancient times.

Kautilya (p 236) compared merchants to thieves and suggested imposing hefty fines for paying lower prices to the producers and charging higher prices from the consumers. However, just like

Adam Smith, he was not aware of the concept of deadweight loss created by the existence of monopoly and monopsony.

Malpractice: Health care is a private affair. But Kautilya prescribes punishment if the physicians cause any harm to their patients. However, he does not prescribe any physical punishment for the physicians. On the other hand, Robert Lingat (p 303) observes, 'They were not similar to the penalty fixed in other ancient codes, e.g. the Hammurabi's Code, because the Ancient Indian sources of law did not foresee in this case *lex tallionis* but imposed on the physician a fine, the extent of which varied according to circumstances.'

Bankruptcy Protection: Kautilya (p 423) believes that rules should be formulated in such a way that the weak in the society, such as the sick, a minor and an insolvent are protected (there was some bankruptcy protection even at that time).

Protection of Privacy: Kautilya recommends building codes to protect privacy. He (p 371) writes: The doors and windows shall be so made as not to cause annoyance by facing directly a door or a window of a neighbouring house Any window made for lighting shall be high up [so that it does not overlook a room of another house] (3.8).

(iii) *Workers' Right to Negotiate*: He (p 450) recommends: 'The agreement between a labourer and the one hiring him shall be made in public. Labourers shall be paid wages as agreed upon. If there is no prior agreement, the labourer shall be paid in accordance with the nature of the work and the time spent on it at customary rates.' He continues, 'The customary rate can be modified by prior agreement (3.13).' He (p 451) recommends: An employee shall have the right, if he is ill, in distress, incapable of doing the work or if the work is vile: to have his contract annulled or to have it done by someone else. An employee shall not be obliged, against his will, to continue working for his previous employer if he has completed the task allotted to him and already accepted employment under another. An employee shall have the right to additional compensation if he does more work than agreed upon (3.14).

Workers' Right to Form a Union: In those times, there was no restriction on forming labour groups.

Kautilya (p 452) explains: The rules about rights and obligations of individual labour also apply to groups of workmen who contract collectively to do a specified task. Workmen belonging to collective groups shall divide the earnings among themselves either equally or according to shares agreed upon earlier (3.14).

(iv) *Help the Helpless*: Kautilya was concerned about the well-being of the poor, who couldn't pay any tax and needed help.

In his view, there is a very clear demarcation of responsibilities between the individual and the state. According to him (p 182): 'Every man has an obligation to maintain his wife, children, parents, minor brothers and dependent (unmarried or widowed) sisters. No man shall renounce the life of a householder in order to become an ascetic without providing for the maintenance of his wife and children (2.1 The head of the household was in those days primarily responsible for the family and there was a punishment of 12 panas (p 194) for the failure (2.1). However, he (p 182) suggests: 'King shall maintain, at state expense, children, the old, the destitute, those suffering from adversity, childless women and the children of the destitute women (2.1).'

Caring Administration: He believes that a king should take care of his subjects like a father takes care of his children. He (p 128) writes, 'Whenever danger threatens, the king shall protect all those afflicted like a father [protects his children] (4.3)'. He (p 180) adds: 'He shall, however, treat leniently, like a father [would treat his son], those whose exemptions have ceased to be effective (2.1).'

The above statements indicate a comprehensive package of benefits: disability payments to those suffering from adversity, social security to the old, supplemental security income to the children and welfare payments to the poor.

2.3 Concluding Observations

Kautilya advanced a people-centric, proactive and progressive approach to engineer shared prosperity. There was dynamism in ancient India. For example, sage Punarvasu Atreya initiated a well-organised study of medicine in India called Ayurveda (science of life) during the seventh century BCE. This may be considered a paradigm shift in human thinking since it was realised that good health and longevity depended on human efforts, and diseases were not caused by any supernatural powers.

Thus, even before Kautilya, the idea of progress had entered the Indian mind. Robert Nisbet (1980) explored the history of the idea of progress but unfortunately, he limited his search only to the occidental culture. Ideas were flowing from east to west right up to the 17th century and Nesbit's exploration does not add much to our knowledge.

Kautilya did not believe in economic growth just for a few. In his people-centric approach, there is never a helpless and stressed out Rudkus whereas there is nothing in *The Wealth of Nations* to prevent it. According to Kautilya, good governance creates opportunities and existence of good institutions allows individuals to avail of those opportunities. Kautilya, by suggesting that the producers are helped through tax incentives, workers' rights to negotiate wages and form unions are respected and that consumers are protected against monopoly prices, implicitly proposes a genuine stakeholders' model.

Foresight, Oversight, Regulations, Ethics and Systemic Risk

THE SEVERITY of financial crisis of 2008 and its spread throughout the world at an alarming speed shocked everyone. The precipitous fall in equity and real estate prices, the home foreclosures, the fear of a looming deeper and longer recession and the worsening of job markets caused almost an unbearable level of anxiety among workers, manufacturers, homeowners and investors all over the world. A considerable amount of intellectual effort has been devoted to defining, measuring and preventing systemic risk.

Various measures by governments all over the world also have been undertaken to prevent the reoccurrence of such near disaster. For example, in the US, the Dodd-Frank Act established the Financial Stability Oversight Council (FSOC) to identify risks and suggest measures to prevent another financial crisis.

Kautilya had argued that maintenance of both peace and prosperity, to a large extent, depended on preparedness and that required foresightedness. Also, oversight without foresight can be sightless and consequently might be close to being useless. According to Kautilya, the decision-makers must be foresighted. Section 3.1 contains this discussion. *For over two hundred years, an economic system has been compared to a machine. Such comparison is inappropriate since parts of a machine do not negotiate with each other the terms and conditions of engagement and similarly, no part of a machine ever displays moral hazard or strategic behaviour but people, who are the primary constituents of an economic system, do.*

Anyhow, such comparison was harmless, although inappropriate, to treat the baker, the barber and the butcher as parts of a machine but now it can be disastrous since it diverts attention away from the source of systemic risk. On the other hand, Kautilya believes that a kingdom or a system consists of people (policy-makers and others) and things. Such characterisation of a system allows a more meaningful analysis of systemic risk. Kautilya's ideas on economic system and systemic risk are discussed in Section 3.2.

Establishment of the FSOC is a step in the right direction since by adding oversight to complement the regulatory approach reduces the probability of another financial crisis. Historically speaking, legislations creating FDIC and the unemployment compensation, to some extent, have stopped runs on otherwise healthy banks and helped the unemployed pay their bills. But these legislations have created the moral hazard problem.

The depositors of small amounts do not feel the need to pay attention to the risky behaviour of bankers and the unemployed do not feel the pressure to actively search for jobs.[1] Tax-payers bailed-out the troubled Savings &Loan Associations during the 1980s and 1990s and the big financial institutions during the Great Recession (in the USA). That has created a built-in expectation that the tax-payers will bail-out if there is another financial crisis. Consequently, the shareholders and creditors, most probably have become lax and not keen on guarding against the risky behaviour of bankers and others. That is, it has become, in addition to FDIC and unemployment compensation, another case of moral hazard problem.

FSOC has been assigned the task of promoting market-discipline to eliminate such expectations, that is, to drive home the point that tax-payers will not come to their rescue. However, market discipline, would most likely powerless in preventing another financial crisis[2] Perhaps that was the most important lesson learnt from the great depression of the 1930s. Therefore, a trillion dollars question is: are FSOC's two objectives, promoting market discipline and prevention of another financial crisis, compatible with each other? Relevance of Kautilya's insights to answer this question is presented in Section 3.3.

Kautilya was not religious but was ethical and secular.

He strongly believes in *the link between good character and good behaviour.* [1] Samuel Buell (2016) claims that situation and context are more relevant than a person's character in explaining his/her behaviour. Similarly, [2] Eugene Soltes (2016) casts doubt on the link between good character and good behaviour. Unknowingly perhaps, he uses Adam Smith's concept of self-command to conclude that character is not important in explaining one's behaviour. In practice, the concept of self-command is useless in dealing with greed or moral hazard, the underlying factor for committing majority of the white-collar crimes in today's age.

On the other hand, Kautilya's concept of self-discipline is most appropriate in controlling vices such as greed, lust and moral hazard. Keeping this in view, he recommends 'ethical mooring' of the children. This discussion is presented in Section 3.4. Final section contains some concluding observations.

3.1 Kautilya on the Role of Foresight

Kautilya's predecessors considered *possession of foresight as a life saver*. They wrote animal fables to teach the young to develop this component of wisdom. [3] Kautilya (p 205) also warned a would-be adviser to the king: 'A wise man makes self-protection his first and constant concern (5.416.17).'

However, he extends the role of foresight in many directions. If a ruler (CEO) does not foresee a threat, he will not be prepared to take any preventive or remedial measures. According to Kautilya, foresightedness is required in undertaking both preventive and remedial measures to handle a potential threat arising from an attack, occurrence of a famine or moral decay. He (p 116) writes: In the interests of the prosperity of the country, a king should be diligent in foreseeing the possibility of calamities, try to avert them before they arise, overcome those which happen, remove all obstructions to economic activity and prevent loss of revenue to the state (8.4).

Qualification of an Adviser: Kautilya (p, 120) writes: A councilor or minister of the highest rank should be a native of the state, born in a high family and controllable [by the king]. He should have been trained in all the arts and have logical ability to foresee things. He should be intelligent, persevering, dexterous, eloquent, energetic, bold, brave, and able to endure adversities and firm in loyalty. He should neither be haughty or fickle. He should be amicable and not excite hatred or enmity in others (1.9).

The Financial Stability Oversight Council, established by the Dodd-Frank Wall Street Reform and Consumer Protection Act (Dodd-Frank Act), is charged with three primary purposes:

1. To identify risks to the financial stability of the United States that could arise from the material financial distress or failure, or ongoing activities, of large, interconnected bank holding companies or nonbank financial companies, or that could arise outside the financial services marketplace.

2. To respond to emerging threats to the stability of the US financial system.

3. To promote market discipline, by eliminating expectations on the part of shareholders, creditors, and counterparties of such companies that the US government will shield them from losses in the event of failure.

A few remarks are in order. Perhaps for the first time in US history, in 2008, the authorities appreciated the importance of foresight in identifying the threats to financial stability. Secondly, policy-makers realised the inadequacy of regulations and therefore, added oversight to complement regulations in reducing the probability of another financial crisis (see more in Section III). That implies that Buell's concerns have been addressed.[3] Kautilya had emphasises that an adviser must have the 'logical ability to foresee'. However, members of the FSOC are not required to be foresighted.

3.2 Kautilya on an Economic System and Systemic Risk

Adam Smith compared an economic system to a machine and despite its inappropriateness, this metaphor has not lost its appeal.[4]

For example, according to [4] Jean-Pierre Zigrand (2014):A social system on the other hand must be *functioning*, or as Vining (1984) says, it must be a *working thing*, a machine functioning towards accomplishing an aim, an aim embedded in the principle of deductibility from the axiom of economicity. It may not be perfect, but it possesses some minimal requirements, not least consistency, coherence and an ongoing goal.

A few remarks are in order. First, an economic system consists of decision-makers and things. Zigrand and others focus only on the things and leave out the people, who make policies, oversee, regulate and manage the things. That is, a mechanistic definition of an economic system leaves out its core, the people. On the other hand, Kautilya focuses primarily on people.

He (p 116) writes: 'It is the people who constitute a kingdom (7.11.24).' He lists seven elements or constituents of a state. According to him, these are (i) the king, (ii) councilors, ministers and other high officials (iii) public and the territory (iv) the fortified towns and cities (v) treasury (vi) army and (vii) allies, that is, a kingdom or an economic system consists of people and things.[5]

Secondly, a machine does not have any emergent properties. It has merely predictive and repetitive movements. Thirdly, a high degree of linkages among financial firms needs to be seen as a sign of high degree of specialisation and of a vibrant economy and not merely as a propagating mechanism of systemic risk.

A machine does not care who gets the produce and does not understand the pain and hardship. In fact, Kautilya (p 122) defines a calamity as: 'That which deprives a person of his strength and goodness is a vyasana (a vice, adversity orcalamity. 8.1.4).'People are deprived of 'strength and goodness', implying that a mechanistic definition of a system cannot capture the impact of a crisis on an individual's emotional and physical health. Incidentally, Kautilya includes addiction, such as to opioids or narcotics, as a calamity since that too 'deprives a person of his strength and goodness'.

Systemic Risk: According to [5] Zachary Feinsteina, Birgit Rudlob and Stefan Weber (2016): Systemic risk refers to the risk that the financial system is susceptible to failures due to the characteristics of the system itself. The tremendous cost of this type of risk requires the design and implementation of tools for the efficient macro-prudential regulation of financial institutions. The current paper proposes a novel and general approach to systemic risk measurement.

Almost all the academicians and policy makers consider the characteristics, such as leverage, size, mismatch between the maturities of assets and liabilities, and asset prices etc., of the system as the source of systemic risk. Accordingly, managing the characteristics through regulation and supervision is recommended to prevent another financial crisis. But that is a misdiagnosis of the source of systemic risk. Suppose a person has low hemoglobin, boosting it through an iron-rich diet or blood infusion may seem appropriate. However, if hemoglobin is low due to blood cancer, these remedies will be only of temporary help and will not reduce the probability of a health disaster. Similarly, if moral hazard problem is system-wide like the blood cancer, raising the capital requirement might seem appropriate but will not reduce the probability of a financial disaster.

That means, moral hazard, not the characteristics, is the real source of the systemic risk. In other words, characteristics of the system depend on the character of the policy-makers, bankers and hedge fund managers etc., implying that the decision-makers' behaviour is the real source of systemic risk. It is generally acknowledged that moral hazard problem is widespread and the S & L crisis, and the 2008 financial crisis, may be attributed to it, -implying so far as the source of systemic risk is concerned 'too big to fail' is not that big a problem but ethical failing can be a very big problem.[6]

Kautilya on the Link between Moral Decay and Systemic Risk: Kautilya was the first economist, who nderstood the link between ethical conduct and prosperity.

He believes that the survival as well as prosperity of a kingdom depends on the ethical conduct of both the ruler and public. He (pp, 107–08) surmises: 'For the world, when maintained in accordance with the Vedas, will ever prosper and not perish. Therefore, the king shall never allow the people to swerve from their dharma'. He (p 141) writes:A king who flouts the teachings of the *Dharamshastras* and The *Arthashastra*, ruins the kingdom by his own injustice (8.2).

He believes that ethical decision-makers do not fail in their duties and do not promote their private interests at the expense of public interest. Similarly, he believes that 'greed clouds the intellect', implying that a greedy person cannot figure out the consequences of his/her actions. According to him, moral hazard problem and greed will be non-existent in an ethical society. In fact, Kautilya's predecessors had emphasised the foundational role of dharma (ethics). For example, according to [6] *Atharva Veda* (12-1-17), 'This World is Upheld by Dharma'. Kautilya wholeheartedly accepts and promotes the secular virtues (dharmic duties). He (1992, 107) writes: Duties common to all: Ahimsa [abstaining from injury to all living creatures]; satyam [truthfulness]; cleanliness; freedom from malice; compassion and tolerance (1.13).

However, 'too big to fail' plays an important role in the propagation of systemic risk. Input-output matrices are constructed to trace the impact of a change in one industry on other industries. Until the oil shock of 1973, energy cost was so insignificant that no one felt the need to keep records. As a result, no one knew at the time what would be the impact of the oil shock. Although inter-financial linkages are not the source of systemic risk, but it is helpful in understanding the strength of linkages. Dodd-Frank Act has established the OFR to collect data on inter-linkages among financial firms. Something similar to the following matrix:

Matrix 3.1: Inter-linkages among Financial Institutions

	Banks	**Brokerage Firms**	**Hedge Funds**
Banks	B_{11}	B_{12}	B_{13}
Brokerage Firms	B_{21}	B_{22}	B_{23}
Hedge Funds	B_{31}	B_{32}	B_{33}

It will be useful to construct appropriate input-output tables that incorporate the financial sector. It can reveal all the linkages among the financial firms for understanding the domino effect and between the financial sector and the other sectors for gaugng the liquidity effect.[7]

3.3 Relevance of Kautilya's Insights to Prevent Financial Crisis

Businesses are averse to both oversight and regulations, implying concave indifference curves, such as ARB curve in figure 3.1 below. Secondly, if they have a choice, they prefer either but not a combination of them. That is, Point A or B being on a lower Iso-probability curve touching at point T (not shown to avoid cluttering), would be preferred to point R. However, from a policy perspective, a combination of both oversight and regulation would be more effective in preventing another financial crisis since the regulatory approach has serious limitations. First, rules and regulations are usually reactive, dealing with fixing the problem/s and not proactive to prevent future ones. Second, note that an ant will succeed in finding a crack even in a magnificent building like the Taj Mahal. If you fill one, it will find another. Similarly, some individuals, within a short period of time, succeed in discovering loopholes in the laws and start exploiting them (known as regulatory arbitrage). However, a legislation like the Dodd-Frank legislation helps to 'identify' and 'respond' to emerging threats to the stability of the US financial system and can do so for other countries also. That removes the deficiencies of the regulatory approach.

As an illustration, suppose the probability of preventing a financial crisis with regulations only is, $P_1 = 0.85$. If both regulation and supervision were introduced, the probability would increase to P2 =0.95. That means any repeal or weakening of the Dodd-Frank legislation will raise the probability of a financial crisis. The following figure may be used to explain the roles of regulation, oversight and ethical grounding.

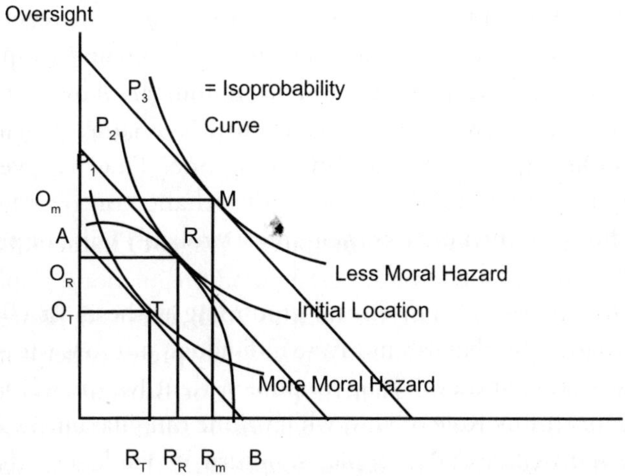

Figure 3.1: P1, P2, and P3 are the Iso-probability curves. Each Iso-probability curve indicates the various combinations of oversight and regulations required for achieving a certain level of probability for preventing a financial crisis.

Kautilya was quite concerned about the possibility of moral decay and its potentially devastating impact on social-fabric, economic growth and stability.

According to him, only self-discipline acquired through ethical grounding, can eliminate the problem of moral hazard, reduce white collar crimes and rent-seeking activities and prevent another financial crisis. That is, without self-discipline, FSOC's twin objectives, prevention of financial crisis and promotion of market discipline, most probably will not be achieved. Moreover, ethical mooring is the most effective and least expensive way to prevent another financial crisis and improve corporate governance.

Regulations and supervision should be perceived as complements to ethical grounding and not as substitutes (see [7] Sihag, 2014, Chapters. 5 and 6). There are no number of rules, regulations, level of supervision or their combination that can effectively tackle the moral hazard problem, which has been the primary source of financial crises. Businesses find ways to circumvent regulations and supervision provisions and policy-makers also help the process by weakening the provisions. This is indicated by a shift of the initial Iso-probability curve P2 to P1. That is, probability of preventing crisis will decline over time. That is, given the predominantly amoral environment, reliance on oversight or regulations or their combination, most probably will not prevent another financial crisis.

On the other hand, ethical grounding is the most effective and reliable tool that can motivate individuals not to waste energy in discovering and exploiting loopholes. Kautilya (p 142) writes: 'Government by Rule of Law, which alone can guarantee security of life and welfare of the people, is, in turn, dependent on the self-discipline of the king (1.5).' With ethical grounding, over time the Iso-probability curve is likely to shift upwards to P3, that is, the probability of preventing a financial crisis may increase. That is, if ethical conduct is also added to regulation and supervision, probability of prevention, most likely will be P3 = 0.999, that is, financial crisis may be almost non-existent.

3.4 Kautilya on Definition and Building of Good Character

Kautilya, just like his predecessors, had a very comprehensive understanding of the concept of good character. According to him, good character means practicing the dharmic (ethical) duties (mentioned above), such as non-violence, compassion, tolerance, truthfulness and freedom from malice and having self-discipline, which also means conquering six enemies 'lust, anger, greed, conceit, arrogance and foolhardiness'. The objective is to promote positive externalities and reduce negative ones. He believes good character leads to good behaviou. The following table presents his views on this relationship.

Table 3.2: Kautilya on the Link between Character and Behaviour

Ethical (Ruler, President, CEO)	Unethical (Ruler, President, CEO)
Kautilya (p 145): A rajarishi [a king, wise like a sage] is one who: has self-control, having conquered the [inimical temptations] of the senses, cultivates the intellect by association with elders, is ever active in promoting the security and welfare of the people, endears himself to his people by enriching them and doing good to them and avoids daydreaming, capriciousness, falsehood and extravagance (1.7). He (p 149) writes: 'In the happiness of his subjects lies his happiness; in their welfare his welfare. He shall not consider as good only that which pleases him but treat as beneficial to him whatever pleases his subjects (1.19).' A king should take care of his subjects like a father takes care of his children. He (p 128) writes: 'Whenever danger threatens, the king shall protect all those afflicted like a father [protects his children] (4.3)'. He (p 180) adds, 'He shall, however, treat leniently, like a father [would treat his son], those whose exemptions have ceased to be effective (2.1)'. Kautilya (p 128) believes, 'It is the duty of the king to protect the people from all calamities (4.3)'. Kautilya (p 182) suggests: King shall maintain, at state expense, children, the old, the destitute, those suffering from adversity, childless women and the children of the destitute women (2.1). He (p 385) states: The judges themselves shall take charge of the affairs of gods, Brahmins, ascetics, women, minors, old people, the sick and those that are helpless [e.g., orphans], [even] when they do not approach the court. No suit of theirs shall be dismissed for want of jurisdiction, passage of time or adverse possession (3.2).	Kautilya (p 133): A decadent king, on the other hand, oppresses the people by demanding gifts, seizing what he wants and grabbing for himself and his favourites the produce of the country [i.e. the king and his coterie consume more than their due share thus considerably impoverishing the treasury and the people.] (8.4). He (p 159) addsthat such a king: Ignores the good [people] and favours the wicked, causes harm by new unrighteous practices; neglects the observation of the proper and righteous practices; suppresses dharma and propagates adharma; does what ought not to be done and fails to what ought to be done; fails to give what ought to be given and exacts what he cannot rightly take; 'indulges in wasteful expenditure and destroys profitable undertakings'; does not punish those who ought to be punished but punishes those who do not deserve to be; arrests those who should not be arrested but fails to arrest who should be seized; 'fails to protect the people from thieves and robs them himself'; 'does not recompense service done to him'; 'does not carry out his part of what had been agreed upon' 'by his indolence and negligence destroys the welfare of his people' (7.5).

On the other hand, [8] Adam Smith (TMS, IV.2.8, p 189) wrote, 'Self-command, in the same manner, by which we restrain our present appetites, in order to gratify them more fully upon another occasion, is approved of, as much under the aspect of propriety, as under that of utility....The spectator does not feel the solicitations of our present appetites. To him the pleasure which we are to enjoy a week hence, or a year hence, is just as interesting as that which we are to enjoy this moment'.

The Impartial Spectator does not discount the future utility, implying absence of time preference. One may call this choice between present-self and the future-self as prudent but in no way ethical. More importantly, the concept of self-command is useless since it does not address the moral hazard problem and greed, which have negatively impacted society. Self-discipline means giving up destructive emotions including greed, implying aversion to white collar crimes. A person may have self-command and still commit white caller crimes. Moreover, this is an overuse of the impartial spectator since he should not be involved essentially in a saving decision

Interestingly, Eugene Soltes (2016) points out that this definition of self-command is still in use. He (p 54) remarks, 'In a well- known set of experiments from the early 1970s, children were given the choice of receiving one marshmallow immediately or two, if they waited until the researcher returned to the room. As adults, those who delayed gratification in childhood exhibited higher educational achievement, had better relationships, and were less likely to be overweight'. Such studies prove that those who have self-command may not be overweight but do not prove that such individuals are ethical.

Soltes (2016, p 63) continues, 'If Judge Hellerstein is correct in suggesting that many of those sentenced for white-collar crimes are actually good people, we need to take a step back from focusing on the characteristics of the individuals involved and focus on the decisions being made by managers instead. Perhaps their failures arise not from "bad character" but, instead, from poor decisions made by otherwise typical individual'. First, it is an untenable assertion to generalise based on a very small sample. Secondly, good people do not make deals with corrupt individuals.[8] Most importantly, a distinction needs to be made between 'poor decisions' and illegal (unethical) decisions. These individuals made illegal (unethical) decisions not poor decisions, and went to jail for doing that.

Samuel Buell (2016) considers context and situation more relevant than character in determining behaviour. He (p 20) remarks, 'Anyone who has taken a course in psychology is familiar with one of the important discoveries of twentieth-century social science: people are wired to understand and explain each other's behaviour with reference to character and disposition (she ran from the police, so she must not be law-abiding) rather than context and situation (if she ran from the police, may be the police have a pattern of wrongful arrests in the area). This is a common mistake. Situation generally has far more influence over people's behaviour than do their prior tendencies'.

A few comments are in order. First, self-protection is a basic instinct and it is hard wired. Secondly, it is an inappropriate way to bring out the importance of character since it is a case of using prior information (related to the past behaviour of the cop) and not the woman's prior disposition. More importantly, this illustration proves the point that character is important: it suggests that cops of bad-character arrest and harass innocent people, that is, they are more likely to do bad things and are feared.

Ethical Education: According to Kautilya, a concerted effort is required for ethical grounding, that is, it is not automatic or easy.[9] He (p 137) believes, 'Vices are due to ignorance and indiscipline; an unlearned man does not perceive the injurious consequences of his vices (8.3)'. He (p 144) states, 'The sole aim of all branches of knowledge is to inculcate restraint over the senses (1.6.3)'. He (pp 155-156) suggests: There can be no greater crime or sin than making wicked impressions on an innocent mind. Just as a clean object is stained with whatever is smeared on it, so a prince, with a fresh mind, understands as the truth whatever is taught to him.[10] Therefore, a prince should be taught what is dharma and artha, not what is unrighteous and materially harmful (1.17).

3.5 Conclusion

Kautilya's *Arthashastra* is a manual on engineering prosperity and preventing crisis. Under the current environment in which heavy emphasis is put on materialism, it is unrealistic to expect people not to exploit loopholes or not harm through their amoral and immoral behaviour.[11] However, according to Kautilya, ethical grounding of children is possible.

Stress test is used to diagnose heart failure, a physical condition, not moral failure, which is a primary source of systemic risk. That is, the stress test is not a reliable guide to predicting financial crisis. Former Federal Chairman Ben Bernanke had repeatedly expressed his concerns about the potential impact of the Great Recession as: 'What was clear to me was that we were at tremendous risk for another Great Depression. If the financial system collapsed, it would bring down everything. It wouldn't just be folks on Wall Street who would be suffering, but it would be people in the heartland who would also be hit.' That implies that systemic risk can end up as *systematic risk*. Therefore, it is desirable to study them together and not separately as currently done by [9] Barro and Urs′ua (2012) and Zigrand (2014).[12]

Relevance of Kautilya's Insights to Corporate Governance & Management

IN MODERN Corporations there is a separation between managers and owners. The managers might become lazy and, also put their own interests ahead of the owners (shareholders). Two types of legalistic approaches have been proposed to mitigate the moral hazard problem. The principal-agent approach essentially focuses on devising incentive-based legal contracts to elicit effort. The other legalistic approach focuses on accountability of the agents' actions to mitigate the moral hazard problem. There has been an intense debate between those who advocate shareholder (principal)-supremacy and others, who advocate Agent-supremacy.

This debate has led to the realisation that there is a trade-off between accountability and authority on the possibility frontier. [1] Zohar Goshen and Richard Squire (2016) argue that just like agency costs, there are principals' costs also. They propose minimisation of the sum of agency costs and principals' costs for determining the division of control between managers and owners. Their suggestion does help in determining a mix of accountability and authority on the possibility frontier. A very brief review of these two approaches is presented in Section 4.1.

Goshen and Squire identify four types of costs: agency costs consisting of conflict costs and competence costs and similarly principals' costs consisting of competence costs and conflict costs. Kautilya's objective was to avoid the avoidable costs.

He believes agent's conflict costs are avoidable costs and he suggestes an effective way to eliminate them. He understood the distinction between constraints and restraints. Constraints are external to the person since these are imposed by the society and are less effective than the restraints since these are internal to the person. Kautilya puts heavy emphasis on internal restraints to eliminate agent's conflict costs. This is presented in Section 4.2.

Limited liability and economies of scale by pooling resources are the two hallmarks of a corporation for an industrial economy.[1] For example, no one can start a steel plant with some pocket change. On the other hand, in the current knowledge-based economy, pooling of information and knowledge is considered the key to survival and growth. Interestingly, Kautilya understood its importance even in his agricultural economy.

Board of Directors is not known to enhance creativity. Kautilya suggests replacing such a Board with three or four full-time experts. His organisational structure is also efficient since agent's competence costs are virtually zero. His insights relating to efficient management are provided in Section 4.3. Final Section contains some conclusions.

4.1 A summary Review of Current State of Corporate Governance

Kautilya understood the principal-agent problem and suggests various measures to eliminate it. However, credit goes to [2] Adolf A Berle and Gardiner C Means (1932) for highlighting the fact that there is a separation of ownership and control in public corporations.[2] Since then, two approaches: (a) principal-agent and (b) agency costs have been proposed to handle the agency/ principal-agent problem. These are presented below in turn.

(a) Principal-Agent Approach: All the research on principal-agent problem assumes that the CEO is competent but is lazy, that is, might not put in full effort. S/he is a utility maximiser and takes care of the shareholders (or stakeholders) only to the extent that promote his/her own interest. Various packages of incentives are suggested to motivate the CEO to reduce shirking and align his/her interest with those of the principals. The following figure captures the most salient feature of principal-agent approach.

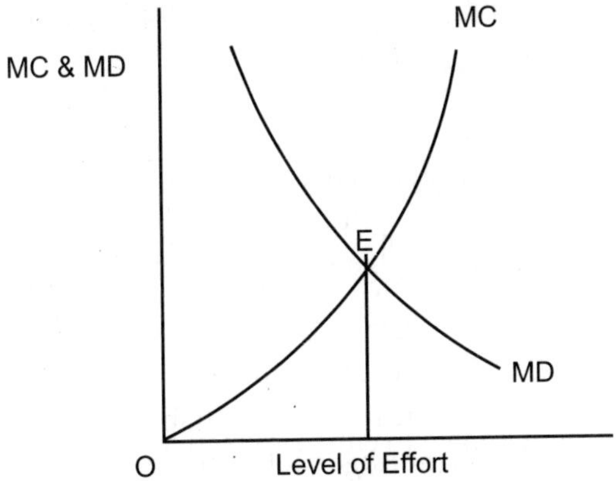

MB=marginal benefit curve of incentive package and MC= marginal cost curve of the incentive package. OE*= optimum level of effort.

Any point to the left of E, Marginal Benefit to shareholders from giving incentives to management > Marginal Cost of the incentive package to it, it is profitable to continue providing additional incentives. Similarly, any point to the right of E, marginal cost of incentives is higher than the marginal benefits to the shareholders, reduce the incentives. The benefits to the shareholders are maximised where Marginal Benefit= Marginal Cost of incentives.

It may be noted that the emphasis is primarily on eliciting effort and not on corporate control as such. More importantly, it may also be pointed out that the additional effort elicited through financial incentives, will most likely be still less than the potential effort.

As an illustration, suppose, the effort level were 80% of the potential level before the provision of incentives. Provision of financial incentives might raise it to 90%, implying that it will still be less than the potential level. It is also possible that sometimes, financial incentives might not work at all. For example, the provision of stock options to management were introduced with an expectation that it would reduce shirking and diversion of assets from the corporation to personal gain. But instead, this led to abuses by backdating the options and focusing on measures for boosting stock price at the expense of long run growth.

(b) Agency Cost Approach: Since the managers are not the owners, they are likely to shirk, that is, likely to put less than the desirable level of effort in managing the company, divert corporate resources to enjoy perks and use defensive measures to stop any value enhancing takeover. These are called agency costs (see below Goshen and Squire's Matrix for a comprehensive definition of agency costs). [3] Arrow (1974) argues that an increase in accountability comes at the expense of authority.[3] [4] Bainbridge (2008) accepts Arrow's argument that there is a trade-off between accountability and authority but still advocates Agent-supremacy. [5] Brett McDonnell (2009) points out that any point on the possibility curve is equally good, implying that Bainbridge's claim regarding Agent-supremacy is not justified. The debate between proponents of shareholder-supremacy and those of agent-supremacy cannot determine the appropriate mix of accountability and authority.

Zohar Goshen and Richard Squire (2016) significantly advance the analysis. They argue that just like the agency costs, there are principals' costs. They explain, 'And in terms of the problem, we distinguish between "competence costs" which we define as "the costs of honest mistakes plus the costs of efforts to avoid such mistakes", and "conflict costs" which we define as "the costs of self-seeking conduct plus the costs of efficient efforts to prevent such conduct". We refer to efficient *efforts* to prevent self-seeking conduct because a cost resulting from, for example, overspending on monitoring – the incurring of \$100 in monitoring costs to prevent only \$50 in misconduct – would constitute a mistake, and thus should be considered a competence cost rather than a conflict cost'. They classify agency costs into two categories as agency conflict costs and agency competence costs and similarly, principals' costs are classified into principals' competence costs and principals' conflict costs. They provide the following matrix (with a slight alteration) of agency costs and principals' costs.

Synthesis: The Control-Cost Matrix

	Principal	**Agent**
Competence Costs	Lack of expertise Inadequate information Lack of intelligence Poor emotional control Coordination problems Cognitive myopia	Lack of expertise Inadequate information Lack of intelligence Poor emotional control Overconfidence bias Optimism bias
Conflict Costs	Collective-action problems Reneging on promises Rational apathy Rational reticence Holdouts Empty voting Different horizons	Shirking (reduced effort) Diverting (self-dealing) Option backdating Entrenchment Merging for size Merging for diversification Excessive or inefficient pay

Source: Zohar Goshen and Richard Squire (2016) Principal Costs: A New Theory for Corporate Law and Governance

They argue that there is a trade-off between principals' costs and agency costs. According to them, minimisation of the sum of principals' costs and agency costs should determine the division of control between the principals and the agents and it is likely to

vary from firm to firm. They say, 'Let us define the "delegation substitution rate" as the ratio of the increase in expected agent costs to the decrease in expected principal costs produced by an incremental transfer of control rights from investors to managers in a firm:
Delegation rate of substitution = increase in expected Agent costs/ Decrease in expected Principal costs'.

For cost minimisation, the rate of substitution should be = 1.
That is,
Increase in expected Agent costs = Decrease in expected Principal Cost
Marginal cost (MC) = Marginal Benefit (MB)
This cost minimisation approach can be used to determine the mix of accountability and authority also. The following Figure 4.2 captures the usefulness of their suggestion.

Figure 4.2: Control Costs

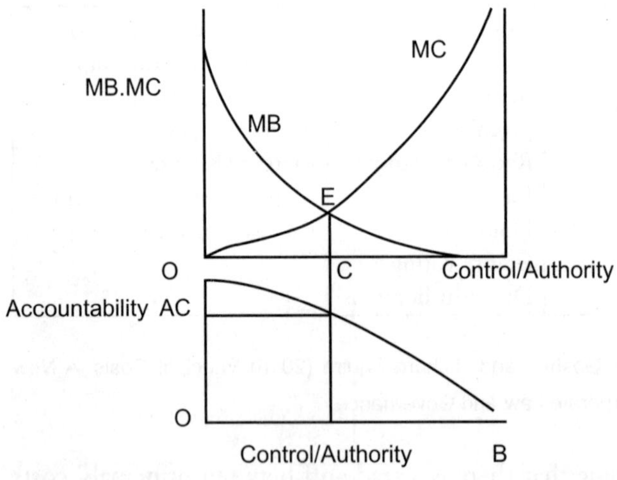

MB curve indicates the decrease in Principals' cost and MC curve indicates increase in Agent's costs as the principals' control/ authority decreases. AB curves indicates the trade-off between accountability and authority/control. Principals have 100% control at point O. At equilibrium point c (MC = MB), Agent's control= OC and the Principals' control = CB.

A couple of remarks are in order. Firstly, as the Principals decrease their control, their competence costs decrease but not necessarily their conflicts costs, such as 'Collective-action problems and different horizons' and actually might increase. Secondly, it may also be pointed out that minimisation of costs does not mean that they are insignificant. In fact, these may be significant. Thirdly, shareholders are not the only stakeholders, knowledge workers have invested as much if not more in human capital as the shareholders have in physical capital.

4.2 Kautilya's Ethics-based Approach to Corporate Governance

Kautilya considered the public as the principals and the king as their agent (CEO), a salaried employee. Someone wrote that according to Kautilya, 'a king is a loyal servant to his royal public'.* Kautilya identified three types of CEOs (rulers): (i) the ethical, (ii) the self-interested (utility maximiser) and (iii) the myopic and unethical. He linked the growth potential to the CEO-type. The following table captures his implicit conceptual framework on the relationship.

Table 4.1: Kautilya on CEO-type and Economic Growth potential

Type of CEO	Agency Costs		Principals' costs		
	Conflict costs	Competence costs	Conflict costs	Competence costs	Economic Growth
Ethical	Zero	Almost Zero	Negligible	Zero	High
Utility-maximiser	Significant	Modest	Modest	Modest	Modest
Unethical	Significant	Significant	Significant	Significant	Negative/ poor

Kautilya on the need to have an Ethical CEO: Kautilya understood the usefulness of backward induction and used it extensively.

He invariably sets up his objective, such as bringing prosperity or providing national security, and explores ways to realise it in the most effective and ethical way. In this case, his objective is to eliminate agent's conflict costs, that is, the moral hazard problems. According to him, these costs can be eliminated only if the agent is ethical. This is so as an ethical agent will not shirk and, also will not turn his office into a museum with expensive artwork/ paintings. [6] Kautilya (p 149) looks at the king as someone: 'In the happiness of his subjects lies his happiness; in their welfare his welfare. He shall not consider as good only that which pleases him but treat as beneficial to him whatever pleases his subjects (1.19).' [7] Drekmeier (1962, p. 175-76) notes, 'Now the king must concern himself directly with the common good, an idea anticipated in the *Arthashastra*.'

There are at least two points worth noting. (i) The Pareto optimality condition is satisfied implicitly. Since the king does what is good for the public and he derives satisfaction from that, that is, both the king and the public are better off. (ii) It seems that Kautilya is trying to ensure that the social welfare function is not imposed or dictatorial, that is, the king does not impose his preferences on the public, rather respects the preferences of his subjects.[4] Obviously, Kautilya did not want to sacrifice individual sovereignty.

According to Kautilya, only an ethical agent will put principals' interest ahead of his own interest.[5] However, he (p, 145) writes: There is no need for such a king to deprive himself of all sensual pleasures and lead a life of total austerity so long as he does not infringe his dharma or harms his own material well-being.

Utility Maximiser (Self-Interested) CEO: Kautilya understood the power of self-interest.

He (p, 159) argues, 'When a people are impoverished, they become greedy; when they are greedy, they become disaffected;

when disaffected, they either go to the enemy or kill their ruler themselves'. Kautilya advises the king (CEO) that it is in his own interest to provide some acceptable standard of living to the people. He writes: Therefore, the king shall not act in such a manne ıs would cause impoverishment, greed or disaffection among the people; if, however, they do appear, he shall immediately take remedial measures.

Unethical CEO: According to Kautilya (p 133), 'A decadent king, on the other hand, oppresses the people by demanding gifts, seizing what he wants and grabbing for himself and his favourites the produce of the country [i.e. the king and his coterie consume more than their due share thus considerably impoverishing the treasury and the people] (8.4)'. He continues that such a king 'fails to give what ought to be given and exacts what he cannot rightly take'; 'indulges in wasteful expenditure and destroys profitable undertakings'; 'fails to protect the people from thieves and robs them himself'; 'does not recompense service done to him'; 'does not carry out his part of what had been agreed upon'; and 'by his indolence and negligence destroys the welfare of his people' (7.5). Actually, Kautilya and Chandragupta Maurya dethroned such a orphan.

[8] Miller (1997) notes, 'As North argued, a ruler generally has incentives to take confiscatory actions which undermine property rights and contract enforcement, and sharply constrain the incentives for productive economic activity by his own subjects. The constitutional problem is to constrain the self-interested activity of the ruler – to commit the ruler to constitutional constraints that are consistent with economic development'. He further adds that 'Efficiency is inconsistent with self-interest by the ruler. In other words, this demonstrates that North's historical observations about tension between profit-seeking rulers and efficiency for the society was not, in fact, accidental, but a manifestation of a logical inconsistency in mechanism design (G Miller and Hammond 1994)'.

Three remarks are in order. Firstly, both framing and upholding of constitution depend on the character of those in power, implying that a constitution is not a fool-proof device against the possible inconsistency between efficiency and self-interest. Secondly, the constitution of conscience is much more effective than the legal document in ensuring efficiency. Thirdly, according to Olson's second law of invisible hand, even a bandit provides some minimum growth opportunities.[6]

Kautilya (p 121) writes, 'The wealth of the state shall be one acquired lawfully either by inheritance or by the king's efforts (6.10)'. He (p 231) adds, 'Water works such as reservoirs, embankments and tanks can be privately owned, and the owner shall be free to sell or mortgage them (3.9)'. He condemned an immoral and shortsighted king, who does not protect private property rights.

Creating Ethical Environment: Kautilya believes that if one entity resorted to undesirable practices, others had no option but to adopt similar practices to survive. That is, people compete in giving bribes or cooking the books. He also believes that moral hazard problems due to agency problems and attempts to search for regulatory arbitrage (looking for gaps or holes in law) cannot be checked by any amount of laws. Existence of political and judicial corruption makes the field uneven and usually, it is at the expense of consumers and workers, diverts resources from productive uses to unproductive ones and makes businesses less competitive.

Kautilya wanted the king to be a role model, earn respect and rule through leadership and not through authority. He (p 147) writes, 'If the king is energetic, his subjects will be equally energetic. If he is slack and lazy in performing his duties the subjects will also be lax and, thereby, eat into his wealth. Besides, a lazy king will easily fall into the hands of his enemies. Hence, the king should himself always be energetic (1.19)'. He (p 121) states, 'A king endowed with the ideal personal qualities enriches the other elements when they are less than perfect (6.1)'. He (p 123) adds, 'Whatever character the king has, the other elements also come to have the same (8.1)'. Thus, according to Kautilya, a king (CEO) should be an impartial, ethical, far-sighted, foresighted, disciplined and energetic action-oriented individual.

4.3 Kautilya on Efficient Corporate Management

Kautilya was an independent thinker. He was not a bureaucrat but understood the important role of an organisational structure. According to Drekmeier, Kautilya linked a man's greatness to his organising abilities. Drekmeier (p, 290) observes: We may surmise that men began to conclude that remaking the world was within the realm of possibility. The ancient belief in the cyclical periodicity of time, the eternal return, was modified or displaced altogether by a sense of continuity and development approximating a historical attitude. Accumulated wealth and the military power and administrative efficiency it made possible could now be used for achieving ambitious, long-range political and social goals. The great man is, in fact, the great organiser. He creates the very conditions that make the hero obsolete, for he imposes an order that limits the unpredictable contingencies against which the hero struggles. The hero was made by his age; the organiser is the maker of his age. Men can now do things that earlier could be accomplished only by the gods.

Kautilya's objective was to maximise efficiency or minimise the agent's competency costs.

He suggests pooling of information and knowledge to arrive at a sound decision. According to Kautilya, if management is wisdom-based, no one will ever ask for any accountability (monitoring). Secondly, since in today's knowledge-based economy, creativity is the mantra for having an edge. Board Directors are only part-timers and therefore, not likely to contribute to creativity. Kautilya recommends a team of three or four full-time highly qualified advisers for enhancing creativity.

The Board of Directors is supposed to reduce the scope for a potential for moral hazard since there is a separation of management from the owners (shareholders) of the company. The underlying assumption has been that irrespective of the fact that the management is ethical and wise, still it needs direction/ supervision from the Board of Directors. If the management team is efficient and ethical, no Board of Directors is needed. Similarly, if management is cooking the books, Board of Directors will not be able to detect inefficiency or fraud, implying it is a useless entity. [9] Eugene Soltes (2016, p 315) points out, 'Dennis Kozlowski, the former CEO of Tyco, described how infrequently he experienced such dissonance as chief executive. "When the CEO is in the room, directors – even independent directors – tend to want to try and please him", Kozlowski explained. "The board would give me anything I wanted. Anything."'

Secondly, the world has changed and continues to change. Now intangible capital is becoming increasingly more important than the physical capital. The skilled employees have as much stake as the shareholders. The Board of Directors is just a relic of the past and for knowledge-based enterprises has lost its relevance.

Thirdly, according to Kautilya, it is difficult to keep a secret if shared with more than four persons. That is, someone from a large number of Directors is likely to divulge the secret. He writes: [There should be no more than four advisers] because, with more than four, secrecy is rarely maintained. [While, normally, the king should consult three or four advisers,] he may, depending on the nature of the work and the special circumstances of each case, take a decision by himself, consult just one adviser, or even two. The opinions of the advisers shall be sought individually as well as together [as a group]. The reason why each one holds a particular opinion shall also be ascertained (1.15).

Thus, according to Kautilya, as the number of advisers increase, the king receives better council which increases the probability of success of a task, but the problem of secrecy might become serious and hurt its chances of success. He (p, 200) also suggests: No one who belongs to the side likely to be adversely affected by the project shall be consulted (1.15).

Fourthly, unless the Board members become hands-on participants in corporate affairs, they will not know the internal working. In this case their role will change from supervisory to managerial. But the law does not allow that.

Kautilya's Ethical and Wisdom-based Model: If management is ethical, far-sighted, foresighted and wise, there is no need for a Board of Directors, since there is no problem of moral hazard. The shareholders will get maximum possible profit, workers decent wages and consumers be treated like real sovereigns.

Emphasis on Team Work: Kautilya (p 177) observes: 'A king can reign only with the help of others; one wheel alone does not move a chariot. Therefore, a king should appoint advisers as councilors and ministers and listen to their advice (1.7)'. Clearly the phrase 'one wheel alone does not move a chariot' indicates a complementary nature of relationship between the king's own abilities and the advice from the advisers, which may be critical in ensuring survival and progress of the kingdom. He (p 196) explains: Because the work of the government is diversified and is carried on simultaneously in many different places, the king cannot do it all himself; he, therefore, has to appoint ministers who will implement it at the right time and place (1.9).

Pooling of Information and Knowledge: Kautilya writes: Vishalaksha says 'never can a single person arrive at the right decision. The work of government is dependent on [complete] knowledge – that which the king personally knows, that which is reported to him and that which he has to infer. To find out what is not known, to clarify doubts when there are alternatives, to obtain more information when only a part is known – all these can be done only with the help of advisers. Hence a king shall conduct his deliberations with advisers of mature intelligence. (As the saying goes:) 'Despise no one, [but] listen to all views; for, wise man pays heed to all sensible advice, even those of a child' (1.15).

Kautilya (p, 120) describes the qualifications of an adviser as: A councilor or minister of the highest rank should be a native of the state, born in a high family and controllable [by the king]. He should have been trained in all the arts and have logical ability to foresee things. He should be intelligent, persevering, dexterous, eloquent, energetic, bold, brave, able to endure adversities and firm in loyalty. He should neither be haughty or fickle. He should be amicable and not excite hatred or enmity in others (1.9). A recipe for the perfect officer, both in government and private entreprise, valid even now.

Maximising Economic Growth: Kautilya (p 149) suggests: Hence the king shall be ever active in the management of the economy. The root of wealth is economic activity and lack of it brings material distress. In the absence of fruitful economic activity, both current prosperity and future growth are in danger of destruction. A king can achieve the desired objectives and abundance of riches by undertaking productive economic activity (1.19).

Minimising threats to Prosperity: He (p 116) writes: In the interests of the prosperity of the country, a king should be diligent in foreseeing the possibility of calamities, try to avert them before they arise, overcome those which happen, remove all obstructions to economic activity and prevent loss of revenue to the state (8.4).

A Summary: Kautilya's approach to corporate governance is far better since:

(i) There is no moral hazard problem implying that there are no agent's conflict costs.

(ii) CEO is ethical, competent, far-sighted and foresighted.

(iii) CEO willingly accepts a minimum subsistence salary, that is, does not behave like greedy Grasso.

(iv) Most importantly, management by pooling information and knowledge raises both the probability of success and output of every carefully chosen project. The following figure may be used to capture the advantage of Kautilya's approach over the existing approaches to corporate governance and management.

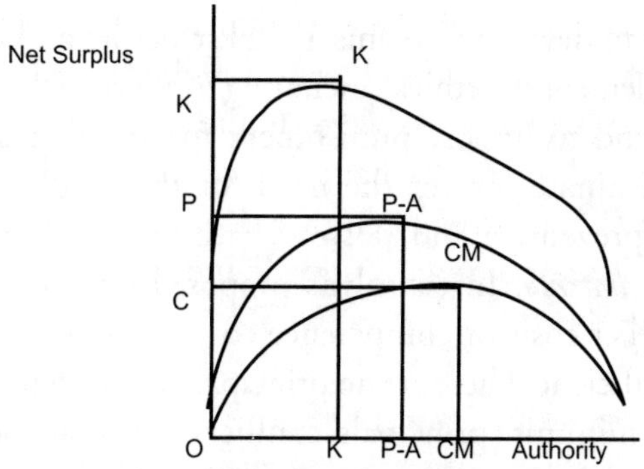

Figure 4.3: Advantage of Kautilya's Approach

OK= net surplus under Kautilya's proposal, OP =net surplus under principal-agent's incentive packages, OC = under cost minimisation suggested by Goshen and Squire (2016). PK = OK - OP=the ethical surplus

Cost-minimisation Approach: The growth potential of this approach is most likely to be less than the principal-agent approach because there are no incentives to motivate the CEO to reduce shirking.

Kautilya's Stakeholders' Model: Kautilya does not believe in the zero-sum game, that is, if the employees are paid decent wages, that does not mean the profit is lower. An ethical CEO takes care of workers and consumers in a fair way. Kautilya argues that satisfied workers produce much more than their compensation, since there is no shirking, stealing, quarrelling or colluding. An employer should learn about the need, nature and qualifications of each employee and compensate him/her accordingly. Kautilya believes that highly qualified individuals have to be paid efficiency (higher than market) wages to attract them and retain them. He thinks, middle and lower level employees are risk-averse and prefer job-security. Similarly, treating the consumers well pays off. Kautilya's Ethics-based Model: Under this approach workers are more satisfied and work harder. Similarly, consumers are more loyal.

4.4 Concluding Observations

Kautilya, being an empiricist, does not believe in fate and asserts that a person's destiny is quite in his own hands. He counts on human ingenuity to devise an organisational structure and a legal structure to complement the ethical anchoring to alleviate the moral hazard problem and to impose punishment for any digressions. His goal is to eliminate forever the need for the Godly *avatar* by internalising preventive and positive measures for imbuing governance with *dharma*. In Kautilya's proposed structure there is no agency conflict costs or competence costs since the agent is both ethical and efficient. There are no principals' competence costs either. He tries to minimise principals' conflict costs by advocating a stakeholders' model.

[10] Williamson, (1985, p 47) characterises the potential behaviour of the other firm as: 'calculated efforts to mislead, disguise, obfuscate, or otherwise confuse' and 'seeking self-interest, but they do so with guile'. He does not realise that such behaviour has created trust deficit within the firm also. Legal contracts, to a large extent, have crowded out the conscience-based commitments. Precious resources are being wasted in devising precautionary measures to protect against perceived (often imaginary) cheating/reneging. Kautilya believes that a Fiduciary duty can never replace the moral duty.

Measurement of the ethical surplus is beyond the scope of this Chapter. World's GDP in 2016 was around $75.4 Trillion (https://www.statista.com). Roughly speaking, if corporate profits were 10 per cent of the GDP and ethical surplus was 10 per cent of the profits, the magnitude of ethical surplus would have been $754 billion. It would be a major contribution if future research could devise a creative methodology to measure Kautilya's ethical surplus.

Establishing Moral Order to Prevent Government and Market Failures

CONFUCIUS (551-479 BCE) WAS a humble, ethical, foresighted, wise and religious person. He might have briefly served as a minister of justice and, also as a Prime Minister but essentially, he was a teacher. He believed in ethical education of the young. Kautilya was simple, foresighted, ethical, secular and wise. According to Indologists, he wrote his *Arthashastra*, a manual on engineering shared prosperity, during the 4th century BCE. However, new research has challenged that view and claims that he lived many centuries earlier than the fourth century BCE.[1] Both Confucius and Kautilya were original thinkers and advocated establishment of a moral order. They did not reject the legalist approach – rather considered it as complementary but not a substitute to the ethics-based approach. They firmly believed that legalist approach alone could not bring peace and prosperity for all the people.

Confucius, Kautilya and Kautilya's predecessors wanted to create a peaceful and harmonious society. They assigned a foundational role to moral order. Although Confucius primarily focused on the ethical approach, but he was not naïve to ignore the relevance of laws. Kautilya, however, along with the ethical approach, also developed cardinal principles of justice, and suggested contract laws, property rules and tort laws (see [1] Sihag 2014, Chapters, 6, 15, 16 and 17). *Both Confucius and Kautilya, believed that law and order, to a large extent, depended on good ethical conduct.* They understood the limitations of a legalist approach that did not emphasise or promote self-discipline, which could be acquired only through ethical anchoring, implying that it could never help in controlling excessive greed, the major source of corruption. *They essentially linked government failure to moral failure and market failure to government failure.* They not only had similar views on the need to establish a moral order but also had similar views on other topics. These are presented in Section 5.1.

Establishment of a moral order is essential to the creation and sharing of knowledge and, also to the reduction of transaction costs. *An opportunistic environment is not very conducive to knowledge creation and its sharing, which are the main characteristics of a knowledge-based economy.* Economists and organisational scholars believe that it is not possible ex ante to differentiate a trustworthy person from an untrustworthy one, so it is prudent to adopt a 'calculative' approach to trust, that is, treat trust as a risk. Complex contracts requiring expensive legal advice, are written to safeguard against the potential harm that might be caused by the partners' opportunism. Section 5.2 presents the need for establishing a moral order for a creative economy.

Adam Smith (1723-1790) lived at least two thousand years later than Confucius and Kautilya. He wrote two books: *Theory of Moral Sentiments* and *The Wealth of Nations*. He, just like Han Feitzu, rejected the possibility of establishing a moral order and advocated a legalist approach. He could not introduce the benevolent man of *The Theory of Moral Sentiments* to the commercial man of *The Wealth of Nations*; although some prominent economists have been trying hard to perform a civil marriage between these two unwilling adults. Recently, [2] Carsten Herrmann-Pillath (2011) compares Confucian thinking to that of Adam Smith and finds 'a number of conceptual family resemblances between the two'. Section 5.3 shows that their conceptual thinking is as much apart as the North Pole from the South Pole.

Transaction cost economics (TCE) approach to trust is a statistical approach to the building or destroying of confidence. Repeated games or familiarity breeds confidence but not necessarily trust. The common definition of trust as a person's vulnerability to the competence and benevolence of another person or party is valid only in the current amoral or legalistic environment but not in an ethical environment. Genuine trust is an ethics-intensive concept since non-violence, truthfulness, honesty and benevolence are the foundation for trust. That is, trust flourishes only in an ethical environment. How to make sure that children grow-up to be ethical adults? Ideas of Confucius and Kautilya on ethical anchoring of children is presented in Section 5.4. Final section contains concluding observations.

5.1 Confucius and Kautilya on Moral Order to Prevent Government Failure

Western countries' legalistic approach has not prevented insider trading, back-dating options, regulatory arbitrage, shadow banking, lobbyists influencing tax laws, environment laws, trade policies and many other policies. In other words, both the formulation and implementation of laws get compromised and thus adversely affect the common good. That is, legalistic approach alone cannot prevent government failure. There are too many instances where the government officers themselves participate in committing economic crimes. Additionally, legalistic approach is almost totally ineffective in preventing crimes resulting from greed, anger or lust. [3] Kautilya observed a long time ago that 'greed clouds the mind' and similarly lust and anger, the other destructive passions, overpower the reasoning faculty.

Confucius's List of Virtues: Speak the truth, do not yield to anger; give, if thou art asked for little; by these three steps thou wilt go near the gods. To practice five things under all circumstances constitutes perfect virtue; these five are gravity, generosity of soul, sincerity, earnestness, and kindness. Virtue is more to man than either water or fire. I have seen men die from treading on water and fire, but I have never seen a man die from treading the course of virtue.

Kautilya's List of Virtues: [4] Kautilya (p 107) listed ethical values as: Ahimsa [abstaining from injury to all living creatures]; satyam [truthfulness]; cleanliness; freedom from malice; compassion and tolerance.[2]

Foundational Role of Ethics: Both Confucius and Kautilya are unique in assigning a foundational role to ethics but were not naïve to ignore the importance of legalistic approach.[3] They wanted the legalistic approach to complement the ethics-based approach, not substitute it. For example, Kautilya argues that ethical environment is essential to the maintenance of law and order. [4] He (p 142) writes: 'Government by Rule of Law, which alone can guarantee security of life and welfare of the people, is, in turn, dependent on the self-discipline of the king (1.5).' He (p 106) adds, '[The observance of] one's own *dharma* leads to heaven and eternal further bliss. When *dharma* is transgressed, the resulting chaos leads to the extermination of this world'. He expands the role of ethics. He argues that ethics is the most effective catalyst in attaining salvation from poverty. He (pp. 107-108) asserts: 'For the world, when maintained in accordance with the Vedas, will ever prosper and not perish. Therefore, the king shall never allow the people to swerve from their *dharma*.'

Similarly, Confucius believes, 'The perfecting of one's self is the fundamental base of all progress and all moral development. He who exercises government by means of his virtue may be compared to the north polar star, which keeps its place and all the stars turn towards it. If the people be led by laws, and uniformity sought to be given them by punishments, they will try to avoid the punishment, but have no sense of shame. If they be led by virtue, and uniformity sought to be given them by the rules of propriety, they will have the sense of shame, and moreover will become good'. On the other hand, both Han Feitzu and Adam Smith rejected the ethics-based approach and advanced only the legalistic approach.

Confucius on Controlling Vices: When anger rises, think of the consequences. There are three things which the superior man guards against. In youth, when the physical powers are not yet settled, he guards against lust. When he is strong and the physical powers are full of vigor, he guards against quarrelsomeness. When he is old, and the animal powers are decayed, he guards against covetousness.

Kautilya on Controlling Vices: [4] Kautilya (p 137) explains,

'Vices are due to ignorance and indiscipline; an unlearned man does not perceive the injurious consequences of his vices (8.3)'. He (p 144) states: The sole aim of all branches of knowledge is to inculcate restraint over the senses (1.6.3). Self-control, which is the basis of knowledge and discipline, is acquired by giving up lust, anger, greed, conceit, arrogance and foolhardiness. Living in accordance with the *shastras* means avoiding over-indulgence in all pleasures of [the senses, i.e.,] hearing, touch, sight, taste and smell (1.6.1, 2).

Confucius on Good Governance: When a country is well governed, poverty and a mean condition are something to be ashamed of. When a country is ill governed, riches and honours are something to be ashamed of. There is good government when those who are near are made happy, and when those who are afar are attracted. To rule a country of a thousand chariots, there must be reverent attention to business, and sincerity; economy in expenditure, and love for men; and the employment of the people at the proper seasons. An oppressive government is more to be feared than a tiger.

Kautilya on Good Governance: Kautilya emphasises the provision of infrastructure, fair, clean and caring administration (see [1] Sihag, 2014, Chapter 8 for details). Kautilya (4th century BCE/2000, p 88) observes: The ruler's duties are stated to be five: punishment of the wicked, rewarding the righteous, development of state revenues by just means, impartiality in granting favours and protection of the state. He emphasises on clean administration. He (4th century BCE/1992, pp 493-494) asserts: Thus, the king shall first reform the administration, by punishing appropriately those officers who deal in wealth; they, duly corrected, shall use the right punishments to ensure the good conduct of the people of the towns and the countryside (4.9).

Confucius on Role Model: By the ruler's cultivation of his own character there is set up the example of the course which all should pursue. When superiors are fond of showing their humanity, inferiors try to outstrip one another in their practice of it. When rulers love to observe the rules of propriety, the people respond readily to the calls on them for service. If a minister makes his own conduct correct, what difficulty will he have in assisting in government? If he cannot rectify himself, what has he to do with rectifying others?

Kautilya on Role Model: He (p 147) writes: 'If the king is energetic, his subjects will be equally energetic. If he is slack and lazy in performing his duties the subjects will also be lax and, thereby, eat into his wealth. Besides, a lazy king will easily fall into the hands of his enemies. Hence, the king should himself always be energetic (1.19).' He (p 121) states: 'A king endowed with the ideal personal qualities enriches the other elements when they are less than perfect (6.1).' He (p 123) adds, 'Whatever character the king has, the other elements also come to have the same (8.1)'.

Confucius on Bounded Rationality: Ability will never catch up with the demand for it.

To know what you know and what you do not know, that is true knowledge. Real knowledge is to know the extent of one's ignorance. The superior man is distressed by his want of ability. He is not distressed by men's not knowing him.

Kautilya on Bounded Rationality: A king can reign only with the help of others; one wheel alone does not move a chariot. Therefore, a king should appoint advisers (as counsellors and ministers) and listen to their advice. Kautilya (p177).

Confucius on the Role of Foresightedness: If a man takes no thought about what is distant, he will find sorrow near at hand. He who does not anticipate attempts to deceive him, nor think beforehand of his not being believed, and yet apprehends these things readily (when they occur); – is he not a man of superior worth?

Kautilya on the Role of Foresightedness: In the interests of the prosperity of the country, a king should be diligent in foreseeing the possibility of calamities, try to avert them before they arise, overcome those which happen, remove all obstructions to economic activity and prevent loss of revenue to the state (8.4). [4] Kautilya (4th Century BCE, p 116).

5.2 Relevance of a Moral Order to a Creative Economy

Trust Key to Creation and Sharing of Knowledge: [5] Lukasz Hardt (2009) discusses the transaction cost economics (TCE) in a knowledge-based economy, which he labels as a second cognitive turn. He (p 44) remarks, 'Therefore, when problems are non-decomposable, searching best takes place within the firm, and when they are decomposable the market will be a more efficient machine for organizing searching. In this approach the firm is able to produce valuable knowledge (or, in other words, to solve problems)'. Note, the above statement explains the efficiency gains in 'organising searching' and producing knowledge by a firm. However, the level of positive gains from creation and sharing of knowledge depend on the level of trust since it is the mutual trust which binds the knowledge workers together.

Characteristics of a Knowledge-based Economy: First, a knowledge-based economy may be characterised as one in which intangibles are more valuable than the tangibles. Innovation is the source of survival and sustainable economic growth, that is, innovate or perish. Knowledge-intensity in almost every product/service is relatively higher and rising. Knowledge has characteristics of a public good and usually there exists more tacit knowledge than explicit knowledge. Second, a creative economy is very different from an industrial economy. Knowledge workers need flexibility and the old assembly line approach, which was labeled as Fordism, does not work. Third, the market for ideas is, at best, imperfect. The buyer does not know what s/he is buying, and the seller does not know what s/he is selling, since the potential of an idea is never known with certainty.

Critical Role of Trust in a Knowledge-based Economy: Trust may be an intangible asset/good but has the most tangible role in creating and sustaining the social, economic, cultural and political structures. It is the brick and mortar to the building of inter-personal relationships. In an industrial economy, trust (a) reduces transaction costs by reducing opportunism, enhances a feeling of wellness by reducing anxiety and (b) also might increase GDP by reducing the demand for lawyers and turning them into engineers.

Emphasis on the Power of Pooling Knowledge and Information: Kautilya's predecessors understood the importance of sharing information and knowledge to arrive at the most efficient decision. However, trust is the most valuable asset in a knowledge-based economy. Both creation and sharing of ideas depend on trust. The distinguishing characteristic of a knowledge-based economy is a frequent sharing of tacit knowledge and exchange of information among the cognitive labour. As soon as a person codifies his/her tacit knowledge everyone has access to it. Knowing this fact, a person will share tacit knowledge only if s/he is sure of not getting fired. It is indicated in section 5.4 below that creating ethics-based trust is the key to realising all the potential gains from creating and sharing of knowledge.

[6] Williamson (1985, p 47) characterises the potential behaviour of the other firm as: 'calculated efforts to mislead, disguise, obfuscate, or otherwise confuse' and 'seeking self-interest, but they do so with guile'. In the prevailing opportunistic and legalistic environment, it is naïve or even foolish to trust anyone since that is too risky. Interestingly, Machiavelli had very similar views. [7] He (1513, p 52) wrote, 'For, of men one can, in general, say this: They are ungrateful, fickle, deceptive and deceiving, avoiders of danger, eager to gain'. He continues, 'Men are less nervous of offending someone who makes himself lovable, than someone who makes himself frightening. For love attaches men by ties of obligation, which, since men are wicked, they break whenever their interests are at stake'. He (p 73) adds, 'This is how it has to be, for you will find men are always wicked, unless you give them no alternative but to be good'.

Trust and Transaction Costs: Compared to a moral society, an amoral or immoral society incurs increasingly burdensome transaction costs as a prudent person or firm cannot afford not to undertake protective measures. Consequently, each firm ends up devoting a considerable amount of resources to protect itself against opportunism. Everyone tries to outsmart the other party to the contract by negotiating and writing a good contract, which leaves no room for conscience or compassion. The increasing share of transaction sector, the rising number of tort cases, increasing cost of defensive medical practice, rising cost of enforcement indicate that, may be in the long run, such rising transaction costs will make the purely contract-based economies lose their competitive edge.

It may also be noted that the relational contracts are experience-based and are not based on any ethical foundation, implying they may not create any trust and thus the possibility of opportune behavior is not precluded. Secondly, relational contract may lead to poor quality as one party may too readily accommodate the requests of the other party. For example, Ford Motors and Firestone Tires Company had almost 100 years of business relationship and consequently Firestone Tires Company was not strict on requiring Ford Motors to maintain the desired air pressure in the tires and thus compromising safety, that is, their relationship had become too cozy. Both companies were sued and the costs of litigation and compensation to the consumers were huge. Additionally, reliance on contracts alone might cause an erosion of ethical values (called crowding out).

5.3 Adam Smith on Infeasibility of Moral Order

Adam Smith's *Theory of Moral Sentiments* has over 400 pages but does not explain the concept of virtue and does not assign any foundational role to virtue ethics.[4] [8] Adam Smith ([1790] 1982, VII.1.2, p 265) states, 'In treating of the principles of morals there are two questions to be considered. First, wherein does virtue consist of? Or what is the tone of temper, and tenour of conduct, which constitutes the excellent and praise-worthy character, the character which is the natural object of esteem, honour, and approbation?[5] And secondly, by what power or faculty in the mind is it, that this character, whatever it be, is recommended to us? Or in other words, how and by what means does it come to pass, that the mind prefers one tenour of conduct to another, denominates the one right and the other wrong; considers the one as the object of approbation, honour, and reward, and the other of blame, censure, and punishment'.

[9] Raphael (2007, pp 71-72) comments, 'Smith gives us a full and clear account of the content of virtue, that is, the cardinal virtues and the relation between them, but fails to provide an enlightening explanation of the concept itself, as he does with the topic of moral judgement. Such an explanation would show how the concept of moral virtue arises and how it distinguishes moral excellence from other forms of human excellence'. Apparently, according to Raphael, Adam Smith's *The Theory of Moral Sentiments* has essentially no theory, implying that the controversy over 'Adam Smith's problem' is a futile one. Also, lack of a theory, perhaps has been one big reason that only economists have shown such an interest in it.

Adam Smith assigned no Foundational Role to Virtue Ethics: Adam Smith ([1790] 1982, II. ii. 3. 3-4) believes, 'Beneficence, therefore, is less essential to the existence of society than justice. Society may subsist, though not in the most comfortable state, without beneficence; but the prevalence of injustice must utterly destroy it'. He added, 'It is the ornament which embellishes, not the foundation which supports the building, and which it was, therefore, sufficient to recommend, but by no means necessary to impose'. Adam Smith ([1790] 1982, II. ii. 3.4) argued, 'Justice, on the contrary, is the main pillar that upholds the whole edifice, if it is removed, the great, the immense fabric of human society must in a moment crumble into atoms.'

According to Adam Smith, 'prevalence of injustice' would destroy the edifice. However, he does not realise that lack of ethics is the sole source of injustice, discrimination, infringement, slavery and suppression. Adam Smith gives justice a foundational status but does not explain how to construct it and what upholds this pillar. A few remarks are in order. First, the pillar must be standing on the solid rock of *dharma*, (ethics) otherwise it will be unstable. That is, justice in an unethical society is unattainable. Second, if justice has to serve as the main pillar, then it must be strong enough to support the edifice. However, it will not be strong unless it is constructed with the bricks and mortar of *dharmic* (ethical) values. Finally, it appears as if the pillar and the edifice are two separate entities and not components of one system. Every society decides both the pillar and the edifice together, but Adam Smith's approach does not allow any possible interaction or interdependence between them.

[10] James Halteman and Edd Noell (2012) explore Adam Smith's ideas on ethics. They (p 76) remark, 'The social passions are generosity, compassion, and esteem. They are inherently good and bring forth virtuous behaviour, but they are also scarce and not prevalent enough in everyday life to serve as the foundation of a successful social order'. Clearly, Smith did not have a positive view of people and did not suggest any ethical education to make them ethical. His approach essentially was legalistic and very similar to that of Han Feitzu (280-233 BCE), another thinker from ancient China.

[11] Chang (1987) explores the contributions of Confucius (551-479 BCE), a moral philosopher and Han Feitzu (280-233 BCE), a legalist. Chang remarks, 'The Confucian state is established on a set of ethical norms and rites – rules, ceremonies, and manners codified by legendry sages – and governed by men through moral influence, rather than law, coercion, or by divine spirits.' Chang adds: Another outstanding legalist was Han-fei-tsu (280-233 BC), a theoretician and a disciple of Hsun-tzu. Following his teacher, Han-fei-tzu believed that basically people were motivated largely by self-interest. For the sake of social order and economic progress, Han-fei-tzu proposed strict and uniform application of rewards and punishments and rejected Confucian egalitarianism. In his view, chances for success under Confucianism were far less than under Legalism. In his assessment, the former would function well only if individuals are guided by morality and rulers are sage kings, but in reality, individuals are guided overwhelmingly by self-interest and rulers are mostly average kings. On the contrary, Legalism, along with its laws and regulations designed for the good of the whole society headed by an average ruler, offers a greater chance of success.

Similarly, [12] Choi (1989) points out, 'Han Feitzu repeatedly argued against Confucians (moralists) and showed that proposals based on moral grounds, though eloquent, inevitably resulted in absurdity if not outright undesirability'.

5.4 Confucius and Kautilya on Ethical Anchoring of the Young

Both Confucius and Kautilya were optimistic and believed that an ethical environment could be created. There was rampant corruption during their times and they were aware of the existing conditions. Their ultimate objective was to establish a moral order, may be in a generation or two, which ensured a richer and fuller life to everyone in the society. They argued that was possible only through ethical grounding of the young. As mentioned earlier, they were not against the legalistic approach for handling the existing situations.

Confucius on Ethical Anchoring: The mechanic that would perfect his work must first sharpen his tools. A youth, when at home, should be filial and, abroad, respectful to his elders. He should be earnest and truthful. He should overflow in love to all and cultivate the friendship of the good. When he has time and opportunity, after the performance of these things, he should employ them in polite studies.

Kautilya on Ethical Anchoring: Kautilya (p 137) believes, 'Vices are due to ignorance and indiscipline; an unlearned man does not perceive the injurious consequences of his vices (8.3)'. He (p 144) states, 'The sole aim of all branches of knowledge is to inculcate restraint over the senses (1.6.3). Self-control, which is the basis of knowledge and discipline, is acquired by giving up lust, anger, greed, conceit, arrogance and foolhardiness. Living in accordance with the *shastras* means avoiding over-indulgence in all pleasures of [the senses, i.e.,] hearing, touch, sight, taste and smell (1.6.1, 2)'. He (p 155-156) adds: 'There can be no greater crime or sin', says Kautilya, 'than making wicked impressions on an innocent mind'. Just as a clean object is stained with whatever is smeared on it, so a prince, with a fresh mind, understands as the truth whatever is taught to him. Therefore, a prince should be taught what is dharma and artha, not what is unrighteous and materially harmful (1.17).

Strengthening and Sustaining Ethical Values: Company of disciplined individuals, particularly of elders was considered important in strengthening ethical values and conduct. Kautilya (p 143) suggests, 'With a view to improving his self-discipline, he should always associate with learned elders, for in them alone has discipline its firm roots (1.5)'. Similarly, Confucius suggests:He who aims to be a man of complete virtue in his food does not seek to gratify his appetite, nor in his dwelling place does he seek the appliances of ease; he is earnest in what he is doing, and careful in his speech; he frequents the company of men of principle that he may be rectified – such a person may be said indeed to love to learn.

5.5 Concluding Observations

Ethical environment encourages both trust and transparency, which help in changing the 'culture of suspicion' and thus in reducing the need to take defensive measures. In recent years the words transparency and accountability have taken hold of our imagination. Transparency is understood as the full and accurate disclosure of relevant information in a simple format and timely fashion. Almost exclusively, the emphasis has been on rule-based transparency, such as 'public's right to know' legislations regarding shareholders' right to know how much a CEO gets paid and consumers' right to know the calories or fat content in the meals, restaurants serve. Similarly, many regulatory agencies have been created to protect against the trust deficit rather than to eliminate the trust-deficit.

There has been very little, if any, emphasis or effort on the ethics-based transparency or trust. Honest, truthful and fair-minded individuals do not see the need to hide any information from any one. Similarly, ethical corporations do not engage in the practices of cooking the books for defrauding the stakeholders. Ethics-based transparency provides two types of benefits: it allows consumers and investors in allocating their resources in an optimal way and governments need not spend any time writing disclosure rules and devoting resources to enforcing them (i.e. it improves efficiency and lowers transaction costs). Rules-based transparency should be considered only as a complement to the ethics-based transparency.

Finally, according to both Confucius and Kautilya, creation of ethical environment may be essential to improving the environment. They would have strongly recommended holding conferences in New Delhi or Beijing, like the one just concluded in Paris, on creating ethical environment for solving problem of global warming fairly and expediently.

Ideas on Curbing Corruption

KAUTILYA WAS deeply influenced by the *Mahabharata* (3102 BCE) and it appears as if it had happened in not too distant a past. Secondly, Rao (1973) points out that the measurements used in the *Arthashastra* are very similar to those prevalent during the Sindhu–Sarasvati Civilisation (2600 BCE-1800 BCE).[1] According to the new research, Chandragupta Maurya ruled around 1534 BCE and not during the 4th century BCE. The preponderance of emerging evidence indicates that Kautilya wrote his *Arthashastra* - science of wealth and welfare – several centuries earlier than the fourth century BCE which has been advanced by western Indologists. They had taken upon themselves the selfless and tortuous task of dating, without any margin of error, all the historical events, such as the Aryan Invasion Theory and providing authentic interpretations of our ancient texts. They really need their well-deserved retirement from this demanding responsibility and leave it to the native amateurs.

Kautilya was far-sighted, foresighted, ethical but not very religious, believed in designing an efficient organisational structure but was not a bureaucrat. According to him, law should promote economic efficiency and ethical conduct. His *Arthashastra* is a world heritage and source of national pride. He believed in flexibility but subject to fairness. He suggested both preventive and remedial measures to handle corruption, any threat to national security or threat arising from natural calamity, such as famine, flood or fire.

His insights, such as an ounce of ethics is better than a ton of laws; market failure is bad, government failure is worse, but the moral failure is the worst, are as relevant today as they were in his time.

North (1990, 1995) defines institutions as rules of the game, that is, formal rules and regulations, such as a Constitution and informal rules, such as social norms, which constrain the socially unacceptable behavior of individuals.[2] Since the '90s, a considerable amount of intellectual effort has been devoted to study the relationship between institutions and economic growth. Some economists claim that institutions are the most important determinant of economic growth. In fact, these economists call institutions as the 'deep determinants' of growth. However, Kautilya argues that dharmic (ethical) conduct, not institutions, is the 'deep determinant' of economic growth, since, according to Kautilya, only ethical decision-makers create good institutions by putting public interest at par or ahead of their own personal interests. We are indebted to the framers of our democratic Constitution. However, the Constituent Assembly could have benefited from Kautilya's advice in several other respects. He sugests that (i) all possible preventive and remedial measures be undertaken to handle the ever-present threat of corruption, (ii) keeping an eye on heads of villages and departments to prevent them from extracting bribes, (iii) one should learn even from a child, implying that the framers of the Indian Constitution should have paid attention to the experiences of other countries, and (iv) try to eliminate avoidable conflicts of interest situations. This is presented in Section 6.1.

The Constituent Assembly copied the western legalistic approach that has essentially eliminated the role of conscience.

Kautilya emphasises that legalistic approach is only to complement the ethics-based approach and not to substitute it. His ideas for making provisions for ethical, not religious education of children should have been incorporated into the Constitution, and they are presented in Section 6.2. He understood the power of incentives, interests and institutions and how each one influenced the others and how in turn each one was influenced by them. His ideas on motivating the decision-makers to do the right thing are collected in Section 6.3. The final Section contains concluding observations.

6.1 Kautilya's Legalist Approach to Improving Institutions

> The ruler's duties are stated to be five: punishment of the wicked, rewarding the righteous, development of state revenues by just means, impartiality in granting favors and protection of the state.
>
> **—Kautilya**

Kautilya's *Arthashastra* is a manual on how to promote *Yogakshema* – peaceful enjoyment of prosperity – of all the people. Kautilya put heavy emphasis on building infrastructure, such as roads, water works to promote growth in the private sector. He believes in raising the tax revenue by increasing income through expanding the productive capacity of the economy rather than by raising the tax rate. The increased tax revenue is to be used to further increase the productive capacity of the economy and consequently income and that in turn tax revenue. In other words, he believes in the virtuous cycle: higher income resulting in higher tax revenue and that in turn to higher income by building infrastructure with the tax revenue. He understood that the virtuous cycle happens only if the taxpayers pay their taxes fully and the government officials put the tax revenue to the most productive projects and do not siphon off the tax revenue for personal uses. According to him, corruption is a major threat to bringing prosperity and should not be taken lightly. His observations related to corruption are truly insightful. Some of those are:

(a) *Resisting the temptation to embezzle is hard*: If you put halva (pudding) or honey at someone's tongue, it is hard not to swallow it. He insists on appointing individuals of impeccable character to posts that handle revenue to minimise the threat of corruption. Kautilya (p 281) writes: Just as it is impossible not to taste honey or poison that one may find at the tip of one's tongue, so it is impossible for one dealing with government funds not to taste, at least a little bit, of the King's wealth (2.9.32).

(b) *Its detection is even harder*: Note, there were no Swiss banks at the time, yet it was not easy to detect corruption. Kautilya (p 283), observs: It is possible to know even the path of birds flying in the sky but not the ways of government servants who hide their [dishonest] income (2.9.34).

He (p 281) adds, 'Just as it is impossible to know when a fish moving in water is drinking it, so it is impossible to find out when government servants in charge of undertakings misappropriate money (2.9.33)'. In a democratic system like ours, the term 'government servant' should be taken to embrace the political executive (ministers) as well; Supreme Court has treated them under the category 'public servants'.

(c) *Identification of those who could be Corrupt*: Kautilya (p 221) points out, 'There are thirteen types of undesirable persons who amass wealth secretly by causing injury to the population. [These are: corrupt judges and magistrates, heads of villages or departments who extort money from the public, perjurers and procurers of perjury, those who practice witchcraft, black magic or sorcery, poisoners, narcotic dealers, counterfeiters and adulterators of precious metals]. When they are exposed by secret agents, they shall either be exiled or made to pay adequate compensation proportionate to the gravity of the offense (4.4)'.

No one should be surprised at the current level of moral decay and resultant corruption. Kautilya would have predicted it since no effective measures were taken to prevent it. The question boils down to: how we are going to prevent a Chief Minister, Minister or a party chief from becoming a thief? That is, how are we going to take away the key to the treasure from a thief or stop a public servant from causing harm to the system by bending it to accommodate personal interests?

Kautilya on Minimising Scope for Conflicts of Interest: Kautilya proposes the establishment of two very important offices to monitor and manage the financial health of the state: the positions of a Treasurer and a Chief Comptroller-Auditor. They are very well paid, and in turn they must be incorruptible and efficient. Creation of two independent positions reduce the scope for corruption. Suppose the Auditor is subordinate to the Treasure and the Treasurer is corrupt and steals from the Treasury. the Auditor might be too afraid to report to the king. Also, the Treasure might ask the Auditor not to audit certain units. This is precisely the situation faced today. For example, if the Home Minister is corrupt, the CBI as part of Home Ministry, needs his permission to investigate him or any other corrupt person/entity, in the current prevalent system. This is clearly a case of conflicts of interest. Kautilya (p 200) writes: No one who belongs to the side likely to be adversely affected by the project shall be consulted (1.15.46). Our rules stipulate otherwise.

Corruption was rampant in England during the 18th century. Alfred Marshall, a British economist, provided an explanation why it had declined. He (1925, pp 335-336) believed, 'The people are now able to rule their rulers and check class abuse of power and privilege, in a way which was impossible before the days of general education and a general surplus of energy over that required for earning a living'.

Mackenzie and Hafken (2002) describe level of corruption in USA during President Lincoln's time. They (p 10) note, 'The enterprises of fielding, equipping, and supplying the Union forces were littered with payoffs and kickbacks and rip-offs. Middlemen bribed public officials to get contracts for their clients, vessels chartered by the government never left port, and goods delivered under government contract often fell short of the negotiated standards'. They quote the report of a House investigating committee (1862), 'such gross and unblushing frauds would have cost those who participated in them their heads under any system than our own'. They describe the post-Civil war period when the industrial revolution in America was in full swing. They (p 10) add, 'In politics, patronage was king, and government service seemed but one more avenue to the cornucopia of opportunities that filled the era. Historian Vernon Louis Parrington compared the "come and get it" morality of the time to a "Great Barbeque"'.

According to the original American Constitution, which was introduced in 1787, Senate members, just like our Rajya Sabha members, were elected/selected by the State legislatures and that, just like in our country, had allowed all sorts of corruption. Public there could not tolerate the blatant corruption and campaigned successfully to amend the Constitution and introduce direct election of Senate Members. Similarly, under public pressure the primaries for all the legislatures were introduced in the USA.

Political Reforms in India: Framers of our Constitution had this information and could have benefited from it, had they wanted to. The following changes to the Constitution may have reduce the scope for corruption: (i) Public should decide who gets the ticket, not the bosses of political parties in New Delhi or in State capitals. In the short run that is the only (until people become politically mature and discerning) way that criminals can be prevented from getting party tickets by paying crores of rupees to the designated handler. (ii) Rajya Sabha members should also be elected by the public and not by the State legislators, who are openly bought. (iii) CBI and other investigative agencies should be made genuinely autonomous entities under reasonable social control; their Heads should not be civil servants, who were likely to behave like 'caged parrots'. (iv) Any public servant, who receives bribe and / or misuses his authority against public good (not the person who is forced to give bribe), should be prosecuted.

6.2 Character-building Essential to Nation-building

Kautilya put heavy emphasis on ethical environment. According to him, if there are no ethics there is no society and no prosperity. He repeatedly returns to this theme. He (p 142) writes, 'Government by Rule of Law, which alone can guarantee security of life and welfare of the people, is, in turn, dependent on the self-discipline of the king (1.5)'. That is, if rulers are not ethical, there will be no rule of law and it will be unlikely for a country to attain its potential level of prosperity. On the other hand, he asserts, 'For the world, when maintained in accordance with the Vedas, will ever prosper and not perish. Therefore, the king shall never allow the people to swerve from their dharma'. He (p 141) also warns, 'A king who flouts the teachings of the *Dharamshastras* and The *Arthashastra*, ruins the kingdom by his own injustice (8.2.12)'.

However, despite explicit warnings by Kautilya, our Constituent Assembly did not foresee the possibility of moral decay and rampant corruption and consequently, did not include any provision to maintain or strengthen the moral fabric of our society.

Adoption of the western legalistic approach provides some relief but over time, politicians find ways to circumvent the laws as they have done in USA. Clearly, Kautilya's goal of creating a nation free of crimes and corruption cannot be realised with a legalistic approach as such. According to him, crimes of passions arising from anger, greed or lust, can effectively be curtailed only by self-discipline acquired through ethical anchoring and not by laws, even if these were forcefully implemented. For example, he writes, 'Greed clouds the mind', that is, a greedy person loses his logical ability to foresee its destructive consequences. He (p 137) believes, 'Vices are due to ignorance and indiscipline; an unlearned man does not perceive the injurious consequences of his vices (8.3)'.

He (p 144) states: The sole aim of all branches of knowledge is to inculcate restraint over the senses (1.6.3). Self-control, which is the basis of knowledge and discipline, is acquired by giving up lust, anger, greed, conceit, arrogance and foolhardiness. Living in accordance with the *shastras* means avoiding over-indulgence in all pleasures of [the senses, i.e.,] hearing, touch, sight, taste and smell (1.6.1, 2).

Secondly, according to Indian traditions, the emphasis is on (i) that a defendant admitted his guilt in public and (ii) willingly performed penance. Robert Lingat (1967/2004, p 64) notes, 'Penance inflicted on the wrongdoer often provides a kind of public reparation for the victim, sufficient to assuage his desire for vengeance. Occasionally, too, the penance devised takes into account reparation to the victim'. India's current legal system does not allow any role for an apology or repentance. Canada, perhaps, is the only country that has recently started experimenting by incorporating the role of an apology. In India too, emphasis should be put on community service and ethical training.

Thirdly, Kautilya was not religious but very ethical and secular and strongly advocated both since he did not find any conflict between them. Somehow, the framers of India's Constitution incorrectly equated ethics with religion and therefore, believed that these were incompatible with each other and strangely ended up undermining both, the ethical and secular fabric of India's society.

Ethical Anchoring of Children: According to Kautilya, it is better to pass on good values rather than ill-gotten wealth to the younger generation. If we insist on labeling reforms as the 'first generation' reforms and 'second generation' reforms, Kautilya might suggest a more appropriate distinction: to undertake reforms of the 'old generation', which is running the country and whose unethical behaviour is casting a long shadow on the character building of the younger generation.

Kautilya (pp 155-156) writes: 'There can be no greater crime or sin than making wicked impressions on an innocent mind. Just as a clean object is stained with whatever is smeared on it, so a prince, with a fresh mind, understands as the truth whatever is taug'.. .o him. Therefore, a prince should be taught what is dharma and artha, not what is unrighteous and materially harmful (1.17).

In a democratic country every child is a prince. Moreover, Kautilya (p 123) points out, 'Whatever character the king has, the other elements also come to have the same (8.1)'.

Kautilya advocates teaching and practicing of non-violence, compassion, truthfulness, tolerance, malice against none and cleanliness for creating an ethical society in which everyone can enjoy prosperity and security. These are secular values and do not promote or offend any religion. Ethical training should be made mandatory just like other basic subjects.

6.3 Kautilya on Motivating Decision-makers to Do the Right Thing

> The miser should be won over by means of wealth, the proud man by offering respect, the fool by flattery, and the learned one by truthfulness.
>
> **—Kautilya**

Everyone acknowledges Kautilya as the king-maker but hardly anyone knows or acknowledges him as a maker of his age. Kautilya envisioned a prosperous, secure, crime-free and secular nation and his *Arthashastra* is a manual for realising that vision. He does not believe in getting things done by breaking or twisting someone's arm since he knows that the twisted behaviour will come back as soon as the arm is let go. Instead, he believes in the power of persuasion and incentives to harness and channelise the private interest to serve the public interest also.

Actually, understanding the distinction between private interest and public interest goes back, at least, to Lord Rama's times. He often sacrificed his personal interest to protect and promote public interest. At that time, self-discipline acquired through ethical anchoring, was the sole instrument relied upon to put public interest at par or ahead of the private interest.

Ancient sages wanted to create a harmonious, peaceful and caring society. They identified the system-creating virtues and system-destroying vices. For example, Apastamba [Olivelle (1999, p 34)] wrote, 'Refraining from anger, excitement, rage, greed, perplexity, hypocrisy, and malice, speaking the truth; refraining from overeating, calumny, and envy; sharing, liberality, rectitude, gentleness, self-control, amity with all creatures,... benevolence and contentment'. He surmised that if a person wanted to go to heaven, he must lead a virtuous life, perform good deeds and control vices, that is, he could not go to heaven unless he created heaven on earth. Thus, the motivation to go to heaven aligned private interest to public interest (see Sihag, 2014, Chapter 6 for more details). Kautilya extended his approach of aligning private interest to public interest for bringing both peace and prosperity.

Apastamba and other ancient sages essentially focused on identifying and promoting system-building ethical values and controlling system-destroying vices. Kautilya, just like his predecessors, whole-heartedly accepts and promotes ethical anchoring, but complements that with persuasion and material incentives to channelise private interest to serve the public interest.

He adds conflicts of interest to that of his predecessors' list. He realises that certain activities are in public interest, such as making charitable contributions, doing good deeds, taking risks to defend the motherland but not in private interest. And similarly, some activities are in private interest but against public interest, such as insider trading, financial manipulation, regulatory arbitrage and lobbying (see Chapter 1 for an in-depth analysis).

Moral Duty: According to Kautilya, it is the moral duty of the rulers to protect and promote public interest and they will be rewarded with residence in heaven. He (p 377) writes: A king who observes his duty of protecting his people justly and according to law will go to heaven, whereas one who does not protect them or inflicts unjust punishment will not (3.1.42).

The legislators are the trustees and they should devote themselves to advance their voters' interests. Kautilya (p 149) states, 'In the happiness of his subjects lies his happiness; in their welfare his welfare. He shall not consider as good only that which pleases him but treat as beneficial to him whatever pleases his subjects (1.19)'. The older generations got us the freedom and gave India a Constitution. Now it is the moral duty of the current generation of leaders to amend the Constitution and promote Yogakshema for all the people.

Self-interest: According to Kautilya, the public does not tolerate injustice and poverty for too long. CBI prosecuting selectively and similarly, the Income Tx Department auditing selectively and often opponents of the ruling party, will not be tolerated for too long. Additionally, nothing gets done without greasing the palms. This is not a sustainable situation. Kautilya (p 133) described the existing conditions during Nanda's rule as: A decadent king, on the other hand, oppresses the people by demanding gifts, seizing what he wants and grabbing for himself and his favourites the produce of the country [i.e. the king and his coterie consume more than their due share, thus considerably impoverishing the treasury and the people.] (8.4).

He (p 159) adds that such a king: Ignores the good [people] and favours the wicked, causes harm by new unrighteous practices; neglects the observation of the proper and righteous practices; *suppresses dharma and propagates adharma*; does what ought not to be done and fails to do what ought to be done; fails to give what ought to be given and exacts what he cannot rightly take; 'indulges in wasteful expenditure and destroys profitable undertakings'; *does not punish those who ought to be punished but punishes those who do not deserve to be*; arrests those who should not be arrested but fails to arrest who should be seized; '*fails to protect the people from thieves and robs them himself*'; 'does not recompense service done to him'; 'does not carry out his part of what had been agreed upon' '*by his indolence and negligence destroys the welfare of his people*' (7.5).

Situation now may not be much different from Nanda's rule. No one needs reminding as to what happened to Nanda's kingdom. There is only a short window to do the right things. That is, it is a matter of a few years and not decades, people will start agitations against the poor governance and rampant corruption. It may appear calm before a tsunami. No one can predict or control the level of violence and destruction of property from agitations. It is in the interest of sitting legislators to amend the Constitution and protect themselves from the fury of public anger. On the other hand, if they do the right thing, people will honour them and reward them with a lifelong opportunity to maintain their current status.

Incentives: Kautilya believes that those who make sacrifices for a common good or for protecting the country should be showered with honours and awards. He (p 272) writes, 'The King may also ask the rich to give as much gold as they can, either voluntarily or in expectation of favours. Honours and status symbols (umbrella, headgear, decorations) may be bestowed on them in return for gold (5.2.35, 36)'. If the sitting legislators carry out all the necessary amendments to the Constitution, they should be awarded Tamra Patars and may be an extra year of tenure as it will be an historic, courageous and selfless act that will finally liberate us from the colonial mind-set.

6.4 Concluding Observations

Kautilya's goal was to create a society without any crimes and corruption.

According to him, some mandatory courses on ethics should be introduced in the primary and high schools. Secular values, such as honesty, non-violence (both physical and financial), truthfulness, compassion, tolerance and cleanliness should be instilled into our children. That is the most reliable method to eliminate corruption and a purely legalistic approach can never succeed in preventing crimes or corruption. It has not succeeded in the so-called advanced countries, why should anybody think it will in India? Legislators should know agitations for change are inevitable and often involve violence and destruction. Why wait for that to happen? Introduction of primaries, direct election of Rajya Sabha members, ethical anchoring and prosecution of only the official who accepts bribes, and not the person who has to give bribes under pressure or intimidation, are some necessary steps in good governance.

When a drunk driver runs over sleeping children, and where grabbing rather than giving has become a standard practice, that is not the India any one of us want. Let us remove the dust over our *atamans* that has been accumulating for some time. We should not copy the west. We should develop self-discipline to overcome the destructive vices of lust, anger and greed. We are blessed with enormous energy, divine hearts, super intelligence and multiple talents. We can build a spiritually and materially strong Nation that would be an envy of the world. It is doable. But this time, we must be vigilant that no one dares cast an evil eye on our country. Also, we must keep in mind that the current situation did not arise overnight, and it will not improve overnight. It will take several years of sustained effort to get rid of the current unhealthy situation.

PART TWO

Exposing Chauvinism in Euro-Cetric' History of Economic Thought

IT HAS been a standard practice to give credit only to the thinker who originates an idea, and not to the one who copies it and tries to claim proprietorship. Adam Smith's *Wealth of Nations* does not contain a single original idea. There is evidence that he lifted ideas from other works, yet he has been erroneously declared as the founder of economics. Instead of correcting this error, concerted and coordinated efforts have been made over the last two hundred years and are still continuing in perpetuating it. Kautilya established economics as a full-fledged and separate discipline during the fourth century BCE, implying that Economics was older than the great-great grandmother of Adam Smith. How could Smith be the father of economics? Similarly, other outlandish/exaggerated claims, such as that (a) there was no transmission of Kautilya's ideas to Europe, (b) Fibonacci was the first financial engineer, (c) Graunt and Petty were the founders of statistics and (d) mathematical economics is only of recent origin, have been made. It is shown that all these claims are patently false. An attempt is made to set those records straight.

Fairness requires that acknowledgement be given only to the thinker, who originates an idea and not to the one, who copies it and tries to claim proprietorship. Adam Smith was erroneously declared as the founder of economics and instead of correcting the error, concerted and coordinated efforts have been made over the last two hundred years.

Arthashastra: A Recognisable Source of *The Wealth of Nations*

IT IS truly astounding that there is almost a consensus that the *Wealth of Nations* does not contain anything that may qualify as original. Adam Smith merely collected materials from various sources. Often, he expressed the borrowed material in his own language and, also tried to synthesise it, although with some inconsistencies.[1] Sometimes, he acknowledged his sources, and other times the honorable Doctor concealed them, assuming, perhaps that no one would bother to find that out. That proved to be an unrealistic assumption, particularly when the source was too obvious to be concealed. As an illustration, in emphasising the importance of division of labour, he used the example of the pin-factory, that *Wealth of Nations* did not acknowledge but reproduced from the French *Encyclopédie* (1755).[2]

Adam Smith borrowed key ideas both from western and non-western sources but avoided acknowledging them.[3] If his borrowed feathers were returned to the owners, the unearned title of 'father of economics' would also fly away with the feathers.

Adam Smith personally supervised the burning of his confidential papers to destroy not just his incomplete manuscripts but also evidence related to his sources. Nevertheless, at least in three areas, Adam Smith's debt to Kautilya is clearly recognisable: (a) identification of land, labour and capital as the sources of economic growth; (b) the four canons of taxation: (i) certainty of tax liability, (ii) tax liability in proportion to benefit (income), (iii) economy in collection, and (iv) convenience to the tax payer in making payment; and (c) undesirability of monopolies.

Section 7.2 presents paragraphs related to the sources of growth from Kautilya's *Arthashastra* and from Adam Smith's *Wealth of Nations*. Paragraphs related to the four canons of taxation are presented in Section 7.3. Kautilya's and Adam Smith's views on the undesirability of monopolies are presented in Section 7.4. Final Section contains some concluding observations. Section 7.1 briefly presents the respective scopes of *The Arthashastra* and *The Wealth of Nations*.

7.1 Kautilya and Adam Smith on the Scope of Economics

Scope of The Arthashastra: Kautilya considered his *Arthashastra* as a manual on engineering *Yogakshema* – peaceful enjoyment of prosperity – for all the people. The concept of *Yogakshema* is much broader and holistic than the currently used concept of 'human security'. Capitalism was emerging, and both urbanisation and monetisation were increasing in the Indian subcontinent at Kautilya's time.[4] Keeping those trends in view, Kautilya proposed a judicious mix of visible and invisible hands.

He understood the allocative role of prices.[5] He suggests incentives to promote economic growth in the private sector. At that time, Kings used to spend most of the tax revenue on building luxurious palaces and very little on building infrastructure. However, Kautilya (p 149) suggests, 'Hence the king shall be ever active in the management of the economy. The root of wealth is economic activity and lack of it brings material distress. In the absence of fruitful economic activity, both current prosperity and future growth are in danger of destruction. A king can achieve the desired objectives and abundance of riches by undertaking productive economic activity (1.19)'.

He suggess building roads, water works, 'remove all obstructions to economic activity' and create an ethical environment. He identifies (i) capital, labour and land as the sources of economic growth, (ii) suggests incentives to encourage supplies of these inputs, (iii) devises a tax system that includes not only the principles of taxation and a piecewise linear income tax but also measures for compliance and (iv) formulates laws that promote economic efficiency and the ethical fabric of the society. He believes that ruler's ethical conduct, and not institutions, is the 'deep determinant' of economic growth. According to him, a king should be a rajarishi, ethical and wise like a sage and create an ethical environment.

Until recently, Kautilya has been the only economist who suggested both preventive and remedial measures to handle threats of an aggression, occurrence of a famine and moral decay to prosperity and national security. He (p 116) states: In the interests of the prosperity of the country, a king should be diligent in foreseeing the possibility of calamities, try to avert them before they arise, overcome those which happen, remove all obstructions to economic activity and prevent loss of revenue to the state (8.4).

The Arthashastra consists of three reasonably developed but inter-related parts.

(a) Economic Issues: This part deals with Principles and policies related to economic growth, taxation, international trade, efficient, clean and caring governance, moral and material incentives to elicit effort and preventive and remedial measures to deal with famines and other calamities and Accounting Methods.

(b) Law and Economics: Kautilya devotes the second part to administration of justice, minimisation of legal errors, formulation of ethical and efficient laws, labour theory of property, regulation of monopolies and monopsonies, protection of privacy, laws against sexual harassment and child labour.[6]

(c) Application of Economic Analysis to National Security: This part discusses all aspects of national security, such as energetic, enthusiastic, well trained and equipped soldiers, most qualified and loyal advisers, strong public support, setting-up an intelligence and analysis wing, negotiating a favourable treaty, military tactics and strategy, and diet of soldiers to enhance their endurance.

Table 7.1: Concepts Developed and Used by Kautilya

Remerged during the period	Concepts Originated and Applied by Kautilya
1700-1850	Gains from Trade, Diversification, Division of Labour, Inter-temporal choice, Labour theory of Property, Law of diminishing returns, Moral Hazard, Regulation of Monopoly, Sources of Economic Growth, Principles of taxation
1850-1900	Distinction short-run and long run, Efficiency Wages, Externality, Duipit-Laffer Curve, Demand-Supply Apparatus, Opportunity Cost, Producer Surplus
1900-1970	Principal-agent Problem, Liquidity, Mean-Variance Approach, Non-cooperative Game
1970-Present	Asymmetric Information, Piece-wise Linear income Tax, Loss-aversion, Information Economics, Self-protection, Self-insurance, Time Inconsistency, Systemic Risk

Scope of The Wealth of Nations: [2] Adam Smith (Book 1, p 394) wrote, 'But the great object of the political economy of every country is to increase the riches and power of that country'. One would expect that *The Wealth of Nations* would cover how a nation should enhance its power and enrich its people. As [3] Prasch (1991) comments:'First, the title of the book, *An Inquiry into the Nature and Causes of The Wealth of Nations*, as well as his lengthy tracts about the mercantilists' confusion with regard to the formation of wealth, lends credence to the view that he shared the mercantilists' goals, namely the development of England's wealth and power as a policy goal. Reviewing book IV of *The Wealth of Nations*, one finds that Smith never raises issue with the mercantilists' policy goals, only with their attempts to achieve them.' However, Adam Smith's discussion on national security was inadequate. He followed Machiavelli, who did not have much to say on national security (See Chapter 8).

Then, in Book IV, Adam Smith (Book IV, p 449) defined, 'Political economy, considered as a branch of the science of a statesman or legislator, proposes two distinct objects: first, to provide a plentiful revenue or subsistence for the people, or more properly to enable them to provide such a revenue or subsistence for themselves; secondly, to supply the state or commonwealth with a revenue sufficient for the public services. It proposes to enrich both the people and the sovereign'. One would expect that he would explain, at the minimum, how to bring prosperity. As [4] Dorfman (1991) notes, '*Wealth of Nations* was primarily a treatise on economic development'. However, Adam Smith borrowed the sources of economic growth from *The Arthaṣhastra* and ignored how to promote growth. Thus, the scope of *The Wealth of Nations* is very limited. On the other hand, Kautilya's *Arthashastra* is comprehensive, consistent, concise, coherent and rigorous.

7.2 Kautilya and Adam Smith on Economic Growth

As mentioned above, Kautilya identifies Land, Labour and Capital as the sources of economic growth. Assembly-type division of labour, what is now called Fordism, was practiced during fourth century BCE in India and Kautilya did not see the need to mention it.[7] The following Table presents their identification of the sources of economic growth.

Table 7.2: Sources of Economic Growth

Sources of Economic Growth	Kautilya	Adam Smith
Importance of Capital	Man, without wealth, does not get it even after a hundred attempts. Just as elephants are needed to catch elephants, so does wealth capture more wealth, Wealth will slip away from that childish man who constantly consults the stars. The only [guiding] star of wealth is itself; what can the stars of the sky do? (9.4.26-27). Kautilya (p 664) observes: On the other hand, one fighting with a tiny army perishes like one trying to cross the ocean without a boat (12.1).	He (p 11) stated that machines 'facilitate and abridge labour and enable one man to do the work of many'. Adam Smith (p 13, ft. 1): Two men and three horses will do more in a day with the plough than twenty men without it. The miller and his servant will do more with the water mill than a dozen with the hand mill, though it too be a machine.
Importance of Labour	He (p 619) states: The value of land is what man makes of it (7.11). He (p 621) adds: A king who trusts in fate and does not believe in human effort will fail because such a king never begins a work and never achieves anything (7.11). He (p 685) states:t is better to have either an army composed of Kshatriyas trained in the use of weapons or a Vaishya or Sudra army with a large number of men (9.2).	Distinction short-run and long run, Efficiency Wages, Externality, Duipit-Laffer Curve, Demand-Supply Apparatus, Opportunity Cost, Producer Surplus.

Importance of Land	Kautilya (p 617) statesAmong the signatories to a treaty for a joint campaign, he who acquires land [whether settled land or virgin land] with [the maximum number of] ideal qualities and with many developed productive facilities outmanoeuvres the others (7.10).	He (p 195) stated: The acquisition of new territory, or of new branches of trade, may sometimes raise the profits of stock, and with them the interest of money, even in a country which is fast advancing in the acquisition of riches.
Role of Institutions	Kautilya (p 108) observes: By maintaining order, the king can preserve what he already has, acquire new possessions, augment his wealth and power, and share the benefits of improvement with those worthy of such gifts. The progress of this world depends on the maintenance of order and the [proper functioning of] government (1.4).	(Bk V, Ch III, p, 445) Commerce and manufactures can seldom flourish long in any state which does not enjoy a regular administration of justice, in which people do not feel themselves secure in the possession of their property, in which the faith of contracts is not supported, and in which the authority of the state is not supposed to be regularly employed in enforcing the payment of debts from all those who are able to pay.

Kautilya in emphasising the contribution of capital writes, 'Man, without wealth, does not get it even after a hundred attempts'. Adam Smith said that as machines 'facilitate and abridge labour, and enable one man to do the work of many'. There is hardly any difference since Adam Smith substituted 'hundred' by 'many'. However, according to Kautilya, all workers contribute to income, whereas Adam Smith did not think so. We may summarise as follows:

(i) Kautilya emphasises the importance of capital to economic growth so did Adam Smith. Both use simple examples to make the point. Industrial revolution was taking hold all around Adam Smith, he still used simple examples. It indicates that he spent twelve years in collecting ideas from existing sources rather than shifting the knowledge frontier outwards.

(ii) Kautilya believes that capital and labour are complements, so did Adam Smith.

(iii) Kautilya believes that use of capital increases labour productivity and saves labour and Adam Smith also believed that. They do not make any distinction between labour-augmenting and labour-saving.

(iv) Interestingly, Kautilya understands that training is labour-augmenting.

7.3 Kautilya and Adam Smith on Principles of Taxation

Kautilya emphasises certainty of taxation, proportional income tax, convenience of payment and economy in the collection of taxes. Additionally, Kautilya is concerned about tax evasion. He equates tax evasion to a theft and recommends strict enforcement. Adam Smith appreciated the tax system in India and other countries. He (1776, part II, p 364) wrote, 'The sovereigns of China, those of Bengal while under the Mahometan government, and those of ancient Egypt, are said accordingly to have been extremely attentive to the making and maintaining of good roads and navigable canals, in order to increase, as much as possible, both the quantity and value of every part of the produce of the land, by procuring to every part of it the most extensive market which their own dominions could afford'. The tax system in Bengal and other parts of India was the one recommended by Kautilya two thousand years ago, before Muslim rule.[8] It is no surprise, that rulers of the middle ages, pre-British rulers of India continued to adopt the tax system of earlier eras, because they were good. Adam Smith recommended the same canons of taxation. The following Table presents their views on taxation.'

Table 7.3: Canons of Taxation

	Kautilya	Adam Smith
Benefit-rule of taxation	(p 820): When there was no order in society and only the law of the jungle prevailed, people [were unhappy and being desirous of order] made Manu, the son of Vivasvat, their king; and they assigned to the king one-sixth part of the grains grown by them, one-tenth of other commodities and money. The king then used these to safeguard the welfare of his subjects.	(Bk. V, Ch. II, p 350): The subjects of every state ought to contribute towards the support of the government, as nearly as possible, in proportion to their respective abilities; That is, in proportion to the revenue which they respectively enjoy under the protection of the state.
Certainty of tax	Income tax rate was proportional and equal to one-sixth of income and was fixed by the tax-payers.	The tax which each individual is bound to pay ought to be certain, not arbitrary.

	Kautilya	Adam Smith
Benefit-rule of taxation	(p 820): When there was no order in society and only the law of the jungle prevailed, people [were unhappy and being desirous of order] made Manu, the son of Vivasvat, their king; and they assigned to the king one-sixth part of the grains grown by them, one-tenth of other commodities and money. The king then used these to safeguard the welfare of his subjects.	(Bk. V, Ch. II, p 350): The subjects of every state ought to contribute towards the support of the government, as nearly as possible, in proportion to their respective abilities; That is, in proportion to the revenue which they respectively enjoy under the protection of the state.
Certainty of tax	Income tax rate was proportional and equal to one-sixth of income and was fixed by the tax-payers.	The tax which each individual is bound to pay ought to be certain, not arbitrary.
Economy	(p 220): A wise Chancellor is one who collects revenue so as to increase income and reduce expenditure. He will take remedial measures if income diminishes and expenditure increases (2.6.28). P 284: He who produces double the [anticipated] revenue eats up the janapada [the countryside and its people, by leaving them inadequate resources for survival and future production] (2.9). Kautilya (p 181) suggests: He (the king) shall protect agriculture from being harassed by (onerous) fines, taxes and demands of labour (2.1).	(p 351): Every tax ought to be so contrived as both to take out and to keep out of the pockets of the people as little as possible, over and above what it brings into the public treasury of the state.

Convenience of payment	(He (p 253) observs: Just as one plucks fruits from a garden as they ripen, so shall a king have the revenue collected as it becomes due. Just as one does not collect unripe fruits, he shall avoid taking wealth that is not due because that will make the people angry and spoil the very sources of revenue (5.2).	(p 351): Every tax ought to be levied at the time, or in the manner, in which it is most likely to be convenient for the contributor to pay.
Compliance	The Record Keepers are responsible for collecting the taxes and there were magistrates to 'inspect their work and to ensure proper collection of taxes' (2.35).	None.

Incidentally, Spengler brings out Kautilya's additional insights on taxation. [5] He (1971, p 72) observes: Kautilya's discussion of taxation and expenditure, apparently in keeping with traditional doctrine, gave expression to three Indian principles: taxation power is limited; taxation should not be felt to be heavy or excessive; tax increases should be graduated. One of his main concerns seems to have been the collection and expenditure of revenue in such ways as to build up the permanent revenue-yielding capacity of the economy. While he manifested little knowledge of tax shifting and incidence, he emphasised the long run, cautioned against too heavy taxation in the short run, and noted that a ruler could not tax at his pleasure, particularly in frontier regions whence disgruntled taxpayers could flee to neighboring countries. (See [6] Sihag 2014, Chapter 12) for an in-depth analysis of Kautilya's ideas on taxation).

7.4 Kautilya and Adam Smith on Undesirability of Monopoly

Kautilya suggests provision of public goods and regulation of externalities, monopolies and monopsonies by the government.

Adam Smith suggested provision of public goods by the government but did not suggest any regulation of externalities and monopolies. However, neither Kautilya nor Adam Smith call them market failures. The following Table presents their view on the undesirability of monopolies.

Table 7.4: Undesirability of Monopoly

Convenience of payment	Kautilya's *Arthashastra*	Adam Smith's *Wealth of Nations*
Monopolies and monopsonies	P 236: Merchants are all thieves, in effect, if not in name; they shall be prevented from oppressing the people (4.1). He (p 134) adds: It is the frontier officer who promotes trade, whereas traders form cartels in order to raise prices [for the goods they sell] or lower them [for the goods they buy]; they are profiteers making one hundred panas on one pana or one hundred measures on one measure of [grain].	(Book 1, Ch. XI, p 278), he wrote: It comes from an order of men, whose interest is never exactly the same with that of the public, who have generally an interest to deceive and even to oppress the public, and who accordingly have, upon many occasions, both deceived and oppressed it.
Regulation of Monopolies and monopsonies	Kautilya (p 250) recommends: Cartelisation by artisans and craftsmen with the aim of lowering quality, increasing the profits or obstructing the sale or purchase and by merchants conspiring to hoard with the aim of selling at a higher price (4.2) would be dealt with stiff punishments of 1000 panas for such offenses. Such a high penalty indicates the perceived seriousness of the offense. He (p 249-250) recommends: punishment for 'adulteration', 'fraud', 'false description in selling', 'showing one product and selling another', and 'stealing precious metal in making new objects', etc. (4.2).	Nothing specific.

Kautilya does not use deadweight loss as the argument for the undesirability of monopolies. Instead he argues that monopoly is undesirable since it oppresses people. Adam Smith also did not argue that monopoly was undesirable because it created a deadweight loss. He, just like Kautilya, argued that monopoly was undesirable because it oppressed people. This is irrefutable evidence that Adam Smith had access to Kautilya's ideas. Interestingly, Kautilya equates charging of high prices through the formation of cartels to theft.

7.5 Concluding Observations

Fairness requires that acknowledgement be given only to the thinker, who originates an idea and not to the one, who copies it and tries to claim proprietorship. Adam Smith was erroneously declared as the founder of economics and instead of correcting the error, concerted and coordinated efforts have been made over the last two hundred years and are still continuing to perpetuate it. Moreover, one cannot extract any butter by churning buttermilk, in this case *The Wealth of Nations*, unless s/he has added butter beforehand.

Kautilya and Machiavelli on Justice, Prosperity and National Security

AS SOON as [1] Machiavelli's *Prince* was indexed in 1559, his name and the word evil, although incorrectly, became interchangeable. Machiavelli advocated a cruel and callous approach as to how a new king should retain his kingdom. First translation of the *Arthashastra* in English by Shamasastry was published in 1915 and almost immediately, its comparison with Machiavelli's *Prince* started in earnest. Numerous political science scholars, apparently without fully understanding/reading [2] Kautilya's *Arthashastra*, have been inappropriately comparing Kautilya to Machiavelli. [3] Kangle (1965/2000, Ch. 12) presents the views of several authors on such comparison.

Most of the western scholars set out to show that Kautilya was as much – if not more – callous than Machiavelli in his approach. Even seasoned [4] Henry Kissinger (2014) has taken the same distorted and beaten track. The primary source of their confusion, misrepresentation or distortion seems to be that all these scholars have focused only on one part, how to protect the nation against traitors and aggressors (national security), of the *Arthashastra* and ignored Kautilya's monumental contributions to economic principles and policies and administration of justice. However, according to Kautilya, traitors, just like filth, must be flushed out of the system and aggressors must be destroyed so that ordinary people can enjoy both peace and prosperity (*Yogakshema*).

Machiavelli, just like Kautilya, was an honest and hard-working individual. So, the intended comparison is not about them as such but related to the approach, purpose, vision, scope and depth of analysis of their works. Kautilya had a long-term horizon, was forward-looking and has been acknowledged as a king-maker. He has a vision of a prosperous, secure and secular nation, and he has developed a conceptual framework and formulates appropriate policies to realise his vision. Everything relevant to the wellbeing of the people is discussed in depth. His *Arthashastra* is comprehensive, coherent, consistent and original. Machiavelli, on the other hand, was seeking a job. He sent his letter and manuscript of his Prince in support of his application for the job. He had a very short-term horizon, was often backward-looking and had no vision. Consequently, he covered very few subjects, did not analyseany topic in depth and was often inconsistent. Also, there is nothing original in the *Prince*. Machiavelli just collected the insights of others. For fuller understanding of these works some background on differences between Kautilya's *Arthashastra* and Machiavelli's *Prince* related to: (a) the vision and scope of their works; (b) their approaches; (c) king's character, (d) human nature and (e) role of advisers are presented in Sections 8.1, 8.2, 8.3, 8.4 and 8.5 respectively.

Kautilya's *Arthashastra* is a manual on how to promote Yogakshema – peaceful enjoyment of prosperity –for all the people (see Chapter 2). On the other hand, Machiavelli mentions that the king should take care of his public but there is absolutely no discussion about any policy or programme to enrich them. This discussion is presented in Section 8.6. Apparently, Machiavelli understood the importance of good laws, but unlike Kautilya, did not discuss how to formulate and implement such laws. Section 8.7 contains their differences related to administration of justice. [5] Sihag (2014a, chap. 18) presents Kautilya's comprehensive, proactive and prudent approach to national security and the link between prosperity and national security. Machiavelli did not offer any comprehensive approach to national security and did not understand the link between prosperity and national security. Machiavelli makes some ad hoc remarks related to making alliances, role of information and public support and these are collected in Section 8.8.

8.1 Comparison of Kautilya's Vision to that of Machiavelli

There are sharp differences related to the vision and scope of their works. Kautilya is focused on nation-building. He has a grand vision of building an empire encompassing the whole of the Indian-subcontinent, with diversified and productive economy in which people are honest and hard-working and enjoy prosperity and security. Machiavelli was desperately looking for a job and could not afford the luxury of entertaining a vision and therefore did not see the need to develop any conceptual framework or programme to bring prosperity or security to the people. The following table 8.1 compares the vision and scope of their works.

Table 8.1: Vision and Scope of the Arthashastra and the Prince

Kautilya	Machiavelli
Kautilya's Vision: Kautilya [pp. 120-121] states his vision as: The kingdom shall be protected by fortifying the capital and the towns at the frontiers. The land should not only be capable of sustaining the [native] population but also outsiders [when they come into the kingdom] in times of calamities. It should be easy to defend from [attacks by] enemies and strong enough to control neighboring kingdoms. It should have productive land (free from swamps, rocky ground, saline land, uneven terrain and deserts as well as wild and [unruly] groups of people). It should be beautiful, being endowed with arable land, mines, timber forests, elephant forests, and good pastures rich in cattle. It should not depend [only on] rain for water. It should have good roads and waterways. It should have a productive economy, with a wide variety of commodities and the capacity to sustain a high level of taxation as well as a [large] army. The people shall be predominantly agriculturists [artisans and craftsman], devoted to work, honest, loyal and with intelligent masters and servants [6.1.8].	Machiavelli on Irrelevance of a Vision: He (513, p 48) wrote:But my hope is to write a book that will be useful, at least to those who read it intelligently, and so I thought it sensible to go straight to a discussion of how things are in real life and not waste time with a discussion of an imaginary world. For many authors have constructed imaginary republics and principalities that have never existed in practice and never could; for the gap between how people actually behave and how they ought to behave is so great that anyone who ignores everyday reality in order to live up to an ideal will soon discover he has been taught how to destroy himself, not how to preserve himself.

Scope: Kautilya (p 100) explains the scope as: By following [the principles set out in] this treatise one can not only create and preserve dharma [spiritual good], artha [material well-being] and kama [aesthetic pleasures] but also destroy [their opposites, ie.] unrighteousness, material loss and hatred. It is a guide not only for the acquisition of this world but also the next (15.1.71-72).	Scope: Machiavelli (p 3) wrote in his letter to Francesco Vettori: I discuss what a principality is, how many types of principality there are, how one acquires them, how one holds onto them, why one loses them.

Dharma and *Artha*: Kautilya gives the highest priority to the preservation and promotion of *dharma*, that is, to the practice of secular virtues, such as non-violence, compassion, tolerance, freedom from malice, truthfulness and honesty. He, just like the Vedic seers, assigns a foundational role to *dharma*. He believes if there is no dharma, there will be no society. According to Kautilya, role of dharma is not only foundational but also instrumental to the promotion of artha (prosperity), that is, *dharma* not only paves the path to bliss but also to prosperity. He (p 142) explains, 'Government by Rule of Law, which alone can guarantee security of life and welfare of the people, is, in turn, dependent on the self-discipline of the king (1.5)'. That is, economic growth depends on rule of law and that, in turn, dependsd on ethical conduct of the king.

He (p. 107-108) emphasises, 'For the world, when maintained in accordance with the Vedas, will ever prosper and not perish. Therefore, the king shall never allow the people to swerve from their *dharma* (1.3.17)'. He (p 177 adds, 'Ever victorious and never conquered shall be that Kshatriya, who is nurtured by *Brahmins*, made prosperous by the counsels of able ministers and has, as his weapons, the precepts of the shastras (1.9.11)'. He (p 141) warns: A king who flouts the teachings of the *Dharamshastras* and the *Arthashastra*, ruins the kingdom by his own injustice (8.2).

Henry Kissinger (2014) remarks: Like Machiavelli's, his (Kautily's) is an analysis of the world as he found it; it offers a practical, not a normative, guide to action. And its moral basis is identical with that of Richelieu, who lived nearly two thousand years later: the state is a fragile organisation, and the statesman does not have the moral right to risk its survival on ethical restraint.

Kissinger is correct in claiming that Machiavelli accepted the world as he found it but is dead wrong about Kautilya. As presented above, Kautilya has a vision of shared prosperity, developed a conceptual framework and offers normative yet actionable guidelines to realise it. [5] Drekmeier (1962, p 76) puts it very aptly as: 'Now the king must concern himself directly with the common good, an idea anticipated in the *Arthashastra*.' He (p 201) asserts, 'There can never be a thoroughgoing divorce of politics and ethics for Kautilya; he never denies that the ultimate purpose of the state is a moral purpose, the maintenance of dharma'. He (p 202) adds: 'For all his commitment to a philosophy of opportunism and force, Kautilya would not have limited might to mere physical mastery. Such may be the primary obligation of warrior and even king, but the ultimate power is spiritual.' He (203) observes: Self-mastery and world-mastery are interdependent.

Richelieu certainly pursued national interest and his own interest by following the maxim: end justifies the means. Attributing the concept of 'moral duty' to Richelieu is incorrect. Richelieu was a religious person but not ethical. He was a self-serving and power-hungry monster in a cardinal's red robe. Kautilya, on the other hand, believed in the concept of moral duty.

Machiavelli (chap. 7, p 27) listed his suggestions as to what a new ruler needed to do to stay in power. These were: 'So anyone who decides that the policy to follow when one has newly acquired power is to destroy one's enemies, to secure some allies, to win wars, whether by force or by fraud, to make oneself both loved and feared by one's subjects, to make one's soldiers loyal and respectful, to wipe out those who can or would want to hurt one, to innovate, replacing old institutions with new practices, to be both harsh and generous, magnanimous and open-handed, to disband disloyal troops and form new armies, to build alliances with other powers, so kings and princes either have to win your favour or else think twice before going against your wishes – anyone who thinks in these terms cannot hope to find, in the recent past, a better model to imitate than Cesare Borgia.'

He does not offer any policy or programme to achieve any of his suggestions. Use of 'force or fraud' implies no role for ethics. Cicero had remarked that fear was incompatible with love so how can one accomplish to be 'loved and feared' at the same time?
We may summarise that dharma and artha form the core of Arthashastra and Roger Boesche, Henry Kissinger and many others have an inadequate understanding of Indian culture and of economics, and therefore, fail to appreciate and acknowledge Kautilya's unique contribution and keep comparing Kautilya to some mediocre writers. Machiavelli provided inadequate analysis and the *Prince* has a very limited scope.

8.2 Comparing Kautilya's Approach to Machiavelli's

Kautilya and Chandragupta Maurya inherited an economy in shambles. At that time, there was no such thing as live and let live and threat of an aggression by unscrupulous, murderous and neurotic rulers like Alexander was real. Kautilya wrote the *Arthashastra*, a manual on promoting *Yogakshema* – peaceful enjoyment of prosperity – for all the people. That is, (i) how to engineer prosperity, (ii) how to ensure security and (iii) of all the people. Kautilya realised that one uniform set of values or one single approach would not help in realising his vision. Keeping that in view, Kautilya suggests a people-centric, ethical and proactive approach towards king's own subjects but proactive and a mix of ethical approach and pragmatic approach towards other rulers. In other words, idealism for the domestic affairs and a mix of idealism and realism for international affairs.

David Wootton (p xxii) believes, 'Machiavelli may appear to teach the immoral pursuit of power by any means. In fact, he clearly teaches two sets of moral values: one deals with relations between states, where only success counts; the other much more complex, concerns one's dealings with one's fellow citizens, where the means must be justified by the purposes they serve'. Actually, Machiavelli's approach towards own subjects and towards others was practically the same: king-centric, proactive and pragmatic. Machiavelli does not assign any role to moral values – whether the king was dealing with his own subjects or others, that is, there was only one set of immoral values and not two sets of moral values. The following Table 8.2 is intended to capture these differences.

Table 8.2: Comparison of the Approaches

Kautilya's Approach	Machiavelli's Approach
People-centric: (a) In the happiness of his subjects lies his happiness; in their welfare his welfare. He shall not consider as good only that which pleases him but treat as beneficial to him whatever pleases his subjects (1.19). (b) He (p 128) writes: Whenever danger threatens, the king shall protect all those afflicted like a father [protects his children] (4.3). 2 (c) He (p 180) adds: He shall, however, treat leniently, like a father [would treat his son], those whose exemptions have ceased to be effective (2.1). (d) Kautilya (p 182) suggests: King shall maintain, at state expense, children, the old, the destitute, those suffering from adversity, childless women and the children of the destitute women (2.1). (e) Kautilya (p 128) believes: It is the duty of the king to protect the people from all calamities (4.3).	King-centric: Page 31: Do all the harm you must at one and the same time, that way the full extent of it will not be noticed, and it will give least offense, one should do good, on the other hand, little by little, so people can fully appreciate it. Page 49: Above all, do not be upset if you are supposed to have those vices a ruler needs if he is going to stay securely in power, for, if you think about it, you will realise there are some ways of behaving that are supposed to be virtuous [che parra vjtu], but would lead to your downfall, and others that are supposed to be wicked, but still lead to your welfare and peace of mind.

Ethical: He (p 180) writes: or, when adharma overwhelms dharma, the King himself will be destroyed (3.16.42). He (p 639) states: Wealth is like a tree; its roots are dharma and the fruit is pleasure. Achieving that kind of wealth which further promotes dharma, produces more wealth and gives more pleasure is the achievement of all gains (sarvarthasiddhi) (9.7.81).	Unethical: page 55: A ruler, and particularly a ruler who is new to power, cannot conform to all those rules that men who are thought good are expected to respect, for he is often obliged, in order to hold on to power, to break his word, to be uncharitable, inhumane, and irreligious. So he must be mentally prepared to act as circumstances and changes in fortune require. As I said, he should do what is right if he can; but he must be prepared to do wrong if necessary.
Proactive: He (p 116) writes :In the interests of the prosperity of the country, a king should be diligent in foreseeing the possibility of calamities, try to avert them before they arise, overcome those which happen, remove all obstructions to economic activity and prevent loss of revenue to the state (8.4).	Proactive: Page 11: It is necessary not only to pay attention to immediate crises, but to foresee those that will come, and to make every effort to prevent them. Page 35: They all have appropriate moats and ramparts, and more than enough artillery. They always keep in the public stores enough food and drink, and firewood, to be able to hold out for a year.
Pragmatic: (p 541): An enemy's destruction shall be brought about even at the cost of great losses in men, material and wealth (7.13).	Pragmatic: Page 55: So if a ruler wins wars and holds on to power, the means he has employed will always be judged honourable, and everyone will praise them.

According to Kautilya (p 182), 'Every man has an obligation to maintain his wife, children, parents, minor brothers and dependent (unmarried or widowed) sisters. No man shall renounce the life of a householder in order to become an ascetic without providing for the maintenance of his wife and children (2.1)'. The head of the household is primarily responsible for the family and there is a punishment of 12 panas (p 194) for the failure (2.1).[1] Kautilya also suggests remedial measures if a famine or flood occurres despite efforts to prevent them.

We may conclude that Kautilya equates moral duty of the king to his subjects like a father to his children. He envisioned a well governed, well organised, prosperous and progressive state but not a welfare or centrally planned one. His approach is definitely people-centric. On the other hand, Machiavelli focused exclusively on the self-interest of the king.

8.3 Their Relative Views on King's Character

Machiavelli's king was more like a stationary bandit whereas Kautilya's king is a rajarishi whose goal is to uplift people out of poverty. According to Kautilya, a king is a faithful servant of his subjects. This concept is alien to the west. Kautilya believes that only a rajarishi can follow a people-centric and ethical approach. Drekmeier (1962, p. 25) notes, 'In conclusion, we may say that early Indian kingship was broadly contractual, conceived of as a trust, subject to popular approval, and, most important, subject to higher law and certain other restraints, normative and practical. It was basically a secular institution'.

Table 8.3: Differences Regarding the Character of the King

Kautilya's Approach	Machiavelli
(p 145): A rajarishi [a king, wise like a sage] is one who: has self-control, having conquered the [inimical temptations] of the senses, cultivates the intellect by association with elders, is ever active in promoting the security and welfare of the people, endears himself to his people by enriching them and doing good to them and avoids daydreaming, capriciousness, falsehood and extravagance (1.7).	(Chap. 18, p 54): So you see a wise ruler cannot, and should not, keep his word when doing so is to his disadvantage, and when the reasons that lead him to promise to do so no longer apply. Of course, if all men were good, this advice would be bad; but since men are wicked and will not keep faith with you, you need not keep faith with them.

Kautilya's Approach	Machiavelli
(p 169): Unless there are dangers in it, succession of the eldest son is praiseworthy. An only son, if he is wicked, shall not [under any circumstances] be installed on the throne. A king with many sons acts in the best interests [of the kingdom] only if he removes a wicked one from succession (1.17). He (p 144) states: The sole aim of all branches of knowledge is to inculcate restraint over the senses (1.6.3). Self-control, which is the basis of knowledge and discipline, is acquired by giving up lust, anger, greed, conceit, arrogance and foolhardiness. Living in accordance with the shastras means avoiding over-indulgence in all pleasures of [the senses, i.e.,] hearing, touch, sight, taste and smell (1.6.1, 2).He (p 144) writes, A king who has no self-control and gives himself to excessive indulgence in pleasures will soon perish, even if he is the ruler of all four corners of the earth (1.6.4).	Page 55: So you should seem to be compassionate, trustworthy, sympathetic, honest, religious, and indeed, be all these things; but at the same time you should be constantly prepared, so that, if these become liabilities, you are trained and ready to become their opposites. Page 56: You become hateful, above all, as I said, if you prey on the possessions and the women of your subjects.
Why a King should be Ethical: (p 121): A king endowed with the ideal personal qualities enriches the other elements when they are less than perfect (6.1). (p 123): Whatever character the king has, the other elements also come to have the same (8.1).	Why a King should be Ethical: (Discourse, p 204): Princes should not complain of any failings to be found in the people over whom they rule. For such failings are likely to be caused either by their own negligence or they themselves have the same faults. (Discourse, p 205): And Lorenzo de' Medici made the same point, remarking: 'What the ruler does one day, many others do the next, for they all have their eyes on him'.

Thus, according to Kautilya, a king must have a good knowledge of philosophy, but should not be an idle philosopher, or a dictator. Rather, he should be an impartial, benevolent, far-sighted, foresighted, disciplined and energetic doer. On the other hand, Machiavelli suggested that a king should pretend to be ethical but need not behave ethically, that is ready to cheat. Then in his other writing, he suggested that a king should be a role model.

8.4 Their Underlying Assumptions regarding Human Nature

Kautilya believed that there were moral, amoral and immoral types of people whereas Machiavelli believed that all people were amoral or immoral.

Table 8.4: Differences Related to Human Nature

Kautilya's Approach	Machiavelli
Page 124: For the fort, the treasury and the army all depend on the people; so do the reservoirs. All economic activity has its source in the countryside. Bravery, stability and cleverness are also found among the country people (8.1.28-31). P 169: Sons are of three kinds: a wise son is one who understands dharma and artha when taught and also practices these. A lazy son is one who understands what he is taught but does not practice them. A wicked son is he who hates dharma and artha and [therefore] is full of evil. Page 664: There are three types of aggressors: (i) The righteous aggressor is satisfied with submission. (ii) The greedy aggressor is satisfied with seizing land and goods. (iii) The monstrous aggressor is satisfied only when he takes the land, goods, wives, sons and [even the] life of the defeated.	Page 52: For of men one can, in general, say this: They are ungrateful, fickle, deceptive and deceiving, avoiders of danger, eager to gain. He adds: Men are less nervous of offending someone who makes himself lovable, than someone who makes himself frightening. For love attaches men by ties of obligation, which, since men are wicked, they break whenever their interests are at stake. But fear restrains men because they are afraid of punishment, and this fear never leaves them. Still, a ruler should make himself feared in such a way that, if he does not inspire love, at least he does not provoke hatred. For it is perfectly possible to be feared and not hated. You will only be hated if you seize the property or the women of your subjects and citizens.

Kautilya believes in ethical anchoring of young children. He (pp. 155-156) writes: There can be no greater crime or sinthan making wicked impressions on an innocent mind. Just as a clean object is stained with whatever is smeared on it, so a prince, with a fresh mind, understands as the truth whatever is taught to him. Therefore, a prince should be taught what is dharma and artha, not what is unrighteous and materially harmful (1.17).

In conclusion we may say that Kautilya understood the link between character-building and nation-building. Clearly, he wanted to create a more harmonious and caring world and did not accept the existing one as claimed by Henry Kissinger.

8.5 Role of Advisers

There are sharp differences regarding the role of advisers. According to Kautilya, due to bounded rationality a king cannot solve complex problems alone by himself. So, Kautilya advises appointment of advisers and pooling of their information, knowledge and wisdom with that of the king to arrive at the best possible decision. According to Kautilya, as the number of advisers increase, the king gets better advice due to the increase, pooling of information and knowledge but as the number of advisers increasethe probability of keeping it confidential is low.Thus, Kautilya analyses the trade-off between efficiency and confidentiality and concluds that the optimum of advisers should not be higher than four (see Sihag, 2014a, Chap. 10 for a detailed presentation).

Table 8.5: Differences over the Role of Advisers

Kautilya's Approach	Machiavelli
Bounded Rationality: He (p 177) observes: A king can reign only with the help of others; one wheel alone does not move a chariot. Therefore, a king should appoint advisers as councilors and ministers and listen to their advice (1.7).	Page Chap 23, 72: For the emperor is a secretive man, he keeps things to himself and never asks anyone's advice. But, when his decisions begin to be discovered, which is when they begin to be put into effect, he begins to be criticized by those who are close to him, and, as one might expect,

Emphasis on pooling of Knowledge and Information: Kautilya states: Vishalaksha says 'never can a single person arrive at the right decision. The work of government is dependent on [complete] knowledge – that which the king personally knows, that which is reported to him and that which he has to infer. To find out what is not known, to clarify doubts when there are alternatives, to obtain more information when only a part is known – all these can be done only with the help of advisers. Hence a king shall conduct his deliberations with advisers of mature intelligence. (As the saying goes :) 'Despise no one, [but] listen to all views; for, wise man pays heed to all sensible advice, even those of a child' (1.15).	he is persuaded to change his mind. The result is that he undoes each day what he did the day before; that nobody ever knows what he really wants or intends to do; and that one cannot rely upon his decisions. Chapter 23, Page 72: A ruler, therefore, always take advice, but only when he wants to, not when others want him to; he should discourage everybody from giving him advice without being asked; but he should be always asking, and, moreover, he should listen patiently to the answers, provided they are truthful. 'For this is a general rule without exceptions: A ruler who is not himself wise cannot be given good advice.' Page 73: This is how it has to be, for you will find men are always wicked, unless you give them no alternative but to be good. So we may conclude that good advice, no matter who it comes from, really comes from the ruler's own good judgment, and that the ruler's good judgment never comes from good advice.
Qualification of an Adviser: He (p 120) definesacouncilor or minister of the highest rank as someone who: Should be a native of the state, born in a high family and controllable [by the king]. He should have been trained in all the arts and have logical ability to foresee things . He should be intelligent, persevering, dexterous, eloquent, energetic, bold, brave, and able to endure adversities and firm in loyalty. He should neither be haughty or fickle. He should be amicable and not excite hatred or enmity in others (1.9).	Qualifications of an Adviser: Chapter 22, page 71: For there are three types of brains: One understands matters for itself, one follows the explanation of others, and one neither understands nor follows. The first is the best, the second excellent, the third useless.

How many Advisers: He concludes: [There should be no more than four advisers] because, with more than four, secrecy is rarely maintained. [While, normally, the king should consult three or four advisers,] he may, depending on the nature of the work and the special circumstances of each case, take a decision by himself, consult just one adviser, or even two. The opinions of the advisers shall be sought individually as well as together [as a group]. The reason why each one holds a particular opinion shall also be ascertained (1.15).	No discussion.
Conflicts of Interest, Kautilya (p, 200) also recommendes: No one who belongs to the side likely to be adversely affected by the project shall be consulted (1.15).	Conflicts of Interest: Page 71: When you see your adviser give more thought to his own interests than yours, and recognise everything he does is aimed at his own benefit, then you can be sure such a person will never be a good adviser.

Machiavelli thought, in the absence of an adviser the king may change his mind due to the influence of his near and dear ones and appear to be inconsistent. It is not a convincing argument for hiring advisers. Firstly, if the king is wise, then he will realise the inadequacy of his capabilities and also anticipate the reactions of his near and dear ones and consult them before taking a decision. Secondly, the near and dear ones, according to Machiavelli, most likely were protecting their own interests. So, the king may ignore their suggestions. Moreover, the king can still change his mind even if he consults an adviser, that is, Machiavelli could not justify the hiring of an adviser.

However, Machiavelli, just like Kautilya, did understand the principal-agent problem, and the role of efficiency wages. For example, he (p 71) wrote:On the other hand the ruler, in order to get the best out of his adviser, should consider his adviser's interests, heaping honors on him, enriching him, placing him in his debt, ensuring he receives public recognition, so that he sees that he cannot do better without him, that he has so many honors he desires no more, so much wealth he desires no more, so much status he fears the consequences of political upheaval. When a ruler has good advisers and knows how to treat them, then they can rely on each other; when it is otherwise, either ruler or adviser will suffer.

Kautilya, in addition to paying decent wages, suggests moral incentives also to elicit effort (see Sihag (2014a, Chap.11).[2]

Kautilya considered advisers as prized employees since he understood the concept of bounded rationality and the importance of pooling information and knowledge whereas Machiavelli could not justify the need to hire advisers as he was ignorant of the importance of pooling information.

8.6 Kautilya and Machiavelli on Economic Growth

Kautilya, just like his predecessors, believes that ethical conduct paves the way to bliss, but he adds that it also paves the way to prosperity, that is, it is the 'deep determinant' of prosperity. He believes in the power of persuasion and moral and material incentives but never in coercion. According to him, the king is a role model to his employees and public. If he is ethical, all elements will also behave in the same manner. Ethical decision-makers place public interest ahead of their own interests in formulating laws and policies and in their effective implementation. He argues good institutions will lower risk and good governance will raise the rate return on private investment and that will encourage increases in the supplies of labour, capital and land under cultivation. That willl, in turn, lead to a higher economic growth (see Chap. 2 for an in-depth analysis). Kautilya devotes more than a third of his book to economic policies and economic administration.

Machiavelli has just one paragraph that may be somewhat relevant to economic wellbeing. He (p 70) wrote: A ruler also should show himself to be an admirer of skill [virtue] and should honour those who are excellent in any type of work. He should encourage his citizens by making it possible for them to pursue their occupations peacefully, whether they are businessmen, farmers, or engaged in any other activity, making sure they do not hesitate to improve what they own for fear it may be confiscated from them, and they are not discouraged from investing in business for fear of losing their profits in taxes; instead, he should ensure that those who improve and invest are rewarded, as should be anyone whose actions will benefit his city or his government.

Machiavelli did not offer any growth theory. However, he deserves credit for understanding the role of institutions and, to some extent, the role of incentives. Interestingly, [7] Adam Smith understood the importance of institutions but not of incentives, that is, he did not add a whole lot to Machiavelli's insights.

8.7 Machiavelli and Kautilya on Administration of justice

Kautilya's *Arthashastra* contains detailed discussion on administration of justice, contract laws, property rules and tort laws (see Sihag (2014a, Chapters 15, 16 1nd 17)). Kautilya believes that only an ethical king, a rajarishi, can enact laws that will promote both efficiency and ethical conduct. Secondly, Kautilya's goal is to develop the cardinal principles of justice, such as punishment should be certain, in proportion to the crime and imposed impartially. Thirdly, too severe or too lenient punishment will erode public's confidence in law, implying the administration should impose a reasonable (an internal optimum) level of punishment. Finally, and most importantly, the statement 'In the presence of a king maintaining just law, the weak can resist the powerful', connects justice to personal security. Particularly, the phrase 'the weak can resist the powerful', indicates protection of the liberty of the weaker segments of the society. Unlike Mill's negative liberty, the emphasis is on the positive liberty and empowerment of the weak. What Kautilya conveys in one sentence, Mill could not convey in his whole book on liberty.[3]

Table 8.6: Differences related to Crime and Punishment

Kautilya	Machiavelli
Kautilya (p 108) elaborates on this theme, 'Some teachers say: Those who seek to maintain order shall always hold ready the threat of punishment. For, there is no better instrument of control than coercion.' Kautilya disagrees [for the following reasons]: A severe king [meting out unjust punishment] is hated by the people he terrorises while one who is too lenient is held in contempt by his own people. Whoever imposes just and deserved punishment is respected and honored. A well-considered and just punishment makes the people devoted to dharma, artha and kama [righteousness, wealth and enjoyment]. Unjust punishment, whether awarded in greed, anger or ignorance, excites the fury of even [those who have renounced all worldly attachments like] forest recluses and ascetics, not to speak of householders. When, no punishment is awarded through misplaced leniency and no law prevails, then there is only the law of fish [i.e., the law of the jungle]. Unprotected, the small fish will be swallowed up by the big fish. In the presence of a king maintaining just law, the weak can resist the powerful (1.4). Kautilya (p 377) writes: A king who observes his duty of protecting his people justly and according to law will go to heaven, whereas one who does not protect them or inflicts unjust punishment will not. It is the power of punishment alone, when exercised impartially in proportion to the guilt, and irrespective of whether the person punished is the King's son or an enemy, that protects this world and the next. (3.1).	Pages 9-10: There is a general rule to be noted here: People should either be caressed or crushed. If you do them minordamage they will get their revenge; but if you cripple them there is nothing they can do. If you need to injure someone, do it in such a way that you do not have to fear their vengeance. So, a ruler ought not to mind the disgrace of being called cruel, if he keeps his subjects peaceful and law-abiding, for it is more compassionate to impose harsh punishments on a few than out of excessive compassion, to allow disorder to spread, which leads to murders or looting. The whole community suffers if there are riots, while to maintain order the ruler only has to execute one or two individuals. Chapter 12, page 38: I said above it was necessary for a ruler to lay good foundations; otherwise, he is likely to be destroyed. The principal foundations on which the power of all governments is based (whether they may be new, long-established, or mixed) are good laws and good armies. And, since there cannot be good laws where there are not good armies, and since where there are good armies, there must be good laws, I will omit any discussion of laws, and will talk about armies.

Machiavelli's goal was to create fear in the minds of public and not administration of justice and most likely, his advice would have been ineffective in maintaining law and order. Machiavelli's logic that 'since there cannot be good laws where there are not good armies, and since where there are good armies, there must be good laws' is very peculiar.

Laws against Sexual Harassment: Kautilya (p 333) recommends: [The Chief Commissioner shall not misbehave with women with whom he has to deal officially]. For looking at the face of a woman or talking about anything other than work, he shall be punished with the lowest level of fine (2.23). He argued that women were getting paid for doing the work and the officer was not doing any favour to them.

Laws against Child Labour: He (p 449) adds: A minor, below eight years of age and no relatives, shall not be made to work, against his will, in menial jobs or in a foreign country (3.13).

Some of his ideas such as, enacting laws against child labour and sexual harassment truly belong to the later part of 20th century.

Machiavelli (Chapter 25, pages 76-77) remarks: I conclude, then, that since fortune changes, and men stubbornly continue to behave in the same way, men flourish when their behaviour suites the times and fail when they are out of step. I do think, however, that it is better to be headstrong than cautious, for fortune is a lady. It is necessary, if you want to master her, to beat and strike her. And one sees she more often submits to those who act boldly than those who proceed in a calculating fashion. Moreover, since she is a lady, she smiles on the young, for they are less cautious, more ruthless, and overcome her with their boldness.

It is a very offensive analogy, yet, David Wootton offers an apology for Machiavelli. He writes: Machiavelli, however, unlike these aphorisms, is offensive, and deliberately so: Modern readers notice only the violence between man and woman in chapter twenty-five of *The Prince,* but sixteenth-century readers would have been acutely conscious that fortune is a lady and would have been particularly shocked at the violence between social inferior and superior. It would be wrong, I think, to jump too quickly from Machiavelli's gendered language to a simple reading of Machiavelli as a patriarchal chauvinist.

8.8 Kautilya and Machiavelli on National Security

Kautilya argued that national sovereignty was essential to prosperity since a foreign ruler would be interested only in enriching himself. Then he reasoned that prosperity is essential to guarding sovereignty since a poor nation willnot have adequate resources to provide for strong national security. He understood that if a country focuseseither only on prosperity or only on national security, it can lose both, that is, he has an understanding of the inter-dependence of prosperity and security. Also, according to Kautilya, in addition to providing resources, prosperity wins public support (see Sihag,2014a). Machiavelli did not understand such interdependence and, therefore, paid no attention to bringing prosperity.

Kautilya offers a very comprehensive approach to national security. He realized that national security was not an abstract concept. So, he suggests that the very first step is to set up an intelligence agency to identify friends, foes and neutral rulers, know whether they are upright, greedy or wicked and their respective strengths and weaknesses. According to Kautilya, a king's goal should be to reach parity with the potential adversary. Then he proceeds to identify all the factors that are relevant to national security and gives concrete suggestions to achieve their optimum levels. He believes in launching a project/treaty/policy only after undertaking a sound cost-benefit analysis. He asks three questions. (i) Who should decide the desirability and feasibility of a project/treaty? (ii) What should be their qualifications for making a sound decision? (iii) What type of incentives would be required to elicit optimum effort from them? [4]

Machiavelli was supposedly involved with national security for fourteen years but still did not develop any comprehensive approach to it. He made just a few remarks and only those are compared with those of Kautilya.

Forming Alliances: Kautilya provides an in-depth analysis on why to form alliances, with who, equal, weaker or stronger, upright or otherwise, and how to extract maximum benefits but never to compromise with national security. As an illustration, he (p 616) suggests: between joining forces with a ruler who is stronger than the king or with two rulers of strength equal to the king, it is better to join two equal kings. For with one ruler, the stronger ruler will have the upper hand during the campaign, whereas with two equals, the king can keep control. If one of them turns treacherous, it will be easy for the other two to suppress him and make him suffer the consequences of the dissent (7.5).

Table 8.7: Respective Advice on Forming Alliances

Kautilya's Approach	Machiavelli
(p 573): Amity with a more powerful monarch carries great danger for kings, except when one is actually at war with an enemy (7.2). (p 624): The king may face dangers even from a trusted king of equal power, when the latter has achieved his objective. Even an equally powerful king tends to become stronger after the task is accomplished and, when his power has increased, becomes untrustworthy. Prosperity changes peoples' minds (7.5). Proactive Measures: (p 609): An ally who is likely to grow in power after defeating the enemy and thus become uncontrollable shall be embroiled in a conflict with his own neighbor and his own ally; or, a pretender in his family or an unjustly treated prince shall be encouraged to seize the throne; or such actions shall be taken as would oblige the ally to remain obedient, in return for help received (7.18).	Page 14: He who is the cause of someone else's becoming powerful is the agent of his own destruction; for he makes his protégé powerful either through his own skill or through his own strength, and either of these must provoke his protégé's mistrust once he has become powerful. (Chap. 21, P 69: But when a ruler boldly takes sides, if your ally wins, even if he is powerful, and has the ability to overpower you, he is in your debt and fond of you. Nobody is so shameless as to turn on you in so ungrateful a fashion. (p 69): Here it is worth noting a ruler should never take the side of someone who is more powerful than himself against other rulers, unless necessity compels him to, as I have already implied.

Table 8.7 presents their respective views on forming alliances. Apparently, Machiavelli is inconsistent regarding his views on human nature. He (p 52) wrote: For of men one can, in general, say this: They are ungrateful, fickle, deceptive and deceiving, avoiders of danger, eager to gain. Then a few pages down, he (p 69) wrote: Nobody is so shameless as to turn on you in so ungrateful a fashion. Also, he does not propose any precautionary measures to protect the king in case an ally turned against the king.

Role of Information: Kautilya suggestes three benefits of having informational advantage. (i) That helps the king in negotiating a more favorable treaty. He (p 599) states: He who, gives a treacherous minister or a treacherous son or daughter as a hostage outmaneuvers the other [the receiver]. The receiver is outmaneuvered because the giver will strike without compunction at the weak point - i.e., the trust that the receiver has that the giver let the hostage come to harm (7.17).

Secondly, it provides an advantage if hostility breaks out with another ruler. He suggests establishing a permanent wing for collection and analysis of latest information. His (p 177) advice to a king is: No enemy shall know his secrets. He shall, however, know all his enemy's weaknesses. Like a tortoise, he shall draw in any limb of his that is exposed (1.15).

He (p 506) recommends: A king shall have his own set of spies, all quick in their work, in the courts of the enemy, the ally, the Middle, and the Neutral kings to spy on the kings as well as their eighteen types of high officials (1.12.20). He (p 562) adds: He shall always station envoys and clandestine agents in all states of the circle. These shall cultivate those acting against the interests of the conqueror and, while maintaining their own secrecy, destroy repeatedly such inimical persons (7.13).

Finally, if the king wantsd to get rid of land of poor quality. Kautilya (p 621) states: If a settlement of a tract is likely to entail heavy losses or expenditure, a king shall first sell the land, with the intention of reacquiring it, to one who will fail in the attempt at settlement. Such agreements shall remain verbal (7.11).

On the other hand, Machiavelli had specified a very limited role for information and there was no intelligence gathering unit to update information. He (p 79) wrote: So, since we know the weakness of each of these infantries, we ought to be able to train a new force that will be able to withstand cavalry and will not be afraid of infantry. To accomplish this, we need specially designed weapons and new battle formations. This is the sort of new undertaking that establishes the reputation and importance of a new ruler.

Public Support: Kautilya believes that public support to a ruler is essential but is conditional on removal of poverty and administration of justice. As mentioned above, Kautilya deals with both topics at length. (a) *Removal of poverty*: Kautilya (p 159) explaines: When a people are impoverished, they become greedy; when they are greedy, they become disaffected; when disaffected, they either go to the enemy or kill their ruler themselves (7.5).

Administration of Justice: Kautilya (p 573) observes: When a strong but unjust king is attacked, his subjects will not come to his help but will either topple him or go over to the attacker. On the other hand, when a weak but just king is attacked, his subjects will not only come to his help but also follow him until death (7.5). Machiavelli acknowledges the importance of public support but does not explain why and how to get it. He (p 8) wrote: Even if you have an overwhelmingly powerful army, you will have needed the support of the locals to take control of the province.

Type of Army: Kautilya lists several types of army, such as regular standing army, territorial army, organised militias, friendly troops, alien forces and jungle tribe forces. He examines the desirable attributes, such as training, loyalty and congruence of objectives of each type. For example, he (p 684) describes: Regular standing army – composed of natives of the country, dependent on the king, sharing his interests, constantly trained [owing loyalty hereditarily to the royal family, honored by the king].

Kautilya concludsthat the regular standing army is the best. He (p 684) writes: It is better to mobilise a force earlier in the list than one later. Because the standing army depends on the king for its existence and because it is constantly under training (9.2). He (p 685) remarkes: Alien troops and jungle tribal forces both have plunder as their objective. [They are both equally untrustworthy]. When there is no plunder or when there is a calamity, they are as dangerous as a viper in one's bosom.

Machiavelli (p 43) remarked: A wise ruler, therefore, will always avoid using mercenary and auxiliary troops, and will rely on his own forces. He would rather lose with his own troops than win with someone else's, for he will not regard it a true victory if it is won with troops that do not belong to him. He (p 45) concluded, 'I conclude, therefore, that no ruler is secure unless he has own troops.' We may conclude that Kautilya understood the interdependence of national security and prosperity on each other and developed conceptual frameworks and practical measures to enhance both. On the other hand, Machiavelli had very little to say on enhancing either prosperity or national security.

8.9 Conclusion

Machiavelli's *Prince* is no match to the depth and breadth of Kautilya's *Arthashastra*. It is shown that comparing Machiavelli's Prince to Kautilya's *Arthashastra* is like comparing a candle light to that of sunlight. Kautilya was an action-oriented visionary. Kautilya's *Arthashastra* contains three inter-linked parts:

(a) *Arthaniti*: principles and policies related to economic growth, taxation, international trade, efficient, clean and caring governance, moral and material incentives to elicit effort and preventive and remedial measures to deal with famines, floods and fire;

(b) *Dandaniti:* administration of justice, minimisation of legal errors, formulation of ethical and efficient laws, labour theory of property, regulation of monopolies and monopsonies, protection of privacy, laws against sexual harassment and child labour.

(c) *Videshniti:* all aspects of national security, such as (i) energetic, enthusiastic, trained and well- equipped soldiers, most qualified and loyal advisers, strong public support, setting-up an intelligence and analysis wing, (ii) negotiating a favourable treaty, (iii) military strategy and tactics and diet of soldiers to enhance their endurance.

Machiavelli's suggestions amounted to how a king could change his status from a roving bandit to a stationary bandit. According to him, one should appear to be ethical but need not be ethical and he advanced the maxim: end justifies the means. There is not a single constructive or original suggestion in *Machiavelli's Prince*. Clearly, negative views expressed by Roger Boesche, Henry Kissinger, Max Weber and many others related to Kautilya's *Arthashastra* have been unsubstantiated.

Kautilya, Fibonacci and Samuelson on Discounting

FISHER (1931) ACKNOWLEDGED the contributions of John Rae and of Eugen von Böhm-Bawerk. Fredrick, Shane, George Loewenstein and Ted O'Donoghue (2002) credit John Rae (1834) for introducing inter-temporal analysis. Apparently, William Goetzmann (2004) is the only one, who claims that Fibonacci (1202/2002) introduced discounting. In fact, Kautilya, more than a thousand years before Fibonacci and two thousand years earlier than Rae, introduced the concept of discounting.

He was concerned not just with the time dimension of an investment but also with its return and risk. Section 9.1 presents Kautilya's ideas on discounting.

There are essentially two examples in Chapter 12 of *Liber Abaci* that form the basis of Goetzmann's conclusion. It is shown that Fibonacci understood neither the concept of discounting nor its significance and his *Liber Abaci*, as he intended, is a book only of calculations and not of concepts. This is discussed in Section 9.2.

Kautilya argues that projects that enhanced national security reduce the probability of political instability and that lowers the risk premium. Samuelson (1964), perhaps, is the only other economist who suggested giving preference to projects that enhance national security. It is pointed out that Jensen and Bailey (1972) misunderstand Samuelson's core argument. This is discussed in Section 9.3.

9.1 Kautilya on Discounting

A pigeon today is better than a peacock tomorrow.

—Kautilya

One may wonder why anyone would need the concept of discounting during the fourth century BCE. Kautilya believed that poverty was death while living. He wrote *The Arthashastra* as a manual on engineering shared prosperity (see Chapter 2 for an in-depth analysis). It contains a conceptual framework along with operational details to promote *Yogakshema* – peaceful enjoyment of prosperity – for every citizen. He introduces not just the concept of discounting but more than a score of other key concepts to operationalise his vision of alleviating poverty (see Chapter 7).

Kautilya knows that selection of most productive projects is essential to bring prosperity. He realises that selection or evaluation of projects is not possible without the availability of accounting methods. He developed reasonably advanced accounting methods.[1] Then, he identifies the concepts of discounting and opportunity cost which are also considered essential to the selection of projects.[2]

There are at least two paragraphs in *The Arthashastra* where inter-temporal arbitrage is discernible. (i) Kautilya (p 636) suggests:When the gains from two campaigns are equal, the king shall compare the following qualities and choose the one which has more good points: place and time; the power and the means required to acquire it; the pleasure or displeasure caused by it; speed or slowness of getting it; the proximity or distance, the immediate and future consequences; its high value or constant worth; and its abundance or variety (9.4).

Discounting: Although Kautilya did not make the Fisherian distinction between impatience and investment opportunity, but he understans the concept of discounting and suggests its application. However, he concentrates only on the *investment opportunity* since he needs it for the selection or evaluation of projects.

Kautilya (p 635) writes: A great gain is a substantial gain available immediately (9.4). However, if the gains from the two campaigns are spread over time, selection should depend on '*speed or slowness of getting it*'. As an illustration, suppose the gains from two campaigns are equal, say $1500. The gains from one campaign accrue at a rate of $500, $500 and $500 over three periods and the gains from the second campaign accrue at the rate of $300, $300, $300, $300 and $300 over five periods. According to Kautilya, the king should prefer the first one. It is obvious that Kautilya introduces the concept of discounting and initiates the discussion on making inter-temporal choices.

Importance of Place: He explains, in addition to the time dimension, the other attributes and why they were relevant to the decision. For example, he prefers a safer location of the relevant piece of land. He (p 618) asks: Which is better – a rich land with permanent enemies or poor land without permanent enemies?

He answers it as follows: Some teachers say that, because a rich land enables one to get wealth and an army with which to destroy the enemies, a rich land with permanent enemies is preferable. Kautilya disagrees. Acquiring land with such enemies, one only adds to one's number of enemies; and an enemy remains an enemy whether he is helped or harmed: on the other hand, a temporary enemy can be made to be quiet through favours or at least by not harming him (7.10).

Again, he prefers an irrigated piece of land to a dry piece of land. He (p 619) states: As between land dependent on rain and land with flowing water [i.e. a river], a smaller tract with flowing water is preferable to a larger drier one because with flowing water, which is always available, the production of crops is assured. As between two irrigated tracts, one on which cereals can be grown is preferable. (7.11).

He was clearly aware of the risk-return trade-off. According to him, if the gains from two campaigns are the same, the one which has a stable worth, and is available quickly, is preferable. Incidentally, the phrase 'the immediate and future consequences' indicates that he makes a distinction between short-run and long run.

Another example of Inter-Temporal Analysis: He explicitly incorporates both risk and return in making a choice. He (p 617) asks: Which is preferable – an immediate small gain or a large gain in the future? According to him, the answer depended on two factors: A large gain in the future is preferable if it is like a seed [yielding fruit in the future] and if it is not likely to disappear [before fruition]. Otherwise, [if there is no growth and if there is a danger of it not fructifying] the small immediate gain is preferable (7.9).

He explains that the choice between accepting a small gain immediately and a large gain in the future depended on two factors. First, what is the nature of the gain? Is it like a seed, which has a potential for growth? Secondly, how certain it is? Is it likely to disappear before it materialises?

9.2 Fibonacci on Discounting

Liber Abaci was written in 1202 and for the next 800 years no one found the concept of discounting in it. Fisher dedicated his *Theory of Interest* to 'the memory of John Rae and of Eugen von Böhm-Bawerk, who laid the foundations upon which I have endeavored to build'. There are two problems and their solutions in Chapter 12 of *Liber Abaci*, which give the false impression that Fibonacci understood the concept of discounting.

However, based essentially on Fibonacci's solutions to these two, specifically the second problem, Goetzmann credits him for introducing the concepts of discounting and present value. He claims, 'This problem alone is unmatched in the history of financial analysis. Although the mathematics of interest rates had a 3,000 year history before Fibonacci, his remarkable exposition and development of multi-period discounting is a quantum leap above his predecessors'. It is shown that this is really a case of 'irrational exuberance' (an exaggerated claim).

Problem 1: Fibonacci (1202, p 372) asks: A certain man proceeding to Lucca on business to make a profit doubled his money, and he spent 12 denari. He then left and went through

Florence; but there doubled his money; and he spent 12 denari. Then he returned to Pisa, doubled his money, and spent 12 denari, and it is proposed that he had nothing left. It is sought how much he had at the beginning?

Fibonacci's Solution: Fibonacci provides two methods to solve the above problem.[3] He (p 372) describes the first method (problem 1) as: Because it is proposed that he always doubled his money, it is clear that 2 will be made from one. Whence it is seen what fraction 1 is of 2, namely ½, which thus is written three times because of the three trips he made: (1/2) (1/2) (1/2), and the 2 is multiplied by the 2 and the other twos that are under the fraction; there will be 8 of which you take ½, namely 4, of which you take1/2, namely 2, and of the 2 you take ½, namely 1. After this you add the 4 to the 2 and the 1; there will be 7 that you multiply by the 12 denari which he spent; there will be 84 that you divide by the 8; the quotient will be (1/2)10, and the man had this money.

Laurence Sigler describes Fibonacci's methodology for solving the problems. He (8-9) writes: The method of single false position solves which are equivalent to linear equations of the simple type Ax=B, and double false position which is used problems leading to equations of the type Ax + B=C. Double false position problems are found in Chapter 13. Besides the method of false position Leonardo solves problems using what he calls the direct method. This, method involves calling the sought quantity the thing and creating an equation containing the thing. The equation is stated in sentences and not written symbolically as we do today. The equation is then solved step by step for the thing. This is, of course, algebra as we know it, and is precisely the method described by al-Khwarizimi in his book on algebra.

According to Laurence Sigler, Fibonacci chose to use sentences instead of algebra to find solutions to the problems. In all probability, Fibonacci had an equation in the background. It does not require any stretch of imagination that he used the following method to find the answer. Suppose the merchant starts with X number of denari. His money doubles at Luca, that is, he has 2X.

He spends 12 denari. He is left with 2X–12. His money again doubles, that is he has 2 (2X–12). He spends 12 denari, he is left with (2 (2X–2)–12). He again doubles his money, that is, he has 2 (2 (2X –12)–12). He spends 12 denari and he is not left with any money. That means:

$$2 (2 (2X-12)-12)-12 = 0$$

$$2x2x2\ X-x2x12-2x12-12=0$$

By rearranging we get

$$X = 12 (1/2 +1/4 + 1/8) = 84/8 = 0.5 \qquad (9.1)$$

In general, this may be written as:

$$X= Y1/ (1+r) + Y2/ (1+r) 2 + Y3/ (1+r)3 \qquad (9.2)$$

We can recognise that X is the present value, but Fibonacci did not know that it was the present value and also did not understand its relevance. Why did the Italian mathematician not report the underlying equation? Charles Burnett (2005) believes that Fibonacci did not want to give credit to anyone so that he could claim this as his own original contribution.

He observes: By the end of the twelfth century, the 'algorismus' was widespread and it would certainly have been known to Fibonacci. In fact, he refers specifically to the 'algorismus', in the preface to his *Liber abbaci*, as we have seen. But it is difficult to see why he should criticise it alongside the '*Gerbertian abacus*' and state that the 'method of the Indians' is better, when the 'algorismus' is precisely 'the method of the Indians'. I suspect that his reason is that he thinks that, or wants to give the impression that, his own work is truly innovatory, for he scrupulously avoids mentioning the name of al-Khwarizmi. (In Chapter 15 he uses only al-Khwarizmi's first name (ism), 'Maumeht'). Are we to suppose that Fibonacci was, in fact, ignorant of this Latin tradition of Indian arithmetic, and re-introduced the place-value numerals afresh from the Arabs?

There could be another more compelling reason. Fibonacci dedicated the second edition of *Liber Abaci* to Michael Scott. Fibonacci, in his Dedication and Prologue to his *Liber Abaci* wrote, 'You, my Master Michael Scott [1], most great philosopher, wrote to my Lord [2] about the book on numbers which sometimes ago I composed and transcribed to you, whence complying with your criticisms, your more subtle examining circumspection, to the honor of you and many others I with advantage corrected this'.

Michael Scott worked as an official astrologer to Emperor Frederick II (the Roman emperors of the time) and was also in the good books of two popes, who recommended him for 'preferment'. That is, he was closely connected to the Church. Fibonacci could not have afforded to displease Michael Scott or the two popes. As pointed out by Burnett, that Fibonacci 'scrupulously avoids mentioning the name of al-Khwarizmi'. But why? Raju (2013) offers a reason as to why Fibonacci did not want to acknowledge al-Khwarizimi's work. Raju (p 129) points out, 'The Crusades (12th and 13th century) had aroused intense hatred of Muslims among Christians of Europe. So, the priests who had so long been preaching Christian Supremacy felt a strong sense of shame in acknowledging the reality that Christians were learning from books written by Islamic scholars.'

Problem 2: The Original Contract: Fibonacci (1202/2002, p 392): A certain soldier because of his fief received from a certain king 300 bezants, and it is satisfied in IIII (IV) payments, and in each payment, he takes 75 bezants; this is a payment for three months which by necessity is collected together.

Modified Contract: [H]e asks for a certain compensation in order to accommodate himself for interest because he accepts the 300 bezants instead of the 75 bezants of each payment, namely payment to payment, of capital and profit. Voluntarily acquiescing to this, he invests the bezants at a profit of two bezants per hundred in each month. It is sought how many bezants he makes in his investment.

Fibonacci's Solution: First indeed you strive to reduce this problem to the method of trips, and it is reduced thus; because in each month the profit from the 100 bezants is 2 bezants, the profit for the one hundred is 6 bezants in the three months, namely at the time of each payment; therefore from each payment of 100 bezants is made 106, that is 53 is from 50, and because there are IIII payments , IIII trips are similarly carried, and because the payment is 75 bezants, this is had for the expense of each trip.

Fibonacci thought that the modified contract was similar to the traveling trader's example. But they were different. The trader had some capital (10.5 Bezanets) when he started on the journey. On the other hand, the soldier had nothing. According to the original contract, the soldier received his first installment after 3 months and according to the modified contract, only interest payment at the end of second quarter. So, Fibonacci should not have, but still used the same technique to solve this problem, that is:

Balance after the first period = X (1 +.06)–75

Balance after the second period = [X (1+ 0.06)–75)] (1+0.06)–75

Balance after the third period = [(X (1+ 0.06)–75) (1+0.06) –75] (1+.06)–75

Balance after the fourth period ([(X (1+ 0.06)–75) (1 +0.06)–75] (1+.06)–75)) (1+0.06)–75=0, that is,

$X (1+0.06)4–75(1+0.06)^3–75(1+0.06)^2–75(1+0.06)–75=0$

1.26247696 X=75–(1.191016 +1.1236 + 1.06 +1)

Solving for X gives

X=7500(4.374616)/ 1.26247696=328.212/1.26247696 =259.882921 (9.3)

Fibonacci, just like before, has the following equation in the background.

X=75 (1/ (1+0.06) + 1/ (1+0.06)2 + 1/ (1 +0.06)3 + 1/ (1 +0.06)4) = 259.882291 (9.4)

Clearly, if discounting is not discernible in the first problem, it is neither in this problem.

Goetzmann claims: The discounted annual value of the 300 bezants paid in the last period is 259 and change. As before, Fibonacci explains how to construct a multi-period discount factor from the product of the reciprocals of the periodic growth rate of an investment, using the model developed from mercantile trips in which a percentage profit is realised at each city. In this problem, he explicitly quantifies the difference in the value of two contracts due to the timing of the cash flows alone. As such, this particular example marks the discovery of one of the most important tools in the mathematics of Finance – an analysis explicitly ranking different cash flow streams based upon their present value.

Apparently, Goetzmann in his excitement jumped over some crucial details. All his claims are false. First, his claim that the 'discounted value of 300 bezants is 259 and change' is not correct since the discounted value of 300 bezants is 237.628099 [present value of 300 paid at the end=237.628099=300/ (1 +0.06)4 and not 259.882921].

Secondly, Goetzmann's claim that Fibonacci 'explicitly quantifies the difference in the value of two contracts due to the timing of the cash flows alone' as explained below, is also not correct.

Potential Value of the Original Contract: Apparently, the soldier wanted to invest his money as soon as he received it. In that case the potential value of his original contract, X0 would have been:

$X0=75 (1/(1+0.06) + 1/(1+0.06)^2 +1/ (1+0.06)^3 + 1/(1 +0.06)^4)$ $+ 75 (.06)/ (1+0.06)2 + 150 (0.6)/ (1+0.06)3 + 225 (0.6)/ (1 +0.06)^4$

X0= 259.882921 (the discounted value of the capital)+ 22.254822 (discounted value of interest)=282.137743 (9.5a).

Value of the Modified Contract: According to the modified contract, the soldier was to be paid interest on 75 bezants at a rate of 6 per cent per quarter at the end of second quarter, that would be 4.5 bezants (75x (0.06)), interest on 150 at the end of third period, that would be 9 bezants (150x (0.06)) and interest of 13.5 (225x (0.06)) bezants on 225 at the end of fourth period along with 300 bezants. We may write as:

Present value of interest payments=

$75 (.06)/ (1+0.06)2+ 150 (0.6)/(1+0.06)3 + 225 (0.6)/ (1+0.06)^4$

$= 4.5/ (1+0.06)2 + 9/ (1+0.06)3 + 13.5/ (1+0.06)^4$

=22.254822

Present value of 300 paid at the end =237.628099=300/ $(1 +0.06)^4$

Present value of modified contract= interest + capital= 22.254822 +237.628099 = 259.882921 (9.5b)

Certainly, not only the respective cash flows of the original contract and that of the modified contract were different but also as shown above, the true value of the original contract was higher than that of the modified contract. However, Fibonacci did not quantify the difference between the original and the modified contracts and could not have done that.

Actually, Fibonacci was not looking for a difference since he provided only one number (259.882921). He thought that the soldier was adequately compensated by allowing the interest payments and it did not matter whether the 300 bezanets were paid at the end or in four quarterly installments. He did not realisee that the modified contract was less generous to the soldier than the original contract. It is clear that Fibonacci did not understand the concept of discounting or of present value.

9.4 Kautilya and Samuelson on Discounting for National Security Projects

Kautilya believed that a foreign ruler would ruin the economy. He (p 175) argues: A foreign king, on the other hand, is one who has seized the kingdom from a legitimate king still alive; because it does not belong to him, he impoverishes it by extravagance, carries off its wealth or sells it. If the country becomes too difficult for him to handle, he abandons it and goes away (8.2).

He (132) adds: Harassment by the enemy's army [not only] affects the whole country but also ruins it by plunder, slaughter, burning and destruction (8.4).

Kautilya also believes that a foreign ruler can cause instability. He (p 176) writes: A new king who has acquired the kingdom by his own might [usually] does as he pleases, as if it was his personal property. If he has been helped by others in the takeover, he has to tolerate them [even] if they oppress the country. [There is also the danger of instability] a usurper, with no firm roots among the people, is easily overthrown (8.2).

Kautilya (p 179) suggests: The king shall avoid [settling] any part of the country which is liable to attack by enemies or jungle tribes and which is likely to be affected by disease and famine. He shall avoid excessive expenditure (2,136).

Kautilya strongly recommends that before an enemy gets a chance to ruin the economy and create instability, (it)must be destroyed. He (p 541) writes: An enemy's destruction shall be brought about even at the cost of great losses in men, material and wealth (7.13). If that is not possible, a king should try to acquire power to prevent an aggression. He developes a comprehensive approach to national security. His ideas can be represented by the following power equation (see Sihag 2014, Ch. 18 for details):

S = A (J, H) (K)l (E Lm) (1–l) (9.6)

R = S1 / S2 (9.7)

Where S_1 and S_2 = powers of king one and king two respectively, A= efficiency parameter, H= experience and analytical skills of the advisers in utilising the information made available through intelligence, K= horses, elephants, chariots and armaments, E= enthusiasm and training, L_m = military strength, J = level of public support for a just and kind-hearted king and R= relative power of nation one. Kautilya believed that H was the most important factor in enhancing national security.

Thus, according to Kautilya, (i) probability of an aggression is negatively related to the relative power and there is always a potential threat to a nation, so long as its relative power is less than one. (ii) A foreign ruler was interested in promoting only his own well-being and could be a source of political instability and (iii) instability would lead to a higher risk premium.[4]

Kautilya's advice to the king is to take precautionary measures to reduce the probability of any man-made or natural disaster and if despite preventive measures, it still happens, remedial measures should be in place to reduce the potential loss. He (p 116) writes: In the interests of the prosperity of the country, a king should be diligent in foreseeing the possibility of calamities, try to avert them before they arise, overcome those which happen, remove all obstructions to economic activity and prevent loss of revenue to the state (8.4).

It may be noted that, according to Kautilya, the probability p of an attack is a policy variable.

Incidentally, Ehrlich and Becker (1972) label 'try to avert them before they arise' as self-protection and 'overcome those which happen' as self-insurance. Equation (8) in Barro and Urs′ua (2012) may be used to express Kautilya's ideas:

$$re - rf = \gamma\sigma + p \cdot E\{b \cdot [(1-b)^{-\gamma} - 1]\} \quad (9.8)$$

Where re= is the expected rate of return on equity, and *rf* = is the risk-free rate.

Kautilya argues that the risk premium (re–*rf*) can be lowered by reducing the probability, p of a disaster, such as a war.[5]

Similarly, according to Samuelson, national security projects, such as nuclear treaties are very different from other projects since they lower the probability of a war and consequently lower the risk premium for all ventures/stocks. Additionally, Samuelson suggests that fiscal policies could be used to reduce the probability of a depression and the loss of income. He (1964, p 95) wrote, 'A private investor faces depression risk in every venture. It would be a blessing if the government incurred dollar losses at such times. Only those huge decisions that bring on serious results to all citizens – atomic bombs treaties, and not regional dams - need strong discounting for risk dispersion'. Jensen and Bailey (1972) did not understand the importance of national security. They wrote, 'Thus, Samuelson notwithstanding, it is precisely "regional dams" and not "atomic bomb treaties" that are more likely to need "strong discounting for risk" when undertaken in the public sector'.

9.5 Conclusion

Kautilya was the first economist who introduced the concept of discounting. He needed this concept along with other concepts to give shape to his vision of building a prosperous, secular, safe and secure nation. He introduces the concept of risk premium, particularly associated with insecurity caused by a foreign aggressor or a local intruder. Most importantly, he justifies giving preference to projects that enhance national security. On the other hand, as shown above, Fibonacci did not understand the concept of discounting. He was simply trying to hide his sources by using sentences instead of an equation.

Grampp (2000) is concerned about the possibility of excessive imagination on the part of some researchers in interpreting earlier writers. Accordingly, he lays some ground rules to avoid such tendencies.[5] Any claim that Fibonacci even remotely could have conceived the concept of discounting would fall under Grampp's (e) and (f) categories. Also, there is no evidence to support the claim that Fibonacci created a financial revolution.[6] Europe was in a deep slumber at least for another three hundred years and Fibonacci's *Liber Abaci* was unsuccessful in waking it up.

Arthashastra: The Origin of Statistical Economics

SINCE THE end of colonialism, the true history of ideas has started to emerge. Recently, Chandrakant Raju (2011) explored the *origin of probability* in ancient India. He shows that the concept of probability first appeared more than four thousand years ago in the Rig Veda and was further developed in the epic Mahabharata. [1] Rajaram and Frawley (2001) have convincingly challenged the fictitious Aryan Invasion theory. Similarly, Sihag (2014) shows that Kautilya established economics as a separate discipline during 4th century BCE, implying that economics already, way before Adam Smith, had its founder.

Peter Bernstein (1996, p 77) claims that both Graunt and Petty may be considered as the co-fathers of statistics. He limits his search only to western contributors and does not see the need to look beyond Europe. Inferential statistics was introduced in India by Vishalaksha, a predecessor of Kautilya, that is, before 4th century BCE. In fact, Vishalaksha not only emphasised the critical role of *inferential statistics* to sound decision-making but also of cognitive division of labour.[2] However, Kautilya was the first economist, who introduced statistics to economics and may be considered as the founder of statistical economics.

India's golden age started in antiquity, about six thousand years ago and continued at least for five thousand years. It began with the composition of Vedas, their mathematical appendices called *Sulvasutras* and *Upanishads*.[3] Then medicine, surgery, prosody, logic and the *Arthashastra* literature were developed during 7th century BCE to 4th century BCE. Kautilya was one of the contributors to the dynamism of the golden age and essentially a maker of his age.

The Vedas and the epic Mahabharata were definitely available to Kautilya. He lists prosody as one of the auxiliary subjects, implying that most likely Pingala's *Chandasutras* was also available to him. Kautilya understands the concept of risk and incorporates it into decision-making. More specifically, he understands the concepts of risk-return trade-off, risk premium, loss-aversion, diversification and analysis of variance and applies them appropriately. Section 10.1 presents his forward-looking ideas for bringing a brighter future to every citizen.

Kautilya proposes population census with its age-distribution (old, young and working), occupation, income and expenditure of each person (something like the modern National Sample Survey parameters in India). Similarly, he proposes a complete census of land-use: crop-pattern, how much land is under cultivation and whether dependent on rain or is irrigated. This proposal is presented in Section 10.2. Kautilya emphasis clarity of expression and efficiency of policy recommendations. He understands the relevance of the first two moments of a probability distribution to decision-making when faced with risky situations. This is presented in Section 10.3. According to Kautilya, at the time, market for high valued products was very thin and their export was very risky. He, thus, suggests precautionary measures to provide security to the traders and their merchandise. Also, he limits the proportion of 'high value' products in the total consignment to reduce the probability of getting robbed, that is, he suggests *diversification* to reduce the risk. This is presented in Section 10.4.

At the time, foreign trade was very risky. Since a trader might get robbed, killed, settle abroad or not make any profit, implying a very high probability of a default on a loan. Kautilya knew people had varying degrees of tolerance for risk-bearing and similarly they had differing levels of capabilities for undertaking productive activities. He understands the basic economic principle that efficient allocation of resources depends on proper allocation of risk-bearing. He adopts a balanced approach in which the lender is compensated adequately for bearing the risk and at the same time, the borrower is protected from being charged excessively high interest rate due to the imperfections in the capital market. Section 10.5 presents Kautilya's ideas on efficient allocation of resources under risky situations. Final Section provides some concluding remarks.

10.1 Dynamism in Ancient India: A Pre-requisite to Risk Analysis

Peter Bernstein (1996) explains why, up to the time of Renaissance, the concept of risk in Europe was not incorporated into decision-making. He believes so long as people are living close to subsistence, they do not have time to think about the future. Unless they can spare some time over and above meeting their survival needs, they are limited to the present conditions. He (p 18) observes: That the push did not occur was not an accident. Before a society could incorporate the concept of risk into its culture, change would have to come, not in views of the present, but in attitudes about the future.

Up to the time of the Renaissance, people perceived the future as little more than a matter of luck or the result of random variations, and most of their decisions were driven by instinct. When the conditions of life are so closely linked to nature, not much is left to human control. As long as the demands of survival limit people to the basic functions of bearing children, growing crops, hunting, fishing, and providing shelter, they are simply unable to conceive of circumstances in which they might be able to influence the outcomes of their decisions. A penny saved is not a penny earned unless the future is something more than a black hole, Says Bernstein.

It is important to point out that India did not experience any Dark Age until the last few centuries. So, the term 'Renaissance' is irrelevant in the case of India. In fact, it is incorrect to use it even for Europe, since knowledge was flowing from east to west during the so-called Dark Age. India experienced dynamism at least two thousand years earlier than Europe.[4] There was dynamism in every sphere of human activity. For example, Kautilya was a great organiser, ethical, and an empiricist, who did not believe in fate. He offers a totally new perspective by linking a man's destiny to his own efforts. He identifies the formation of capital (wealth) and human exertion as the most important source of economic growth. He understands the virtuous cycle: wealth creates prosperity and that in turn creates more wealth (see Chapter 2). Keeping that in view, he devises ways, both to create more wealth and preserve the existing one.

Importance of Wealth (Capital): Kautilya understands the role of capital formation to economic prosperity. He (p 637) explains: Wealth will slip away from that childish man who constantly consults the stars. The only [guiding] star of wealth is itself; what can the stars of the sky do? Man, without wealth, does not get it even after a hundred attempts. Just as elephants are needed to catch elephants, so does wealth capture more wealth (9.4.26-27).

Creation of Wealth: He suggests ways to increase wealth. He (p 149) advises: Hence the king shall be ever active in the management of the economy. The root of wealth is economic activity and lack of it brings material distress. In the absence of fruitful economic activity, both current prosperity and future growth are in danger of destruction. A king can achieve the desired objectives and abundance of riches by undertaking productive economic activity (1.19.35-36).

Preservation of Wealth: Kautilya was farsighted as well as foresighted. He suggests preventive measures to reduce the probability of occurrence of a calamity and to keep ready the remedial measures, if despite efforts, a calamity still occurs so that the loss is kept to the minimum. He suggests measures to prevent an attack by a foreign king, he creates traffic codes to prevent accidents, suggests establishment of industrial zones to prevent fires, advises appropriate measures to prevent famines, floods, fire and epidemics. Kautilya (p 116) suggests: In the interests of the prosperity of the country, a king should be diligent in foreseeing the possibility of calamities, try to avert them before they arise, overcome those which happen, remove all obstructions to economic activity and prevent loss of revenue to the state (8.4.50, 8.5.21). Kautilya is focused on making tomorrow better than today and no wonder, he incorporatesrisk-analysis into decision-making.

Importance of Human Exertion: According to Kautilya, human effort not fate is the key to success. He (p 619) states: The value of land is what man makes of it (7.11.9). He (p 621) adds: A king who trusts in fate and does not believe in human effort will fail because such a king never begins a work and never achieves anything (7.11).

Drekmeier (1962, 290) summarises this period as: We may surmise that men began to conclude that remaking the world was within the realm of possibility. The ancient belief in the cyclical periodicity of time, the eternal return, was modified or displaced altogether by a sense of continuity and development approximating a historical attitude. Accumulated wealth and the military power and administrative efficiency it made possible could now be used for achieving ambitious, long-range political and social goals. The great man is, in fact, the great organiser. He creates the very conditions that make the hero obsolete, for he imposes an order that limits the unpredictable contingencies against which the hero struggles. The hero was made by his age; the organiser is the maker of his age. Men can now do things that earlier could be accomplished only by the gods.

10.2 Kautilya Proposed the very first Population Census

Kautilya identifies land, labour and capital as sources of economic growth. However, no acurate information is still available on these factors of production. He believes that *information* is a critical input in arriving at informed choices and therefore, is obsessed with the collection of information on economic as well as non-economic variables. He recommendsd the appointment of a Record Keeper for every five to ten villages, who keeps detailed records on households and land-use in the villages.

Information Collection about the Village: He (p 220) suggests: The villages shall be classified as best, average or lowest. They shall also be classified according to whether they are [tax paying or] tax exempt, whether they supply soldiers [in lieu of tax], and whether they supply [fixed amounts of] grain, cattle, gold, forest produce, labour or other commodities. [Within each village,] every plot of land shall be numbered, and its use recorded according to the classification: cultivated or fallow, dry or wet cultivation, park, vegetable garden [and orchard], enclosed area, forest, sanctuary, temple, water works, cremation ground, rest-house, public drinking-water facility, holy place, pasture and roads. These records shall be used for determining the location of fields, forests and roads [in case of boundary disputes] and to record transactions such as gifts, sales, charitable endowments and tax exemptions.

This provide information about the crop-pattern, land-use, and land under irrigation to allow estimation of assured agricultural output. Apparently, in those times, there was a lot of flexibility in paying taxes. It could be paid in grain, gold or labour. This information was necessary for building required storage and in determining how many additional soldiers were to be recruited. The information on taxes helped in more realistic budgeting.

Household Census: Kautilya continues: [Likewise,] each house shall be numbered and classified as whether taxpaying or tax-exempt. Records of the inhabitants shall also be kept under the following headings: (i) the varna; (ii) occupation such as farmer, cowherd, trader, craftsman, laborer or slave; (iii) the number of males and females as well as the number of children and old people, their family history, occupation, income and expenditure; (iv) livestock and poultry owned; (v) the amount of tax payable in cash or in free labor; and (vi) tolls and fines that may be due (2.35.1-7).

It should be pointed out that Kautilya did not want to use manpower for collecting useless information. The above information made it possible to calculate the labour participation rate (number of adults/ total population), saving rate, taxes and tax expenditures (tax exemptions). Record Keepers were responsible for collecting the taxes and there were magistrates to 'inspect their work and to ensure proper collection of taxes'.

Similarly, Kautilya suggests a detailed record keeping of government's budget: sources of its revenue and its uses. Mattessich (2000, p 203) remarks: Kautilya's *Arthashastra* is not merely significant for only for business accounting but also government accounting, with some stretch of imagination it may be regarded as a forerunner of national income accounting since the ultimate purpose of Kautilya's work was to strengthen the economy of the entire nation.

Bernstein (p 81) remarks: Among his more ambitious efforts, Graunt made the first reasoned estimate of the population of London and pointed out the importance of demographic data for determining whether London's population was rising or falling and whether it be grown big enough, or too big. Graunt (1662) collected data on mortality rates and causes of death in seventeenth century London and used that to estimate the population of that city and that was considered adequate in bestowing on him the title 'father of statistics'. This is as arbitrary as conferring a sainthood on a priest for performing miracles. Origin of statistics and its useful applications by Kautilya had occurred in India more than two thousand years earlier than Graunt.

10.3 Kautilya on the Relevance of First Two Moments of a Distribution

Kautilya understood the concept of probability since he had access to the Rig Veda and the epic Mahabharata. He understood the importance of the first two moments of a probability distribution to decision-making under risky situations. He introduced many statistical concepts and incorporated them into economic analysis. He was way ahead of his time.

Kautilya on the Necessary Condition for Undertaking a Project: He (p 634) recommends: The king shall undertake a march when the expected gain outweighs the losses and expenses (9.4.3). This indicates that he had some idea of a probability distribution. Otherwise, he could not have used the expression 'expected gain'.

That implies that he did not rely on what Biddle (1999) calls 'eye-balling'.

Second, he suggests that a project must not be undertaken unless the net expected gain is positive.

Kautilya on the Role of Expected Value and Variability: If a king is to participate in a joint-campaign, he should negotiate for a piece of land that has irrigation facilities since the variability in crop-yield on that land would be negligible. He (p 619) states: As between land dependent on rain and land with flowing water [i.e. a river], a smaller tract with flowing water is preferable to a larger drier one because with flowing water, which is always available, the production of crops is assured (7.11.3). It appears that he preferred an irrigated piece of land with lower expected value and lower variance to a larger dry piece of land with higher expected value and higher variance.[5]

$\sigma 1 = \sigma 2$ and $\mu_1 > \mu_2$: If the variability in yield on two pieces of land is the same, that is, $\sigma 1 = \sigma 2$, then the decision should be based only on expected return. Kautilya provides two situations. (i) He (p 619) states: "As between two irrigated tracts, one on which cereals can be grown is preferable (7.11.5). That is, $U(\mu_1, \sigma 1) > U(\mu^2, \sigma^2)$ if $\sigma 1 = \sigma 2$ and μ_1 the expected return from the first piece of land $> \mu_2$, the return on the second piece of land.

$\sigma 1 = \sigma 2$ and $\mu_1 < \mu_2$: Kautilya (p 619) states: [However], if one of them is larger, the larger one unsuitable to the cultivation of cereals is preferable to the smaller one, which is suitable. For, not only can different types of wet crops, dry crops and medicinal plants be grown in [different parts of] a large area but also many forts and defensive works can be built. The value of land is what man makes of it (7.11.6-9). Again, the variability iss the same, but the second piece of land being larger, offers a higher return and should be preferable (see Sihag 2014, Chapter 19) for additional applications).

10.4 Kautilya on Risk Reduction through Diversification

Kautilya believes that the market for high-value products is thin and is more likely to attract robbers/pirates. He is concerned about the safety of the traders and protection of their merchandise and suggestsd undertaking precautionary measures.

Thin Market for High-Value Products: Kautilya believes that the market for high-value products is thin. He (p 623) explains: Some teachers say that a small production of high value minerals is preferable [to a large production of inferior products] because valuable products (such as diamonds, precious stones, pearls, corals, gold and silver) are worth much more than a large amount of inferior products. Kautilya disagrees. Buyers of high-valued products are rare and are found after a long search; there are many buyers and a steady demand for products of small value (7.12).

Export Risk of High-Value Products: According to Kautilya, high-value products attracted robbers/pirates. Kautilya (p 238) states: If the Chief Controller of State Trading sends a caravan by a land route, he shall choose a safe route. One quarter of the goods shall be of high value. Jungle chieftains, frontier officers and governors in the City and the countryside shall be contacted beforehand for assuring security. Steps shall be taken to ensure the protection of the members of the caravan and goods of high value (2.16).

Thus, according to him, the probability of getting robbed (π) depends on the fraction of high-value goods (α) and the expenditure on security measures (S). Formally his ideas may be expressed as:

$$\text{Max } Z = \pi(\alpha, S)\, U^1 (W - \alpha G - S) + (1 - \pi(\alpha, S))\, U^2 (W + \alpha G (1 + RH) - S) + U^3 (W + (1 - \alpha) G (1 + RL)) \quad (11.1)$$

By maximising with respect to S we get

$$\pi S\, U^1 (W - \alpha G - S) - \pi\, U^1 1 (W - \alpha G - S) - \pi_S\, U^2 (W + \alpha G (1 + RH) - S) - (1 - \pi(\alpha, S))\, U^2 1 (W + \alpha G (1 + RH) - S) = 0 \quad (11.2)$$

That is,

$$-\pi S\, U^2 (W + \alpha G (1 + RH) - S) = -\pi S\, U^1 (W - \alpha G - S) + \pi\, U^1 1 (W - \alpha G - S) + (1 - \pi(\alpha, S))\, U21 (W + \alpha G (1 + R_H) - S) \quad (11.2')$$

Equation (2') is the usual maximisation condition indicating that marginal benefit =marginal cost. As mentioned above, according to Kautilya, an increase in the proportion of high-valued goods would require higher expenditure on security measures. By differentiating equation (2) with respect to α, we get:

$ds/d\alpha = G [\pi S U11 - \pi U111 + \pi S U^21 (1+R_H) + (1-\pi) U^211 (1+R_H)]/D$ (11.3)

$D = [\partial^2 \pi / \partial S^2 (U^1 - U^2) - 2 \pi S U^11 + 2 \pi S U^21 + \pi U^111 + (1-\pi) U211] < 0$ (11.4)

Where $\partial\pi/\partial = \pi_\alpha > 0$, that is, as α increases, probability of getting robbed also increases. $\partial\pi/\partial S = \pi_S < 0$, that is, as S, spending on security measures increases, probability of getting robbed decrease. Marginal utility of wealth, $U^11 > 0$ and $U^111 < 0$.

Here $ds/d\alpha > o$ since both numerator and denominator in equation (11.3) are negative, implying that a relatively smaller proportion of high-value products might be more profitable than a larger proportion. Kautilya does not explicitly indicate as to how he arrives at the conclusion that 25 per cent of the consignment should consist of high-value goods. But this could be justified by using a simple numerical example. Suppose the rate of return is 100 per cent on high-value goods and 20 per cent on low-value goods and total value of consignment= 100.

Table 11.1= Optimal Mix of High-Value and Low-Value Goods

Value of High-value goods (X)	Expected Loss from getting robbed π X	Profit from low-value goods (100–X) R_L	Expected Revenue from high-value goods (–π) X	Cost of Protection	Net expected Profit
100	–100 (0.6) = –60	0	(0.4).100 = 40	15	–35
50	–50 (0.35) = –17.5	50.(0.2) =10	(.65) 50=32.5	10	15
25	-25 (0.05) = -1.25	75 (0.2) =15	(.95) 25=23.75	3	34.50
0	0	100 (0.2) = 20	0	0	20

As an illustration only four possibilities are presented.

Possibility (i): If the high-value goods are 100 per cent of the consignment, there will be a loss of 35. Kautilya would never consider that.

Possibility (ii): If the high-value goods are 50 per cent of the consignment, variance of profit=2275, standard deviation=47.7 and expected net profit=15.

Possibility (iii): If the high-value goods are 25 per cent of the consignment, variance=118.75, standard deviation=10.9 and expected net profit=34.5.

Possibility (iv): If no high-value goods, profit= 20.

Possibility (iii) in which high value products consisted of 25 per cent of the consignment provide the highest profit. Kautilya was the first economist, who advocated diversification.

10.5 Kautilya on Efficient Allocation of Resources under Risky Situations

Kautilya on Risk Premium: Kautilya understood the basic economic principle that efficient allocation of resources under risky situations required an efficient allocation of risk. This was truly a unique insight. That is, someone who is most willing and able to bear risk, should assume most of the risk. He says that a producer (trader) might be good in producing goods (export-import business) but unwilling or unable to bear risk. Similarly, a money-lender might be willing and able to bear risk but inexperienced in undertaking any productive activity. Kautilya separates the value-creating activities from bearing risk.[6] The second important issue is the determination of the magnitude of the risk-premium and Kautilya somehow figures that out too.

He (p 426) suggests: 'The lawful rates of interest (on money lent) for different purposes shall be:

Normal transactions Commercial transactions:

Normal	15% per annum
Risky travel:	60%
Through forests	120%
By sea	240%

No one shall charge or cause to be charged a rate higher than the above, except in regions where the King is unable to guarantee security; in such a case, the judges shall take into account the customary practices among debtors and creditors (3.11).'

Travel as such was risky in those days and as Kautilya points out, travel by sea is riskier than travel on land. He (p 623) explains: 'Some teachers say that a trade-route by water is preferable to one on land because water routes can be used to transport a large quantity of goods at less expense and exertion. Kautilya disagrees. A water route is not usable at all times, accessible at only a few places, full of dangers and indefensible in contrast to land routes. Among water routes, a coastal route is better than one on the high sea because there are a large number of ports along any coast. A river route is also good because it poses less serious dangers and is more constantly in use (7.12).'

It is obvious that Kautilya recommends a higher risk premium for undertaking the extra risk. In today's notations: $r = r_n + \pi$. Where r = rate of interest on a risky loan, r_n = normal (prime) rate (which was suggested to be 60%), π = risk premium. Apparently, most of the risk is borne by the financier (more like today's venture capitalists) of the loans and not by the merchant. The financier is capable of bearing the risk, but the borrower must pay the risk premium. Also, the suggestion that the interest rate could be higher 'where the King is unable to guarantee security' is quite significant, implying the importance of law and order in reducing risk and promoting economic activity.

10.6 Conclusion

Arrow (1971) remarks: Insurance is an item of considerable importance in the economies of advanced nations, yet it is fair to say that economic theorists have had little to say about it, and insurance theory has developed with virtually no reference to the basic concepts of utility and productivity.

Firstly, Arrow is describing this situation for 1971, that is, for a very recent period. Secondly, economics of risk, ambiguity and fundamental uncertainty is still in a flux. Kautilya understood the link between risk-premium and productivity (efficiency) during 4th century BCE and appropriately applied the concept of risk premium. It shows how advanced Kautilya was since his insights are as relevant today as they were in his time.

Last sixty years or so have been devoted to the construction, demolition and resuscitation of the Expected Utility Theory (EUT) for studying individual behaviour under risk and uncertainty. Machina (1987) remarks: 'To a growing tension between those who view economic analysis as the description and prediction of what they consider to be rational behavior and those who view it as the description and prediction of observed behavior.'

Kautilya emphasisesd the role of education in making an individual rational, implying that at least one controversy whether to study rational behaviour or the actual behaviour might get resolved and help in restoring EUT.[7]

Kautilya considers information critical to sound decision-making. He was the first economist who proposed taking of population census. It is also clear that he iss as concerned dealing with risk and uncertainty as we are. His predecessors concentrated only on expected return, but he considers both risk and expected return in making a choice. His other insights, such as how to evaluate a policy or determine liability are presented in Sihag (2014, Chapters 5, and 17). Kautilya, essentially, performs a civil union between statistics and economics.

Arthashastra: The Origin of Mathematical Economics

IN RECENT years[1] Ingrao and Israel (1990), [2, 3] Mirowski (1989, 1991) and [4] Weintraub (2002) have explored the why and how of the emergence of mathematical economics in the western world during the last two centuries. These works have been reviewed extensively and have generated both heat and light. Unsurprisingly, all of them are Euro-centric. Weintraub argues that the image of economics changed as the image of mathematics changed but without realising that the image of mathematics in the west might have changed with the change in the theology/ philosophy of the church. It sounds strange, but logically that means that the image of economics has changed as the theology/ philosophy of the church changed. Economics has been criticised for lack of bonhomie but surprisingly no one has ever realised or criticised it for being religion-based.

Mathematics and economics neither originated in the western world, nor during the 17th or 18th century, implying that the scope of current studies on the emergence of mathematical economics is very limited. According to [5] Seidenberg (1962), mathematics originated in India earlier than Babylonia, Egypt or Greece.[1] Similarly, Kautilya was the first economist, who established economics as a separate discipline, developed a score of economic concepts and understood *economy as a system* with its inter-linked elements (see [6] Sihag 2014)).[2] [7] Kautilya's *Arthashastra* contains two parts: the exchange theory and the conflict theory but both use mathematics to enhance clarity of expression and statistical analysis for arriving at the best possible policy-decisions under risky situations and evaluations afterwords.[3] Secondly, there existed some knowledge of astronomy (physics) in ancient India, but economics did not imitate its methodology.

Weintraub applies Corry's distinction between the body and the image of mathematics to economics and devotes his entire book to show that the image of economics changed as the image of mathematics changed. However, neither Corry nor Weintraub explore: why did the image of mathematics change? [8] Raju has researched this subject quite extensively. He links the changes in the image of mathematics in the west to changes in the theology/ philosophy of the church. According to him, during ancient times, (i) mathematics was considered as 'mathesis' and was thought to arouse the soul and make people virtuous to lead a 'blessed life', (ii) became useless during the dark age, (iii) was resurrected as reasoning and proof during the middle ages and (iv) changed to formal representation during the twentieth century. Section 11.1 summarises Raju's findings and concludes with a major implication that economics in the west is religion-based.

On the other hand, mathematics in India has been developed to solve practical problems and its role and image have not changed since the Harappa Civilisation (2600 BCE-1800 BCE) or even earlier. This is presented in Section 11.2. Kautilya applies discrete marginal analysis as a gside to maintaining parity with a potential adversary.[4] In fact, Kautilya shows awareness of some elements of a *prospect theory*. These are presented in Section 11.3. Kautilya counts all possible choices before examining the pros and cons of each one of them. Section 11.4 presents two examples in which Kautilya uses *combinatory* rules to list all possible options so that no option is left out and also the order in which to examine the implications of each option. Kautilya is aware of the functional relationships between variables. This is provided in Section 11.5. Final Section provides some concluding remarks.

11.1 Raju on Images of Mathematics in the West since 5th Century BCE

According to Weintraub (2002, p. 2): 'If economics is intertwined with mathematics in the twentieth century, in order to understand the history of economics we need to understand the history of mathematics. However, the history of mathematics involves the history of both changes in mathematical knowledge and changes in the images of that mathematical knowledge. Thus, in what follows I will refract economics through the prism of changing images of mathematics.' He explains that the image of economics changed as the image of mathematics changed. But he does not explain why did the image of mathematics change? However, Raju explains why the image of mathematics has been changing in the west.

Mathematics as Mathesis from 500 Century BCE to 500 CE: According to [8] Raju, Socrates believed that (i) soul was immortal and (ii) learning was mere recollection. He tried to prove that by asking questions related to geometry from an uneducated slave boy. (iii) Socrates also believed that learning was essential to making people virtuous. (iv) Mathematics was defined as 'mathesis', that is, as learning and it incorporated eternal truths. (v) Mathematics was assigned the role of arousing the soul and making people virtuous. Apparently, mathematics had a metaphysical origin in the west and was not considered useful to science. From Socrates to Proclus, study of mathematics was considered to arouse the soul and essential to a 'Blessed life'.

Darkest Image of Mathematics from 500 CE to Crusade (15th century CE): The Christian priests tasted some power and riches during the reign of Constantine and aspired to have more power. According to Westfall (quoted in [8] Raju, p 77), Newton pointed out, 'It's plain therefore that not a few irregular persons, but ye whole clergy began at this time to be puft up, to set their hearts upon power and greatness more than upon piety & equity, to transgress their pastoral office & exalt themselves....' Socrates' belief of teaching mathematics to arouse the soul became a hurdle in their pursuit of power. They modified incarnation to resurrection, created fear in the minds of believers by introducing the concepts of heaven and hell and sin. There was no role left for mathematics in this modified theological doctrine. A Christian mob burned the library in Alexandria. Hypatia, who tried to teach the elements, was raped and lynched. Proclus was declared a heretic and the church banned the study of mathematics and philosophy. During the dark age of Christendom, the image of mathematics also became dark in the west.

Mathematics as Reasoning and Proof from Crusade to 1900 (400 years): The church tried to convert people to Christianity by force but that did not work against the Muslims. So, it modified its approach and thought of converting them by soft power, that is by reasoning. Accordingly, *the church* brought back mathematics but with a changed image based on its theological philosophy of reason. The church performed a miracle by creating Euclid out of uclides (translation from Arabic as: the key to geometry) and declared him as the author of *Elements*. In fact, there is absolutely no evidence that there was a historical Euclid and the *Elements*, most probably, was written by Theon and his daughter Hypatia around 500 CE.[5] *Elements* was hailed as a paradigm shift in mathematics and the church claimed that for the first time in human history, proofs were derived from a few axioms. Thus, there were two changes of Biblical proportions: one in the image of mathematics and second in church's theology. Although it was still metaphysical, [9] Ferreiros incorrectly equates Gauss's image of mathematics to that of Plato. According to Plato, mathematics was supposed to arouse the soul. On the other hand, Gauss was following the 'reasoning and proof' image of mathematics as propagated by Descartes (b 1596).

Attempt to Rescue eternal truth during 1900-1950: Hilbert and others discovered that *Elements* contained some empirical means for proving certain theorems. As a consequence, two things happened: first, image of mathematics as an eternal truth could not be sustained. Secondly, an attempt to replace eternal truth by consistency through formal mathematics also failed. The following Table summarises the changes in the image of mathematics.

Table 12.1: Images of Mathematics in West over the last 2,500 years

West		
Time-Period	Author	Image
5th century BCE to 4th Century CE	Plato	To arouse the soul, 'God does Geometry', as Eternal Truth, a priori reasoning
5th century CE	Theon and his daughter Hypatia and Proclus	Essential to a 'Blessed life'
5th century CE to Crusade		'Anathemas against pre-existence'
Post-Crusade to 1900	Descartes	'Reasoning and Proof' to align with post-crusade Christian 'theology of reason', Deductive proofs
	Newton	'Mathematics as the perfect language in which God had written the laws of nature'
	Gauss	'God does Arithmetic', still metaphysics
1900-1950	Hilbert	Failed Attempt to replace Eternal Truth by consistency, formalism
1950-Present		It is still metaphysical

Raju points out that the theologically based two-valued logic approach to mathematics cannot be justified as universal since it is religion-based and deductive proofs are not superior to empirical proofs. [8] He (p 159) argues: 'The Buddha, for example, used the logic of catuskoti (four alternatives). Likewise, his contemporary, Mahavira, and the Jains used a logic of three alternatives or perhaps-ism (syadavada). Many mathematical proofs today use a technique called proof by contradiction. These proofs would all fail with Buddhist or Jain logic.'

The above discussion may be summarised as: the image of mathematics in the west has changed as the theology/philosophy of the church changed and it still has religious bias. Logically, that means that the image of economics has changed as the theology/philosophy of the church changed, implying that economics also is religion-based.

11.2 Unchanging Image of Mathematics since Antiquity in India

> In all those transactions which relate to worldly, Vedic or other affairs, mathematics is employed. In the science of love, in economics, in music and in drama, in the art of cooking and similarly in medicine and in things like the knowledge of architecture, the science of computation is held in high esteem. Whatever is there in all the three worlds, which are possessed of moving and non-moving beings all that indeed cannot exist without mathematics.
>
> —[10] Mahavira (c 817-c 875)

Since antiquity, mathematics in India has been developed to solve practical problems related to agriculture, trade, construction, navigation and engineering to enrich human life materially, culturally and in developing rhythms for music. In fact, mathematician Mahavira claimed its usefulness to all areas of human activity. Interestingly, he included even the 'science of love', perhaps he was referring to *Kamasutra*. Whereas, according to [11] Edna St Vincent Millay, 'Euclid alone has looked on beauty bare'. No Indian mathematician has been so lucky to experience anything like that. They instead used mathematics to create beautiful and enjoyable structures. Irony is that there is no record of any historical Euclid and let alone seeing any beauty. And still, this fictitious story has been repeated a million times. Theon, the true author of the Elements, was looking for a 'blessed life' and not beauty, bare or clothed.

Mathematics and Construction: More than five thousand

years ago, Sindhu-Sarasvati Civilisation (populary known as Harappa Civilisation) had introduced standardised weights and measurements to facilitate trade. It developed mathematics to solve architectural and engineering problems. Bricks were designed to provide maximum stability to the structures. The dimensions of the bricks in inches were 11x 5.5 x 2.75, that is, in the ratio of 4:2:1. [12] Jagatpati Joshi (2008, p 157) observes, 'There are quite a few buildings in Mohenjodaro, Harappa, Lothal and Kalibangan which have steps. In the construction of steps on the stairs, one must know how to divide height and length in equal parts. The construction of such a structure involves summation, subtraction, multiplication and division of fractions, which the Harappans apparently used'. He (p 164) adds, 'The Harappans followed the decimal system of measurement, which was used by the Indus masons.'

Harappans devised astronomical calendars to monitor the arrival of monsoons. [13] Vahia and Menon (2013) conclude, 'It can be safely assumed that astronomers in the intellectually advanced Harappan Civilisation had detailed knowledge of positional astronomy'. They add, 'Finally, we should mention that since the Dholavira was an important centre of trade and commerce, keeping track of time would have been crucial, but to date no structures that absolutely served this purpose have been identified'. *Mathematics and Sanskrit*: If mathematics is the language, then Sanskrit is the language of mathematics. [14] Rachel Hall (2007) observes: The Search for ways to list and classify meters led to important mathematical discoveries: Pascal's triangle, the Fibonacci numbers, and even the rudiments of the binary number system. The discoveries of these structures in India predated those in the West, sometimes by several centuries.[6]

Mathematics and Music: Rachel Hall (2007) notes, 'They used recursion and iteration – essential computer programming techniques – to generate lists of rhythms. The fact that several authors solved the same problem in different ways reveals the depth of Indian mathematical development at the time. These discoveries also apply to rhythm patterns in traditional and popular music'. She adds, 'The poetic meters that Pingala and Hemachandra studied have an analogue in music, and indeed, many of the rhythms used in classical Indian music have been deeply influenced by the meters of Sanskrit poetry'.

Kautilya wrote his *Arthashastra* during the fourth century BCE. He listed agriculture, trade and cattle-rearing as the three main enterprises at that time. Agriculture has been dependent on monsoon rains. An accurate prediction of the arrival of monsoon has been a top priority. Similarly, navigation was essential to trade.

Mathematics and Navigation: [15] Raju (2011) summarises his findings as: To summarise the new history, the calculus originated in India for its practical value (for agriculture and navigation) and was brought to Europe also for its practical value (for navigation, and especially the problems of determining the three ells – loxodromes, latitude, and longitude.

Development of mathematics in India has had no religious leanings and has been user-friendly to solve problems related to trade, agriculture, construction, navigation and music.

11.3 Kautilya's Psychological Theory of Risk-taking

Kautilya criticisesYudhisthira, a crown prince who lived around 3100 BCE, for his gambling habit. Yudhisthira put his kingdom, his four brothers, himself and his wife as wagers and lost all the bets. The whole family was exiled for 13 years. He was quite naïve in this game, did not win even a single hand and yet continued until he lost everything. [16] Sebastian Ebert and Philipp Strack (2015) call this 'until the bitter end' and explain this by adopting the *dynamic prospect theory*. However, equally important question is: why did the winner also not stop? Kautilya offers a psychological explanation for this behavior.

Kautilya's *Arthashastra* is a manual on engineering *Yogakshema* – peaceful enjoyment of prosperity – for all the people. Kautilya argues that national sovereignty is essential to prosperity since a foreign ruler would be interested only in enriching himself, that is, prosperity and slavery are mutually exclusive. Then, he reasons that prosperity is essential to guarding sovereignty since a poor nation cannot have adequate resources to provide for strong national security, that is, for achieving and maintaining balance of power. Sihag (2014, Chap18) presents Kautilya's balance of power equation as follows:

$$P = A\,(J, H)\,(K)^{\lambda}\,(E\,Lm)^{(1-\lambda)} \qquad (1)$$

$$RP1 = PE / PC \qquad (2)$$

Where P=power, P_C and P_E = powers of conqueror and potential adversary respectively, A= efficiency parameter, H = experience and analytical skills of the advisers in utilising the information made available through intelligence, K = horses, elephants, chariots and armaments, E = enthusiasm and training, L_m = military strength, J = level of public support for a just and kind-hearted king and RP_1 = relative power of the potential adversary. Kautilya believes that H is the most important factor in enhancing national security.

Kautilya on the Role of Expected Value and Variability: If the variability in yield on two pieces of land is the same, that is, $\sigma 1 = \sigma 2$, then the decision should be based only on expected return. Kautilya (p 619) states: 'As between two irrigated tracts, one on which cereals can be grown is preferable (7.11.5).' That is, $U(\mu_1, \sigma 1) > U(\mu_2, \sigma 2)$ if $\sigma 1 = \sigma 2$ and μ_1 the expected return from the first piece of land > μ_2, the return on the second piece of land.

Preservation of Wealth: Kautilya is farsighted as well as foresighted. He suggests preventive measures to reduce the probability of occurrence of a calamity and to keep ready the remedial measures, if despite efforts, a calamity still occurres, preventive measures will keep the loss to the minimum. He suggests measures to prevent an attack by a foreign king, developes traffic codes to prevent accidents, suggests establishment of industrial zones to prevent fires, appropriate measures to prevent famines, floods, fire and epidemics. Kautilya (p 116) suggests, 'In the interests of the prosperity of the country, a king should be diligent in foreseeing the possibility of calamities, try to avert them before they arise, overcome those which happen, remove all obstructions to economic activity and prevent loss of revenue to the state (8.4.50, 8.5.21)'. Kautilya is focused on making tomorrow better than today and no wonder, he incorporates risk-analysis into decision-making. *Expansion, subject to Preservation*: Kautilya (p 108) observes: By maintaining order, the king can preserve what he already has, acquire new possessions, augment his wealth and power, and share the benefits of improvement with those worthy of such gifts. The progress of this world depends on the maintenance of order and the [proper functioning of] government (1.4).

He (p 629) states:A conqueror, having assured himself about his superiority in power, place and time, shall first leave behind a third or a quarter of his army to protect his capital, the rear, the forest regions and the borders; he shall then march towards the enemy taking with him enough wealth and forces to help him achieve his objective (9.1). Kautilya wants territorial expansion, but subject to the preservation of existing territory.

(1) *Loss Aversion*: Kautilya puts heavier weight on a loss than on an equal size of gain when taking risky decisions. He (p 634) surmises: A small revolt in the rear outweighs a large gain in the front; for, when the king is not there, a small revolt in the rear may be worsened by the anger of the people or by traitors, enemies and jungle tribes. If this happens, a large gain in front, even if actually obtained, will be eaten up by the subjects, allies, losses and expenses. Therefore, a king shall not undertake a campaign when the gain in front is [less than] a thousand times the likely loss due to a revolt in the rear or, at least, a hundred times the loss. A well-known proverb is: 'Misfortunes are, [in the beginning] no longer than the point of a needle' (9.3).

(2) *Emphasis only on Marginal Gains and Losses*: Kautilya considers power almost perfectly correlated with prosperity as he believesthat a richer country can afford a stronger national security. He expects the king to be very vigilant and keep parity

with a potential adversary. He (p 554) explains: It is a decline for the conqueror if the enemy's undertakings flourish; conversely, the decline of an enemy's undertakings is progress for the conqueror. Parity between the two is maintained when both make equal progress. A small gain for a large outlay is decline; the converse is progress. A gain equal to the expenditure on an undertaking means that the conqueror has neither progressed nor declined. Hence a conqueror shall seek to obtain a special advantage by undertaking such works [as building forts] which produce a large profit for a small expenditure (7.12).

Kautilya's advice to the conqueror is to undertake such projects where the net gain (Revenue–cost) is the largest. The above statement implies the following cases:

- $R^0 = W_E / W_C$, (initial reference point)
- $R^1 = (W_E + \Delta W_E)/ (W_C + \Delta W_C)$
- $= R^0 + (\Delta W_E - \Delta W_C)/ (W_C + \Delta W_C)$
- Case (i) If $\Delta W_C = 0$ and $\Delta W_E > 0$, it is a decline in the relative position of the conqueror.
- Case (ii) If $\Delta W_C = 0$ and $\Delta W_E < 0$, it is a progress in the relative position of the conqueror, that is, $R^1 < R^0$.
- Case (iii) If $\Delta W_C = \Delta W_E$, there is no change in the relative position of the conqueror, then $R^1 = R^0$.

Where R^0 = reference point (initial relative position), W_C= Conqueror's own wealth and W_E = enemy's wealth, ΔW_C and ΔW_E are the incremental changes in conqueror's and enemy's wealth respectively.

According to Kautilya, the king (conqueror) requires $RP_1 < 1$ for maintaining sovereignty. Otherwise, there is always a risk of losing it. Kautilya (p 624) states: The king may face dangers even from a trusted king of equal power, when the latter has achieved his objective. Even an equally powerful king tends to become stronger after the task is accomplished and, when his power has increased, becomes untrustworthy. Prosperity changes peoples' minds (7.5).

Two things are obvious from the above statement: Initially, the ally is of equal power (i.e., $R^0 = 1$) and is trustworthy. But after the ally acquires additional power by winning a campaign, $R^1 > R^0$, according to Kautilya, he is likely to become untrustworthy. Why? Kautilya hypothesises that 'Prosperity changes peoples' minds', implying that the ally might not keep his promise not to attack the conqueror, that is, his preferences might change (time inconsistency problem) and also (ii) after accomplishing the task, his aspiration level is likely to rise (a new reference point) and his attitude towards risk-taking may change and is likely to become more assertive. Incidentally, according to the prospect theory, ally is to the left of his new reference point, more like in the domain of loss and is be risk-acceptant. If one looks at the past rulers, Alexander, Napoleon or any other ruler, each win made the ruler more assertive and he kept on attacking other states until he met his Waterloo (losing the battle). It implies that Alexander most likely lost the battle and that is why decided to turn back from the bank of the Indus.

Coercive Diplomacy: In this situation the conqueror is in the domain of loss. Kautilya advises the conqueror to take measures that will stop the ally from placing his sight on the conqueror's kingdom. Kautilya (p 609) advises: An ally who is likely to grow in power after defeating the enemy and thus become uncontrollable shall be embroiled in a conflict with his own neighbour and his own ally; or, a pretender in his family or an unjustly treated prince shall be encouraged to seize the throne; or such actions shall be taken as would oblige the ally to remain obedient, in return for help received (7.18.31-32).

Kautilya on the Importance of Balance of Power: He advises (p 566): The would-be-conqueror shall apply the six methods with the degree to his power. He shall make peace with an equally powerful or stronger king; he shall wage war against a weaker king. [He shall not wage war against a stronger king] because he who fights against a stronger king is crushed like a foot soldier fighting an elephant. A fight with an equal brings losses to both sides, just like the destruction of two unbaked mudpots hitting each other. Like a stone striking a mudpot, a more powerful king gains decisive victory over a weaker one (7.3.1-5). According to Kautilya, balance of power, irrespective of the domain (loss or gain), should not be ignored.

We may summarise this section to say that Kautilya is the first economist, who introduced discrete marginal analysis to offer practical advice. Secondly, he understands the concept of time inconsistency problem and suggests precautionary measures to protect against it. Thirdly, most likely Alexander decided to return back to Greece because of losing the battle to an Indian king named Porus.

11.4 Kautilya on Use of Combinations for Making Policy Choices

Kautilya (p 99) explains his approach to writing his *Arthashastra* as: 'Easy to grasp and understand, free from verbosity, Kautilya has composed this treatise with precise words, doctrines and sense (1.1.19).' Mathematics has been used for precision and not as an ornament. He suggests that decisions must be guided by statistical analysis.

He knows how to calculate combinations. He lists conciliation, placating with gifts, sowing dissension and use of force as the four methods of dealing with conflicts. The first two may be classified under 'riskaversion' and the last two risk aversion 'coercive diplomacy'. Balance of power equation could not be ignored. He (p 115) suggests: 'The methods can be used singly or in combination depending on the seriousness of the situation. There are four ways of using any one method, six ways of using any two at a time, four ways of using three at a time and one way of using all four simultaneously. Thus, there are fifteen ways of using the methods singly or in any of the possible combinations in the *anuloma* [natural] order. Likewise, there are fifteen ways of using them in the *pratiloma* [unnatural] order 9.7.73-77).' He, then, explains which policy is the *appropriate* one to a specific situation. For example, he indicated that using all the four methods simultaneously before considering other possibilities would be unnatural.

Another Illustration of the Use of combinations: Kautilya offers a lesson in human psychology to the king. According to him, the king should anticipate the nature of reaction from his advisers and take appropriate steps so that they will not rebel. Kautilya (1992, 636) explains: The king becomes angry and the counselors afraid when a campaign, undertaken on the advice of the counselors, fails to produce the gain predicted by them, but leads to losses and expenses. Counselors frightened of punishment may rebel. When the king gains from a campaign, disregarding the advice of traitorous counselors, then too the king becomes angry and the counsellors afraid that the successful king will kill them for giving wrong advice. This too may make them rebel. When a campaign undertaken on the advice of trustworthy counsellors achieves the objective or when a campaign undertaken disregarding the advice of untrustworthy counselors fails in both cases the net result pleases all.

Kautilya's ideas on the relationship between accepting advice from trusted or non-trusted advisers and success or failure of a campaign may be expressed by the following matrix:

11.1 Matrix of Anticipated Reactions of (King, Advisers)

		Outcome of the Campaign	
Type of Advisers	Advisers' Recommendation	Success	Failure
Trustworthy	Proceed	(Pleases, Pleases) Case I	(Enrages, Fearful) Case II
	Not to Proceed	(Enrages, Fearful) Case III	(Pleases, Pleases) Case IV
Untrustworthy	Proceed	(Pleases, Pleases) Case V	(Enrages, Fearful) Case VI
	Not to Proceed	(Enrages, Fearful) Case VII	(Pleases, Pleases) Case VIII

According to Kautilya, a king should be aware of the various possibilities so that he can anticipate the possible reactions of the advisers and take the necessary steps to retain these most prized employees. Particularly, he should focus on the possibility of Case II, failure of campaign despite a recommendation from trustworthy advisers and the possibility of Case VII, success of campaign carried out against the advice of untrustworthy advisers. Despite a failure in a campaign, a king should not be angry with the trustworthy advisers. Since not only might he suffer a significant loss of men and material due to the failure, but also might lose his trustworthy advisers, who might be afraid of the king. On the other hand, despite success he should be concerned about the untrustworthy advisers and win them back or remove them. Incidentally, the possibility of Case VIII is interesting, since in this case the king cannot blame the advisers for the failure since he ignores their advice. Therefore, he has no reason to be angry with them.

We may summarise the above analysis as that, Kautilya's goal is to advise the king on realistic possibilities and not to display his knowledge of combinations. Therefore, he ignores the middle four possibilities since the king is likely not to reject the advice of trustworthy advisers and similarly, he is not likely to accept the advice of the untrustworthy advisers. The following quote by Wolters testifies to the practical application of Kautilya's analysis. [17] Wolters (p 49) writes: An inscription states that the 11th century Javanese king named Erlangga subverted his enemy's power 'by the application of the means taught by' the author of *The Arthashastra*, the most famous of all Indian treaties on the policies of a successful mandala manager. *The Arthashastra* also contains many precepts useful for a would-be conqueror. (Wolters cites the inscription translated by B.R. Chatterji, *History of Indonesia*, p 183, verse 29).

11.5 Use of Functional Relationship by Kautilya

It is noteworthy that he implicitly uses functional relationships to make decisions. He identifies the king, the ministers, the public, the fort, the treasury, the army and the ally as the key elements of a state. He compares the seriousness of calamities befalling on these various elements of the state. According to him, if all these elements are not be protected, a ranking of their importance is essential for making choices. Kautilya (p 126) states: When two elements are affected equally, they should be judged according to whether the damage is increasing or decreasing, so long as neither of them affects any other element.

A few remarks are in order. The initial impact on say element X_1 and X_2 is the same, that is CX_1 (t_0) = CX2 (t_0). First, the above statement implies that if no other element is adversely affected, attend to the element where the marginal cost is increasing, compared to the one where the marginal cost is declining. That is if MCX_1 (t) > MCX_2 (t), attend to the first element.

Second, if the calamity to one of these two elements affects the other elements adversely, then that element should be considered more serious. That is, he notes that for valid comparisons, all the damages (i.e. the full impact) caused by the various calamities should be included. Thus, if element X_2 adversely affects element X_3, that should be included in the cost. And if MCX_2 (t) + MCX_3 (X2 (t)) > MCX_1 (t), attend to the second element first.

Third, the very fact that Kautilya made a point by implicitly using a functional relationship is significant. This is particularly significant, since it took the practitioners of the craft more than two thousand years to do so again. As [18] Scherer (2001) remarks: 'The classical economists such as Adam Smith, David Ricardo, Robert Turgot and John Stuart Mill were not inclined to reason in functional terms, let alone in terms of specific volume-dependent cost functions.'

It may be added that sometimes we fail to appreciate the efforts involved in developing even simple concepts, such as, functions.

11.6 Conclusion

In an attempt to make mathematics perfect to conform to the image of God, it has become so complex that majority of the students cannot understand it and are turned off. As a result, they do not get the opportunity to appreciate and use it to solve practical problems. Perhaps, some cost-benefit analysis regarding the continuance of formal mathematics is called for, that is, a choice has to be made whether to serve the students or keep serving the church.

On the other hand, since ancient times, mathematics in India has been utilitarian in nature. Mathematical proofs and theorems were not considered as aesthetically pleasing, rather mathematics has been used to create aesthetically pleasing music and architecture. Mathematical proofs, unlike the deductive ones, are simpler. Kautilya, naturally, understands the importance of mathematics in sharpening his economic analysis. He shows that it ispossible to do meaningful economic analysis without formal mathematics. Formal mathematics has scared many students away from sciences and may be doing the same thing to economics also.

Epilogue

Going back to Kautilya for a Fairer and Fuller Future

Kautilya's Arthashastra is a world heritage. For the first time in human history, the role of the government was expanded to engineer shared prosperity, help the helpless and provide protection to those who cannot protect themselves.

Kautilya provides the very first meaningful definition of justice. He introduces statistics, mathematics and more than a score of basic concepts to economics. However, the most important contribution of *The Arthashastra* is: an ounce of ethics is better than a ton of laws. According to Kautilya, economists and policy makers, in addition to eliminating budget deficit and trade deficit, should also focus on eliminating the trust deficit for making lives richer and fuller. Kautilya's ethical surplus is presented in Section 12.1. It includes a short list of savings from eliminating the moral hazard problem. Some of Kautilya's timeless insights are collected in Section 12.2. Final Section provides some concluding observation.

12.1 Kautilya's Ethical Surplus

Kautilya puts heavy emphasis on Ethical anchoring of the children since that is the only effective way to eliminate moral hazard problem. He promotes the following ethical virtues:

सर्वेषाम् अहिंसा सत्यं शौचम् अनसूय आनृशंस्यं क्षमा च ॥ 1.3.13

(p 107) Duties common to all: Ahimsa [abstaining from injury to all living creatures]; satyam [truthfulness]; cleanliness; freedom from malice; compassion and tolerance. (1.3.13).

Elimination of moral hazard problem through ethical grounding willd lead to significant savings.

A Sample List of the Sources of Kautilya's Ethical Surplus:

(i) No need for supervisors because employees will not shirk work or steal;

(ii) No need for Corporate Board of Directors because there will be no agency costs (management takes care of the stakeholders as expected);

(iii) Doctors need not do any unnecessary operations or prescribe opioids unnecessarily;

(iv) Bank managers need not take excessive risks;

(v) Stock brokers take care of the investors' interest;

(v) No need to write lengthy contracts;

(vi) Drug companies will not push harmful medicines;

(vii) Public servants will formulate and implement good laws and sound policies.

Consequently, demand for lobbyists, used car sales persons, home security companies, antidepressant medicines, doctors, income tax officers, lawyers, judges, jails and police willgo down approximately by thirty percent. All these people are very smart and capable of enriching themselves and the world with new innovations.

12.2 Kautilya's Timeless pearls of wisdom

(1) Kautilya on an Ideal Ruler

प्रजा.सुखे सुखं राज्ञः प्रजानां च हिते हितम् ।

न_आत्म.प्रियं हितं राज्ञः प्रजानां तु प्रियं हितम् ॥ 1.19.34

Kautilya (p 149) to the King: In the happiness of his subjects lies his happiness; in their welfare his welfare. He shall not consider as good only that which pleases him but treat as beneficial to him whatever pleases his subjects.

(1.19.34).

स यत्.शीलस् तत्.शीलाः प्रकृतयो भवन्ति,
उत्थाने प्रमादे च तद्.आयत्तत्वात् ॥

8.1.17

Whatever character the king (p 123) has, the other elements also come to have the same.

(8.1.17).

चलति.शास्त्रस् तु शास्त्राद् अन्यथा.
अभिनिविष्ट.बुद्धिर् अन्यायेन राज्यम्
आत्मानं च_उपहन्तिइति ॥ 8.2.12

(p 141)A king who flouts the teachings of the Dharmashastras and the Arthashastra, ruins the kingdom by his own injustice (8.2.12).

तस्मात् समान.शील.वेष.भाषा.आचारताम् उपगच्छेत् ॥ 13.5.7
देश.दैवत.स्माज.उत्सव.विहारेषु च भक्तिम् अनुवर्तेत ॥ 13.5.8

Kautilya (p 741): The king, shall adopt the way of life, dress, language and customs of the people [of the acquired territory], show the same devotion to the gods of the territory [as to his own gods] and participate in the people's festivals and amusements. He shall ensure that devotions are held regularly in all the temples and ashrams. The ill, the helpless and the distressed shall be helped.

(13.5.7-8).

(2) Kautilya's Concept of Justice

सुविज्ञात.प्रणीतो हि दण्डः प्रजा धर्म.अर्थ.कामैर् योजयित ॥

1.4.11

दुष्प्रणीतः काम.क्रोधाभ्याम् अवज्ञानाद् वा वानप्रस्थ.
परिव्राजकान् अपि कोपयति, किं.अङ्ग पुनर् गृहस्थान् ॥ 1.4.12

अप्रणीतस् तु मात्स्य.न्यायम् उद्भावयित ॥ 1.4.13
बलीयान् अबलं हि ग्रसते दण्ड.धर.अभावे ॥ 1.4.14

Kautilya (p 108): Some teachers say, 'Those who seek to maintain order shall always hold ready the threat of punishment. For, there is no better instrument of control than coercion'. Kautilya disagrees [for the following reasons]. A severe king [meting out unjust punishment] is hated by the people he terrorizes while one who is too lenient is held in contempt by his own people. Whoever imposes just and deserved punishment is respected and honored. A well-considered and just punishment makes the people devoted to dharma, artha and kama [righteousness, wealth and enjoyment]. Unjust punishment, whether awarded in greed, anger or ignorance, excites the fury of even [those who have renounced all worldly attachments like] forest recluses and ascetics, not to speak of householders. When, [conversely,] no punishment is awarded through misplaced leniency and no law prevails, then there is only the law of fish [i.e., the law of the jungle]. Unprotected, the small fish will be swallowed up by the big fish (1.4.11-14).

दण्डो हि केवलो लोकं परं च_इमं च रक्षित ।
राज्ञा पुत्रे च शत्रौ च यथा.दोषं समं धृतः ॥ 3.1.42

Kautilya (p 377): It is the power of punishment alone, when exercised impartially in proportion to the guilt, and irrespective of whether the person punished is the King's son or an enemy, that protects this world and the next.

3.1.42

(3) Kautilya's Idea of Liberty

स तेन गुप्तः प्रभवतिइति ॥ 1.4.15

In the presence of a king maintaining just law, the weak can resist the powerful (1.4.11-15).

According to Kautilya, Liberty means empowering the weak. This one sentence captures the essence of Liberty whereas John Stuart Mills' book on Liberty fails to do it.

(4) Kautilya on the Provision of Yogakshema

तस्माद् दण्ड.मूलास् तिस्रो विद्याः ॥ 1.5.1

विनय.मूलो दण्डः प्राणभृतां योग.क्षेम.आवहः ॥ 1.5.2

[The three sciences [philosophy, the three Vedas and economics] are dependent [for their development] on the science of government. [For, without a just administration, no pursuit of learning or avocation would be possible.] [Government by] Rule of Law, which alone can guarantee security of life and the welfare of the people, is, in turn, dependent on [the] self-discipline [of the king].]

Kautilya on Sources of Economic Growth

कृत्रिमा हि भूमि गुणाः ॥ 7.11.19
Kautilya (p 619) statedThe value of land is what man makes of it.
7.11.9

नक्षत्रम् अति पृच्छन्तं बालम् अर्थो_अतिवर्तते ।
अर्थो ह्य् अर्थस्य नक्षत्रं किं करिष्यन्ति तारकाः ॥ 9.4.26

न_अधनाः प्राप्नुवन्त्य् अर्थान् नरा यत्न.शतैर् अिप ।
अर्थैर् अर्था प्रबध्यन्ते गजाः प्रजिगजैर् इव ॥ 9.4.27

Kautilya (p 637) argues: Man, without wealth, does not get it even after a hundred attempts. Just as elephants are needed to catch elephants, so does wealth capture more wealth. Wealth will slip away from that childish man who constantly consults the stars.

The only [guiding] star of wealth is itself; what can the stars of the sky do?
(9.4.26-27).

अर्थस्य मूलम् उत्थानम् अनर्थस्य विपर्ययः ॥ 1.19.35

अनुत्थाने ध्रुवो नाशः प्राप्तस्य_अनागतस्य च ।
प्राप्यते फलम् उत्थानाल् लभते च_अर्थसम्पदम् ॥ 1.19.36

Kautilya (p 149): Hence the king shall be ever active in the management of the economy. The root of wealth is economic activity and lack of it brings material distress. In the absence of fruitful economic activity, both current prosperity and future growth are in danger of destruction. A king can achieve the desired objectives and abundance of riches by undertaking productive economic activity (1.19.35-36).

(5) Kautilya's Proactive Approach to deal with Calamities and Systemic Risk

पीडनानाम् अनुत्पत्ताव् उत्पन्नानांच वारणे ।
यतेत देश.वृद्ध्य्.अर्थं नाशे च स्तम्भ.सङ्गयोः ॥ 8.4.50

यतो निमित्तं व्यसनं प्रकृतीनाम् अवाप्नुयात् ।
प्राग् एव प्रतिकुर्वीत तन् निमित्तम् अतन्द्रितः 8.5.21

Kautilya (p 116): In the interests of the prosperity of the country, a king should be diligent in foreseeing the possibility of calamities, try to avert them before they arise, overcome those which happen, remove all obstructions to economic activity and prevent loss of revenue to the state (8.4.50, 8.5.21).

(6) Kautilya's Ideas on Corruption

अर्थस् तथा ह्य् अर्थ.चरेण राज्ञः स्वल्पो_अप्य्
अनास्वादयितुं न शक्यः ॥ 2.9.32

Kautilya (p 281) writes: Just as it is impossible not to taste honey or poison that one may find at the tip of one's tongue, so it is impossible for one dealing with government funds not to taste, at least a little bit, of the King's wealth (2.9.32).

मत्स्या यथा_अन्तः सलिले चरन्तो ज्ञातुं न शक्याः सलिलं पिबन्तः ।
युक्तास् तथा कार्य.विधौ नियुक्ता ज्ञातुं न शक्या धनम् आददानाः ॥ 2.9.33

He (p 281) adds: Just as it is impossible to know when a fish moving in water is drinking it, so it is impossible to find out when government servants in charge of undertakings misappropriate money

2.9.33.

अपिशक्या गतिर् ज्ञातुं पततां खे पतत्रिणाम् ।
न तु प्रच्छन्न.भावानां युक्तानां चरतां गितः ॥ 2.9.34

It is possible to know even the path of birds flying in the sky but not the ways of government servants who hide their [dishonest] income (2.9.34).

12.3 Concluding Thought

There is no better way to conclude this book than do it the way Kautilya did his Arthashastra. Sihag (2014) and this book find Kautilya's following claims to be valid and relevant to today's knowledge-based economy as it was more than twenty-three hundred years ago.

एवं शास्त्रम् इदं युक्तम् एताभिस् तन्त्र.युक्तिभ।
अवाप्तौ पालने च_उक्तं लोकस्य_अस्य परस्य च ॥
धर्मम् अर्थं च कामं च प्रवर्तयति पातिच ।
अधर्म.अनर्थ.विद्वेषान् इदं शास्त्रं निहन्तिच ॥ 15.1.72

By following [the principles set out in] this treatise one can not only create and preserve dharma [spiritual good], artha [material well-being] and kama [aesthetic pleasures] but also destroy [their opposites, i.e.,] unrighteousness, material loss and hatred. It is a guide not only for the acquisition of this world but also the next (15.1).

Ethical anchoring will reduce malice from the hearts and minds of people, establish Kautilya's ethical economy and promote green economy. It will be more efficient than the current amoral economy. There is no trade-off between ethics and efficiency. In the long run, if it is not ethical, it will not be efficient.

Appendix: Transmission of Ideas from India to Europe

How do ideas get diffused? The person who has new ideas must be willing to share them and there must be a willing and capable host to receive them, since these may be complementary or substitutes of his existing knowledge. Role of existing institutions and interests becomes very critical in the acceptance or rejection of new ideas. There were both direct and indirect routes for transmission of ideas from India to Europe before the IT age. Roman coins at Pudukottai and at other places in southern India have been found, indicating that there was brisk trade between India and Italy during the first century BCE and thereafter. The Taj Mahal was built by Turkish architects and craftsmen. In all likelihood, not only were there exports of goods from India but also of men and ideas to Europe. (*In An Antique Land*, Amitav Ghosh, is the story of a 12th Century Jewish merchant from the Nile delta, who has two Indian for slave, where Ghosh uses documents from the Cairo Geniza.) Sri Lanka also served as a transfer station for transmission of ideas from India to other countries.

Kautilya's ideas were transmitted to Indonesia. A king explicitly gave credit to Kautilya's ideas for his success. [7] Wolters (p 49) writes: An inscription states that the 11th century Javanese king named Erlangga subverted his enemy's power 'by the application of the means taught by' the author of *The Arthashastra*, the most famous of all Indian treaties on the policies of a successful *mandala manager*. The *Arthashastra* also contains many precepts useful for a would-be conqueror. (Wolters cites the inscription translated by BR Chatterji, *History of Indonesia*, p. 183, verse 29. The eastern conquests of the Chola and Chera naval powers is well chronicled).

It is almost certain that Kautilya's ideas reached Europe also. Use of Indian numerals spread very quickly since they facilitated in conducting commerce and in tracking the movements of stars and planets. (Astronomer-Mathametician Aryabhata, 476-550 AD. Brahmagupta in 628 AD used 0 which was a concept developed by the Babylonians and Mayans independently, Sumerians before that. The migration of ideas was a two-way traffic. Kautilya wrote at lest 800 years earlier. Even Alaexander was counting out soldiers' wages before this.) For example, these numerals were transmitted to Middle-East in a matter of few decades. There was a wholesale translation of Indian books at Baghdad's House of Wisdom. Indian numerals reached Spain in 976. Vasco De Gama travelled to India in 1498, presumably, in search of exploring an alternative route to India that could allow imports of spices directly without any middleman from the Middle-East. He could have filled his boats with spices but instead he chose to take back a boat-load of books from India. Clearly, Indian books were more valuable than spices.

Most likely, Machiavelli also had access to Kautilya's *Arthashastra*. Since he discusses, although without much depth, many of the same topics, such as forming alliances, role of an adviser, role of information, types of army and specifically the delegation of unpopular tasks (as discussed below), as these were discussed by Kautilya. He did not fully understand the *Arthashastra*, was short of time since he was desperate to find work or tried to modify it to make it look original. As noted by [8] Leo Strauss (1987), Machiavelli was very good in imitation. Leo Strauss (p 316) remarks: Almost all those sayings have been borrowed by Machiavelli from Diogenes Laertius' *Lives of the Famous Philosophers*. Machiavelli changes the sayings in some cases in order to make them suitable to Castruccio. In Diogenes, an ancient philosopher is recorded as having said that he would wish to die like Socrates; Machiavelli makes this Castruccio's saying, yet he would wish to die like Caesar.

Machiavelli imitates Kautilya in recommending that a king

should delegate an unpopular task to someone else so that the king does not become object of hatred. The following table presents their views on delegation.

Table 7.5: Kautilya and Machiavelli on Delegation

Kautilya (*Arthashastra*, 4th century BCE)	[9] Machiavelli (*Prince*, 513 CE)
On Vices Page 137: Anger makes one the object of hatred, creates enemies and brings suffering on oneself. Excessive greed and lust bring about humiliation, loss of wealth and association with undesirable persons like thieves, gamblers, hunters, singers and musicians. [While both have had bad consequences,] being hated is worse than humiliation; whereas one humiliated is held in thrall by his own people and by enemies, a hated one is destroyed. **Anticipating and Avoiding Discontent** Page 158: Spies in the guise of ascetics shall find out who among the following are happy and who discontented: Those dependent on the King for grains, cattle or money; those who help the King in prosperity and adversity; those who [help to] restrain an angry relative or region and those who repel enemies and forest chiefs. The contented shall be appreciated by giving them additional honors and wealth. In order to make the discontented happy, conciliation shall be the method used. If [conciliation fails and] they continue to be unhappy, they shall be used to collect taxes and fines so that they may incur the wrath of the public. When the people come to hate them, they shall be eliminated either by inciting a popular revolt against them or by secret punishment. Alternatively, they may be sent to work in mines and factories while keeping their wives and sons under close security in order to prevent them from being used by enemies.	Ch. 19, page 58: For whoever set up the government of that country understood the powerful are ambitious and insolvent, and judged it necessary they should be bridled so they could be controlled, but on the other hand he recognised the hatred most people have for the powerful, whom they have reason to fear, and the consequent need to reassure and protect the great. So, he did not make this to be the responsibility of the king, in order to avoid his alienating the powerful by favoring the people or alienating the people by favoring the powerful, and he established an independent tribunal, whose task it is, without incurring blame for the king, to crush the powerful and defend the weak. This arrangement is as intelligent and prudent as could be, and makes a substantial contribution to the security of the king and the stability of the kingdom. This institution enables us to recognise a significant general principle: Rulers should delegate responsibility for unpopular actions, while taking personal responsibility for those that will win favor. And once again I conclude, a ruler should treat the powerful with respect, but at all costs he should avoid being hated by the people.

This similarity of views on delegation leaves little doubt that Machiavelli had access to *The Arthashastra*. But to Machiavelli's credit, he (1513, Ch. 6, p 18) wrote, 'But you cannot exactly go in the footsteps of those who have gone before, nor is it easy to match the skill [virtu] of those you have chosen to imitate'. Who were the 'many authors' referred to by Machiavelli (p 48)? Possibly Kautilya was one of them. Kautilya had emphasised the critical role of the ethical values in bringing prosperity.

Similarly, Indian methods of navigation were also transmitted very quickly to Europe. There is new research showing the transmission of calculus from India to Europe. Interestingly, even Indian cows have reached Texas, USA through Africa-Europe-Caribbean-Mexico. Given all these facts, it is unthinkable that other Indian thoughts, including Kautilya's *Arthashastra*, had not reached Europe.

Bibliography

An Ounce of Ethics is Better than a Ton of Laws
End Notes

[1]Gita's Sanskrit slokas are taken from the following source: https:// www.gitasupersite.iitk.ac.in

[2]US Congress passed the Employment Act of 1946. At the heart of the act was its 'Declaration of Policy':

> The Congress hereby declares that it is the continuing policy and responsibility of the federal government to use all practicable means consistent with its needs and obligations and other essential considerations of national policy with the assistance and cooperation of industry, agriculture, labor, and state and local governments, to coordinate and utilize all its plans, functions, and resources for the purpose of creating and maintaining, in a manner calculated to foster and promote free and competitive enterprise and the general welfare, conditions under which there will be afforded useful employment for those able, willing, and seeking work, and to promote maximum employment, production, and purchasing power.

[3]Keep in mind that Lord Krishna-Arjuna dialogue took place in a war setting and that was not the time or place to elaborate on how to provide *Yogakshema*. Kangle, R P (1972, PART II, P 9, fn. 3) defines *Yogakshema* as 'yoga is the acquisition of things and *kshema* is their secure possession; the two together convey the idea of security and well-being or prosperity'. L N Rangarajan translates *Yogakshema* as peaceful enjoyment of prosperity.

[4]Sanskrit slokas are taken from the following source https://sanjeev.sabhlokcity.com/Misc/chanakya/arthashastra-kautilya-sabhlok.pdf

[5]Shamasastry (1988/1915, p 11, fn. 1)) remarks, 'These allusions sufficiently establish the historical nature of the Ramayaṇa and the Mahabharata'.

References

1. Kautilya Vishnugupta (4th Century BC). *The Kautilya Arthashastra*, Part II, An English Translation with Critical and Explanatory Notes, R P Kangle, 2000, Motilal Banarsidass, Delhi.
2. Kautilya Vishnugupta (4th Century BC). *The Arthashastra*, Edited, Rearranged, Translated and Introduced by L N Rangarajan,
3. Penguin Books, 1992, New Delhi, New York.
4. Shamasastry R (1988/1915). *Kautilya's Arthashastra*, Ninth Edition, Mysore: Printed by R Ramakrishna Padma Printers.
5. Sihag, Balbir S (2014a). *Kautilya: The True Founder of Economics*, Vitasta Publications, New Delhi.
6. Smith Adam (1776/1976). *An Inquiry into the Nature and Causes of the Wealth of Nations*. Edited and with an Introduction, Notes, Marginal Summary, and Index by Edwin Cannan, The University of Chicago Press, Chicago.

Engineering Shared Prosperity
End Notes

[1]Charles Drekmeier (1962, p 76) states, 'Now the king must concern himself directly with the common good, an idea anticipated in *The Arthashastra*'. He (p 189) adds: 'In the Arthashastra literature the interests of the state, rather than the king's personal fulfillment, are of foremost importance.

[2]In recent years, the old chronology has been challenged. For example, according to Nagarajan (1992, p 18), Kautilya lived several centuries earlier than the generally accepted fourth century BCE.

[3]Drekmeier (1962, p. 290) observes: New controls over the environment sharpened the distinction between physical necessity and necessity that is created by man. We may surmise that men began to conclude that remaking the world was within the realm of possibility. The ancient belief in the cyclical periodicity of time, the eternal return, was modified or displaced altogether by a sense of continuity and development approximating a historical attitude. Accumulated wealth and the military power and administrative efficiency it made possible could now be used for achieving ambitious, long-range political and social goals. The great man is, in fact, the great organiser. He creates the very conditions that make the hero obsolete, for he imposes an order that limits the unpredictable contingencies against which the hero struggles. The hero was made for his age; the organiser is the maker of his age. Man can now do things that earlier could be accomplished only by the gods.

Thapar (1997, p 142) also writes, 'The Mauryan period was the culminating epoch of a few centuries of rational inquiry and cultural advance'.

[4]Sandel (2009, 201) comments, 'Aristotle's own theory of justice provides ample resources for a critique of his own views on slavery'. That is, if Aristotle had followed his own reasoning, he would have rejected slavery.

[5]Drekmeier (p 201) asserts, 'There can never be a thoroughgoing divorce of politics and ethics for Kautilya; he never denies that the ultimate purpose of the state is a moral purpose, the maintenance of dharma'.

[6]Adam Smith ([1790] 1982, p 86) believed, 'Justice, on the contrary, is the main pillar that upholds the whole edifice, if it is removed, the great, the immense fabric of human society must in

a moment crumble into atoms.'

Sihag (2013, p 279) points out, 'That is an insightful metaphor, but Kautilya looked not only at the pillar but at the foundations on which the pillar stood, including the architecture of the structure and the potential internal and external threats to its existence'. He adds, 'According to Kautilya, the pillar (justice) must be standing on the solid rock of ethics, otherwise it will be unstable and wobbly. Weak ethical anchoring isconsidered the source of injustices.

Adam Smith (p 175) asserts, 'The rules of justice may be compared to the rules of grammar; the rules of the other virtues, to the rules which critics lay down for the attainment of what is sublime and elegant in composition'.The concept of justice itself is ambiguous and its rules are often formulated by less than perfect individuals, implying an unavoidable imprecision. Thus, rules of justice can never be like grammar and it is an invalid comparison.

[7]Drekmeier (p 256) points out, 'Restraints on the king were not formal; they were restrictions imposed by the obligation to uphold custom and sacred law and to fulfill the requirements of *rajadharma*'.

[8]Adam Smith ignored the role of ethics and cognitive division of labour to economic growth and concentrated primarily on the role of institutions. He (Bk V, Ch. III, p 445) wrote, 'Commerce and manufacture can seldom flourish long in any state which does not enjoy a regular administration of justice, in which the people do not feel themselves secure in the possession of their property, in which the faith of contracts is not supported by law, and in which the authority of the state is not supposed to be regularly employed in enforcing the payment of debts from all those who are able to pay'.

More recent works, just like Adam Smith, also ignore the role of ethics and cognitive division of labour to economic growth.

Since the 1990s some economists have advanced institutions as the 'deep determinant' of economic growth. For example, Rodrik et al. (2004) claim, 'This exercise yields some sharp and striking results. Most importantly, we find that the quality of institutions trumps everything else'. Some other economists have rejected this claim. Glaeser et al. (2004, p 298) conclude: But institutional outcomes also get better as the society grows richer, because institutional opportunities improve. Importantly, in that framework, institutions have only a second-order effect on economic performance. The first order effect comes from human and social capital, which shape both institutional and productive capacities of a society.

Acemoglu et al (2014, p 25) conclude: In summary, the results from the full 2SLS/LIML models, where both institutions and human capital are instrumented using historical sources of variation, show a fairly robust effect of institutions on current prosperity, and a much more limited effect of human capital.

[9] A L Basham (1959, p. 153) observes: The humane regulations of *The Arthashastra*, probably unique in the records of any ancient civilisation, are perhaps survivals of Mauryan laws, and it is therefore not surprising that Megasthenes declared that there was no slavery in India.

References

1. Acemoglu D and J A Robinson (2012). *Why Nations Fail: The Origins of Power, Prosperity and Poverty*, New York: The Crown Publishing Group.
2. Acemoglu D, Francisco A Gallego and J A Robinson (2014). 'Institutions, Human Capital and Development'; Paper prepared for the Annual Reviews of Economics
3. Barber William J (1967). *A History of Economic Thought,* Penguin Books, Baltimore, Maryland.
4. Basham, A L (1959). *The Wonder that was India*, Grove Press, New York.
5. Besley Timothy and Torsten Persson (2011). *Pillars of Prosperity: The Political Economics of Development Clusters*,

Princeton, Princeton.

6. Chandler Tertius (1987). *Four Thousand Years of Urban Growth: An Historical Census*, Lewiston, New York: Edwin Mellon Press.
7. Drekmeier Charles (1962). *Kingship and Community in Early India*, Stanford University Press, Stanford.
8. Ehrlich Isaac and Garry S Becker (1972). Market insurance, self-insurance and self-protection. *Journal of Political Economy*, 80 (4), 623-648.
9. Glaeser Edward L, RL Porta, F Lopez-de-Silanes and A Shleifer (2004). 'Do Institutions Cause Growth?' *Journal of Economic Growth* 9, 271-303.
10. Kautilya Vishnugupta (4th Century B C). *The Arthashastra,* Edited, Rearranged, Translated and Introduced by L N Rangarajan, Penguin Books, 1992, New Delhi, New York.
11. Lingat Robert (1967). *The Classical Law of India Translated* with additions by J Duncan MDerrett, Oxford University Press, New Delhi
12. MacLeod Bentley (2013). 'On Economics: A Review of Why Nations fail by D Acemoglu and J. Robinson and *Pillars of Prosperity* by T Besley and T Persson', *Journal of Economic Literature*, Vol., LI, No. 1:116-143
13. Nagarajan V (1992). *Evolution of Social Polity of Ancient India*, Vol. 1, Nagpur, India: Dattsons.
14. Nisbet Robert (1980), *History of the Idea of Progress*, New York: Basic Books.
15. Rodrik D, A Subramanian, and F Trebbi (2004). Institutions Rule: The Primacy of Institutions over Geography and Integration in Economic Development, *Journal of Economic Growth* 9, 131-165.

    Sandel, Michael J2009. *Justice*. New York: Farrar, Straus and Giroux.
16. Sihag Balbir S (2013). Ethical Anchoring as Risk Management, Hrishikesh D Vinod (ed.) in The Handbook of Hindu Economics and Business at: https://www.createspace.com/4224711.

17. Sihag Balbir S (2014a). *Kautilya: The True Founder of Economics*, Vitasta Publications, New Delhi.
18. Sihag Balbir S (2014b). 'Kautilya on Selection, Implementation and Evaluation of a Project', Sangeeta Sharma, Pankaj Nagar and Inderjeet Singh Sodhi (eds.) in Governometrics and Technological 19. Innovation for Public Policy Design and Precision, IGI Global, Hershey, PA, USA.
20. Sinclair Upton (1906). *The Jungle*, New York: Doubleday.
Smith Adam (1776/1976). *An Inquiry into the Nature and Causes of the Wealth of Nations.* Edited and with an Introduction, Notes, Marginal Summary, and Index by Edwin Cannan, The University of Chicago Press, Chicago.
21. Smith Adam (1790/ 1982). *The Theory of Moral Sentiments.* Edited by DD Raphael and AL Macfie; Liberty Fund, Indianapolis.
Thapar Romila (1997). *Ashoka and the Decline of the Mauryas*, Second Ed. Oxford University Press, New Delhi.

Foresight, Oversight, Regulations, Ethics and Systemic Risk

End Notes

[1][10] Mark Egan, Ali Hortacsu, and Gregor Matvos (2017) remark, 'Note that the market shares of insured deposits, which should be insensitive to distress, show no such relationship (panel B)'.

[2][10] Christoffer Koch, Gary Richardson and Patrick Van Horn (2016) conclude: The changing behavior of money-center banks is consistent with the theoretical literature on the impact of too-big-to-fail policies and modern prudential policy initiatives, such as procyclical capital requirements and enhanced reliance on market discipline designed to offset moral hazard. Our findings further suggest that scholars and policy makers alike need to be realistic about the potential benefits of institutional and regulatory reforms. While the institutional framework of the 1920s induced money-center banks to hold excessive capital relative to risk, the United

States and international financial systems still collapsed, aggravating the longest, deepest global downturn in modern history.

[3]Samuel Buell (2016, pp 81-82) remarks: Even without the messiness of democracy, law would be a flawed technology. Laws can never quite reach their intended targets, for two reasons. First, human ingenuity and foresight are always limited, especially when predicting the paths that our species will take. Laws must anticipate futures that the people who make laws cannot clearly see. Legal rules will inevitably end up confronting innovations for which they were not designed.

[4]Adam Smith (1795, p 60) wrote: Systems in many respects resemble machines. A machine is a little system, created to perform, as well as to connect together, in reality, those different movements and effects which the artist has occasion for. A system is an imaginary machine invented to connect together in the fancy those different movements and effects which are already in reality performed.

[5]Samuel Buell (2016, p xii) remarks, 'GM is a corporation. It does not think, it can't drive a car, and it can't even really be seen. It's an amalgam of people, factories, vehicles, images, and spread across the globe. GM is an idea as much as it is a thing'.

[6]Kautilya understood the concept of propagation. He (p 634) wrote: A small revolt in the rear outweighs a large gain in the front; for, when the king is not there, a small revolt in the rear may be worsened by the anger of the people or by traitors, enemies and jungle tribes. If this happens, a large gain in front, even if actually obtained, will be eaten up by the subjects, allies, losses and expenses. Therefore, a king shall not undertake a campaign when the gain in front is [less than] a thousand times the likely loss due to a revolt in the rear or, at least, a hundred times the loss. A well-known

proverb is: 'Misfortunes are, [in the beginning] no longer than the point of a needle' (9.3).

[12] Markus K Brunnermeier and Martin Oehmke (2012): For the more recent housing bubble, the triggering event seems clearer. Blame is usually laid on the subprime mortgage market that began to turn sour in late 2006. However, the subprime market constituted only about 4% of the overall mortgage market. This leads to the question, how can such 'small' news cause so much damage? And how can a crisis that originates in the subprime mortgage market propagate across so many sectors of the economy?

[7]In due course, construction of a larger Matrix may be desirable.

Matrix 3.2: Inter-sectoral Linkages

	Financials (banks, brokerage firms, hedge funds, etc.)	Public Sector	Corporate Sector (other than financials)	Household Sector
Financials (banks, hedge funds, brokerage firms etc.)	A_{11}	A_{12}	A_{13}	A_{14}
Public Sector	A_{21}	A_{22}	A_{23}	A_{24}
Corporate Sector (other than financials)	A_{31}	A_{32}	A_{33}	A_{34}
Household Sector	A_{41}	A_{42}	A_{43}	A_{44}

[8]Confucius: To see and listen to the wicked is already the beginning of wickedness.

https://www.brainyquote.com/quotes/authors/c/confucius_2.html

[9]*Development of Self-Command*: According to Smith (TMS III.22, p 145), 'When it is old enough to go to school, or to mix with its equals, it soon finds that they have no such indulgent partiality. It naturally wishes to gain their favour, and to avoid their hatred or contempt. Regard even to its own safety teaches it to do so; and it soon finds that it can do so in no other way than by moderating, not only its anger, but all its other passions, to the degree which its play-fellows and companions are likely to be pleased with. It thus enters into the great school of self-command, it studies to be more and more master of itself, and begins to exercise over its own feelings a discipline which the practice of the longest life is very seldom sufficient to bring to complete perfection'.

First, if it was that automatic and easy to develop self-command, there would be no need to pass legislation to stop bullying in schools or to install metal detectors in many schools. Secondly, socially meaningful role of self-command is to conquer greed but that is left out, implying it serves no purpose.

[10]On the other hand, Eugene Soltes (2016, p 60) remarks, 'WE'RE NOT BORN with a "blank slate", nor do inherited or genetic dispositions entirely determine our behavior'.

[11][13] Williamson (1985, p 47) characterises the potential behavior of the other firm as: calculated efforts to mislead, disguise, obfuscate, or otherwise confuse and seeking self-interest, but they do so with guile.

[12]Jean-Pierre Zigrand, 'Typical examples of systematic risk would

be aggregate technology shocks, aggregate endowment, output, preference or monetary shocks etc. These systematic events may correspond to very large shocks, such as for instance the power-law shocks in Gabaix (2009) and Barro and Urs'ua (2012), but the system is expected to continue functioning normally and properly. This distinction has also been emphasised by Hansen (20 12)'.

References

1. Buell, W Samuel (2016). *Capital Offenses.* New York: Norton & Company
2. Soltes, Eugene (2016), Why They Do it. New York: *Publicaffairs*
3. Kautilya Vishnugupta (4th Century BCE/1992). *The Arthashastra*, Edited, Rearranged, Translated and Introduced by L N Rangarajan, Penguin Books, New Delhi, New York.
4. Zigrand, Jean-Pierre, Systems and Systemic Risk in Finance and Economics.
5. Systemic Risk Centre, London School of Economics, January 20, 2014. www.systemicrisk.ac.uk
6. Feinsteina, Zachary, Birgit Rudlob and Stefan Weber (2016), 'Measures of Systemic Risk' arxiv.org/pdf/1502.07961.pdf *Atharva-Veda Samhita* (3000 BCE/2004). Edited and Revised by K L Joshi, Parimal Publications, Delhi.
7. Sihag Balbir S (2014). *Kautilya: The True Founder of Economics.* Vitasta Publishing, New Delhi.
8. Smith Adam (1790/ 1982). *The Theory of Moral Sentiments.* Edited by D DRaphael and AL Macfie; Liberty Fund, Indianapolis.
9. Barro RJ and Urs'ua J F (2012). Rare Macroeconomic Disasters. *Annual Review of Economics*, 4(1):83–109.
10. Egan Mark, Ali Hortacsu, and Gregor Matvos (2017). 'Deposit Competition and Financial Fragility: Evidence from the US Banking Sector', *American Economic Review*, 107 (1), 169-216

Koch Christoffer, Gary Richardson and Patrick Van Horn (2016). 11. 'Bank Leverage and Regulatory Regimes: Evidence from the Great Depression and Great Recession', *American Economic Review*: Papers & Proceedings, 106 (5): 538-542., 12. Brunnermeie, Markus K and Martin Oehmke (2012). 'Bubbles, Financial Crises, and Systemic Risk' Working Paper 18398, National Bureau of Economic Research. http://www.nber.org/papers/w18398
13.Williamson, O E (1985). *The Economic Institutions of Capitalism*: Firms, Markets, Rational Contracting. London: Collier Macmillan.

Relevance of Kautilya's Insights to Corporate Governance & Management
End Notes

[1]Goshen, Zohar and Richard Squire (2016): The essential problem that Jensen and Meckling used this simple firm to illustrate is the unavoidable tradeoff between economies of scale and agency costs. Both rise as the firm's manager sells more of its cash flows to the investor in exchange for more capital. The optimal division of cash flows between investor and manager is the one that maximizes economies of scale net of agency costs. In this way, the Jensen-Meckling model shows how the tradeoff between economies of scale and agency costs determines the size of a business firm.

[2][11] Sihag (2014, Ch 11, fn. 4): *Reemergence of the Principal-Agent Problem*: Adolf A Berle and Gardiner C Means (1932) observed that there was a separation of ownership and control in public corporations and suggested that incentives were required to induce the CEO, the agent, to adhere to the objective of the shareholders, the principal. Since then a considerable amount of effort has been devoted to exploring a whole set of mechanisms to resolve the principal-agent problem. However, Joseph E Stiglitz (1987, p 966) credits Ross for coining the term principal-agent in 1973. Eric Rasmusen (1994, 209) discusses various mechanisms

such as: piece rates, profit sharing, efficiency wages, bonuses, merit pay, tournaments, deferred compensation, promotions and even boiling-in-oil (i.e. heavy punishments) to induce workers to supply optimum level of effort. Recently, Prendergast (1999) provides a comprehensive survey of the various incentives provided by the firms to elicit effort from workers. The survey concentrates primarily on two issues: (i) 'do incentives matter?' and (ii) are contracts designed to incorporate the trade-off between insurance against risk and incentives for effort? This is an extremely active field of investigation.

[3]McDonnell, Brett H (2009, p, 143). Arrow, supra note 9, at 78 (If every decision of A is to be reviewed by B, then all we have really is a shift in the locus of authority from A to B and hence no solution to the original problem.).

[4][12] Arrow (1973, p, 129) defines the axiom of 'non-dictatorship' as' "There is no individual whose preferences are automatically society's preferences independent of the preferences of all other individuals'.

[5][13] Kenneth Arrow (1968) notes: Because of the moral hazard, complete reliance on economic incentives does not lead to an optimal allocation of resources in general. In most societies alternative relationships are built up which to some extent serve to permit cooperation and risk sharing. The principal-agent relation is very pervasive in all economies and especially in modern ones; by definition the agent has been selected for his specialized knowledge and therefore the principal can never hope completely to check the agent's performance. You cannot therefore easily take out insurance against the failure of the agent to perform well. One of the characteristics of a successful economic system is that the relations of trust and confidence between principal and agent are sufficiently strong so that the agent will not cheat even though it may be 'rational economic behavior' to do so.

[6][14] Olson (2000) calls this 'the second invisible hand'. He (pp 12-13) states: This invisible hand- shall we call it as invisible hand on the left? – that guides encompassing interests to use their power at least to some degree, in accord with the social interest, even when serving the public good, was not part of the intention. This second invisible hand is as unfamiliar and perhaps counterintuitive as the first hidden hand was in Adam Smith's time, but that does not mean it is less important.

References

1. Goshen Zohar and Richard Squire (2016). Principal Costs: A New Theory for Corporate Law and Governance http://www.law.nyu.edu/sites/default/files/Zohar%20Goshen.pdf
2. Berle Adolf A and Gardiner C Means1932. *The Modern Corporation and Private Property*. New York: Harcourt, Brace and World.
3. Arrow Kenneth J (1974). *The Limits of Organsation*, New York: W. Norton.
4. BainbridgeStephen (2008). *The New Corporate Governance in Theory and Practice*, New York: Oxford.
5. McDonnell Brett H (2009). 'Professor Bainbridge and the Arrowian Moment: A Review of The New Corporate Governance in Theory and Practice', *Delaware Journal of Corporate Law,* Vol. 34: 139-190
6. Kautilya Vishnugupta (4th Century BCE/1992). *The Arthashastra*, Edited, Rearranged, Translated and Introduced by L N Rangarajan, Penguin Books, 1992, New Delhi, New York.
7. Drekmeier Charles (1962). *Kingship And Community In Early India*, Stanford University Press, Stanford.
8. Miller Gary J (1997). 'The Impact of Economics on Contemporary Political Science', *Journal of Economic Literature*, p 1173-1204. Soltes, Eugene (2016). Why

They Do it. New York: Publicaffairs.

9. Williamson O E (1985). *The Economic Institutions of Capitalism: Firms, Markets, Rational Contracting*. London: Collier Macmillan.
10. Sihag Balbir S (2014). *Kautilya: The True Founder of Economics*. New Delhi: Vitasta Publishing.
11. Arrow Kenneth J (1973). 'Values and Collective Decision-Making', chapter 4, in *Economic Justice,* edited by Edmund S Phelps, Penguin, Baltimore, USA.
12. Arrow Kenneth (1968). The Economics of Moral Hazard: Further Comment). *American Economic Review* 58. 3: 537-539.

Olson Mancur (2000). *Power and Prosperity*, New York, Basic Books.

*Sangeeta Sharma, Pankaj Nagar and Inderjeet Singh Sodhi (eds.) in Governometrics and Technological Innovation for Public Policy Design and Precision, IGI Global, Hershey, PA, USA. Samuelson .

Establishing Moral Order to Prevent Government and Market Failures

End Notes

[1]In recent years, the old chronology has been challenged. For example, according to [13] Nagarajan (1992, p 18), Kautilya lived several centuries earlier than the generally accepted fourth century BCE.

[2][14] Dhar (2003, pp 156-157) observes, 'Our tradition recognises certain eternal values including love, compassion and non-injury. It underscores the importance of means being right to achieve right ends.'

On the other hand, [15] Staveren (2001, p 153) asserts, 'Central to Aristotle's Nicomachean Ethics is that virtue can only be found by trial and error as a mean between efficiency and excess: virtue depends on deliberation, as I argued in chapter one. It is important to repeat Aristotle's view that virtues are not pre-given,

they are not universals, nor subjectively prescribed in individual objective functions.'
[3] [16] Richard Kraut (2010) observes, 'What Aristotle has in mind when he makes this complaint is that ethical activities are remedial: they are needed when something has gone wrong or threatens to do so. Courage, for example, is exercised in war, and war remedies an evil; it is not something we should wish for'.

[4]Adam Smith could not borrow from the Greek philosophers since they also did not define virtue. [17] Jim Holt (2006) points out, 'Aristotle defined virtue as a quality of character that makes for a life well lived. Then he characterised the good life as a life lived in accordance with virtue. Circular?'

[5]onfucius: 'In ancient times, men learned with a view to their own improvement. Now-a-days, men learn with a view to the approbation of others.' His now-a-days was 2000 years ago. On the other hand, Adam Smith puts too much emphasis on approbation.

References

1. Sihag Balbir Singh (2014). *Kautilya: The True Founder of Economics,* New Delhi: Vitasta Publications.
2. Herrmann-Pillath Carsten, 'A "Third Culture" in Economics? An Essay on Smith, Confucius and the Rise of China' (February 8, 2011). Available at SSRN: http://ssrn.com/abstract=1757833 or http://dx.doi.org/10.2139/ssrn.1757833
3. *Kautilya Vishnugupta* (4th Century BCE. / 2000). *Maxims of Chanakya*, by Subramanian, V K, Shakti Malik, Abhinav Publications, New Delhi.
4. *Kautilya, Vishnugupta,* (4th Century BCE/1992). *The Arthashastra*, Edited, Rearranged, Translated and Introduced by L N Rangarajan, Penguin Books, 1992, New Delhi, New York.
5. Hardt Lukasz (2009), 'The History of Transaction Cost

Economics and its Recent Developments', Erasmus *Journal of Philosophy and Economics*, Vol. 2, Issue 1, pp: 29-51.

6. Williamson O E (1985). *The Economic Institutions of Capitalism: Firms, Markets, Rational Contracting*. London: Collier Macmillan.
7. Machiavelli N (1994/513). *Selected Political Writings*, edited and Translated by David Wootton, Cambridge: Hackett Publishing.
8. Smith Adam (1790/ 1982). *The Theory of Moral Sentiments.* Edited by DDRaphael and AL Macfie; Liberty Fund, Indianapolis.
9. Raphael D D (2007). *The Impartial Spectato*r, Clarendon Press: Oxford.
10. Halteman James and Edd Noell (2012). *Reckoning with Markets*, New York: Oxford University Press.
11. Chang James L Y (1987). '*History of Chinese economic* thought: Overview and recent works', *History of Political Economy*, 19: 3, PP. 481-502.
12. Choi Young Back (1989). '*Political Economy* of Han Feitzu', History of Political Economy, 21: 2, PP. 367-390.
13. Nagarajan V (1992). *Evolution of Social Polity of Ancient India*, Vol. 1, Nagpur, India: Dattsons.
14. Dhar T N 2003. *A Portrait of Indian Culture*. New Delhi: Deemed University.
15. Staveren Irene Van (2001), *The Values of Economics*, Routledge, New York.
16. Kraut Richard 2010. 'Aristotle's Ethics'. In The *Stanford Encyclopedia of Philosophy*, edited by Edward N Zalta, http://plato.stanford.edu/archives/sum2005/entries/aristotle-ethics/.
17. Holt Jim (2006). 'The Bourgeois Virtues by Deirdre McCloskey', *The New York Times Book Review,* July 30.

Ideas on Curbing Corruption

End Notes

[1]D P Agrawal (2009, p 55) notes, 'Rao has also pointed out that the 17.7 mm Harappan division is very near the traditional *angula* measure of 17.86 mm of the *Arthashastra*'.

[2]*Rules of the Game*: North (1995, p 23) defines institutions as, 'nstitutions are the rules of the game of a society, or, more formally, are the humanly devised constraints that structure human interaction. They are composed of formal rules (stature law, common law, regulations), informal constraints (conventions, norms of behavior and self-imposed codes of conduct), and the enforcement characteristics of both'. According to North (1990, p 47), 'Formal rules include political (and judicial) rules, economic rules and contracts. The hierarchy of such rules, from constitutions, to statute and common laws, to specific bylaws, and finally to individual contracts defines constraints, from general rules to particular specifications. And typically, constitutions are designed to be more costly to alter than statute laws, just as a statute law is more costly to alter than individual contracts. Political rules broadly define the hierarchical structure of the polity, its basic decision structure, and the explicit characteristics of agenda control. Economic rules define property rights, that is, the bundle of rights over the use and the income to be derived from property and the ability to alienate an asset or a resource. Contracts contain the provisions specific to a particular agreement in exchange'.

References

1. Agrawal D P (2009) *Harappan Technology and Its Legacy*, Delhi: Infinity Foundation and Rupa.
2. Kautilya Vishnugupta (4th Century B C) *The Kautilya Arthashastra, Part II*, An English Translation with Critical and

Explanatory Notes, R P Kangle, 2000, Motilal Banarsidass, Delhi.

3. Kautilya Vishnugupta Chanakya (4th Century B. C.) *The Arthashastra*, Edited, Rearranged, Translated and Introduced by L N Rangarajan, Penguin Books, 1992, New Delhi, New York.
4. Kautilya ([4th Century BCE] 2000). *Maxims of Chanakya.* Translated by V K Subramanian. New Delhi: Shakti Malik, Abhinav publications.
5. Lingat Robert (1967., *The Classical Law of India* Translated with additions by J Duncan, M Derrett, Oxford University Press, New Delhi.
6. Mackenzie G Galvin and Michael Hafken (2002). *Scandal Proof*, Washington DC: Brookings Institution Press.
7. Marshall Alfred (1925). 'Social Possibilities of Economic Chivalry', in *Memorials of Alfred Marshall*, edited by A C Pigou, London, Macmillan, 332-346.
8. North Douglass C (1990)., *Institutions, Institutional Change and Economic Performance*, Cambridge: Cambridge University Press.
9. North Douglass C (1995). 'The New Institutional Economics and Third World Development', in *The New Institutional Economics and Third World Development* edited by John Harriss, Janet Hunter and Colin MLewis, Routledge: New York.
10. Olivelle Patrick (1999). *Dharmasutras: The Law Codes of Ancient India*, a New Translation, Oxford University Press, Oxford, New York.
11. Rao S R (1973). *Lothal and the Indus Civilization*. Asia publishing House, Bombay
12. Sihag Balbir S (2014). *Kautilya: The True Founder of Economics*, Vitasta Publications, New Delhi, India.

Arthashastra: A Recognisable Source of The Wealth of Nations

End Notes

I am thankful to Prof Anthony Waterman for presenting me with a challenge to show that Kautilya's *Arthashastra* was a source of Adam Smith's *The Wealth of Nations*.

[1][10] Barber (1967, p 51) observes: Little of the content of *The Wealth of Nations* can be regarded as original to Smith himself. Most of the book's arguments had in one form or another been in circulation for some time.

Barber (1967, p 51) notes, 'Smith's talents as a synthesiser, however, were the source of some analytical imperfections in his writing. At a number of points, he offered explanations that were ambiguous or inconsistent'. Similarly, the remarks by [11] Grampp about Adam Smith that 'to make the ideas of Smith consistent, an honor he was not sure he merited' are quite indicative.

[2][12] Murray Rothbard (1995, Chap 16) points out: When Smith upbraided Ferguson for not acknowledging Smith's precedence in the pin-factory example, Ferguson replied that he had borrowed nothing from Smith, but indeed that both had taken the example from a French source 'where Smith had been before him'. There is strong evidence that the 'French source' for both writers was the article on *Epingles* (pins) in the *Encyclopédie* (1755), since that article mentions 18 distinct operations in making a pin, the same number epeated by Smith in the *Wealth of Nations*, although in English in factories, 25 was the more common number of operations. He concluded, 'The problem is not simply that Smith was not the ounder of economics. The problem is that he originated nothing at was true, and that whatever he originated was wrong'.

[3]It appears that the tradition of concealing sources, perhaps started with Fibonacci (1202). [13] Charles Burnett (2005) observes: By the end of the twelfth century the 'algorismus' was widespread and it would certainly have been known to Fibonacci. In fact, he refers specifically to the 'algorismus', in the preface to his *Liber abbaci*, as we have seen. But it is difficult to see why he should criticise it alongside the 'Gerbertian abacus', and state that the 'method of the Indians' is better, when the 'algorismus' is precisely 'the method of the Indians'. I suspect that his reason is that he thinks that, or wants to give the impression that, his own work is truly innovatory, for he scrupulously avoids mentioning the name of al-Khwarizmi. (In chapter 15, he uses only al-Khwarizmi's first name (ism), 'Maumeht'). Are we to suppose that Fibonacci was, in fact, ignorant of this Latin tradition of Indian arithmetic, and re-introduced the place-value numerals afresh from the Arabs?'

[4][14] Drekmeier (1962, p 105) points out: The Ganges valley in the seventh century was the home of a nascent capitalism as well.

[5]According to Spengler (1971), Kautilya understood the role of prices. Spengler (p 74) states: Prices reflected actual or potential scarcity (4.2; 2.21.7-14) as well as the presence of monopolistic arrangements (2.6.10; 4.2.18-19, 28-30).

He (1971, p 74) explains: 'His analysis, of course, was implicit, not explicit; it rested upon the assumption that individual behaviour could be controlled in large measure through economic rewards and penalties, particularly when these were commensurate with the action to be encouraged or discouraged.

He (1971, p 158) concludes: Kautilya was, of course, familiar with the general nature of man's response to changes in price and income as well as to changes in the structure of rewards and penalties.

[6]Adam Smith considered 'justice is the pillar on which the whole

edifice rests' but no discussion on how to build the pillar and its base, was provided. Moreover, he never examined how the rules of justice were formulated, interpreted or implemented. [15] He ((1790/ 1982, p 175) asserted, 'The rules of justice may be compared to the rules of grammar; the rules of the other virtues, to the rules which critics lay down for the attainment of what is sublime and elegant in composition'. The concept of justice itself is ambiguous and its rules are formulated by less than perfect individuals, implying an unavoidable imprecision. Thus, rules of justice could not be like grammar. If they were, would there be any kangaroo courts? Would there be 'black' and 'white' justice? If they were like grammar, would there be need for any lawyers? Thus, it is an inappropriate comparison. *He did not understand justice.*

[7][16] Basham (1959, p 216) notes, 'Though the basis of ancient Indian industry was at all times the individual craftsman, aided chiefly by members of his own family, larger manufactories, worked chiefly by hired labour, were by no means unknown'. Further, 'We read here and there of private producers who had far transcended the status of the small home craftsman, and who manufactured on a large scale for a wide market. Thus, an early Jain text tells of a wealthy potter named Saddalaputta who owned 500 potters' workshops, and a fleet of boats which distributed his wares throughout the Ganges valley; there are a few other references, which confirm that large-scale production for a wide market was not unknown in ancient India'. Basham points out that the existence of co-operatives of workmen were also common. He asserts, 'Their existence tended to encourage division of labour; thus one man would fashion the shaft of an arrow, a second would fix the flights, and a third would make and fix the point'.

[8]John M Keynes worked in the India Office and the following suggestion by Keynes was borrowed from the programme initiated by Nawab Asaf-ud-Daula since there had been no such programme in the whole world. *Nawab Asaf-ud-Daula started a food -for- work*

programme to help the famine-stricken people of Lucknow around 1784. Some workers were employed during daytime to construct a building known as Imambara. Others were hired at night to demolish part of what was constructed during the day time. The objective was to provide employment to as many workers as possible and as long as it was needed.

[17] John Keynes (1936, p 129) wrote:If the Treasury were to fill old bottles with banknotes, bury them at suitable depths in disused coalmines which are then filled up to the surface with town rubbish, and leave it to private enterprise on well-tried principles of laissez-faire to dig the notes up again (the right to do so being obtained, of course, by tendering for leases of the note-bearing territory), there need be no more unemployment and, with the help of the repercussions, the real income of the community, and its capital wealth also, would probably become a good deal greater than it actually is. It would, indeed, be more sensible to build houses and the like; but if there are political and practical difficulties in the way of this, the above would be better than nothing.

References

1. Kautilya Vishnugupta (4th Century B C). *The Arthashastra*, Edited, Rearranged, Translated and Introduced by L N Rangarajan. Penguin Books, 1992, New Delhi, New York.
2. Smith Adam (1776/1976). *An Inquiry into the Nature and Causes of the Wealth of Nations*. Edited and with an Introduction, Notes, Marginal Summary, and Index by Edwin Cannan. The University of Chicago Press, Chicago.
3. Prasch Robert E (1991). 'The Ethics of Growth in Adam Smith's Wealth of Nations' *History of Political Economy*: 23.2, p 337-351.
4. Dorfman Robert (1991). Review Article: Economic Development from the Beginning to Rostow. *Journal of Economic Literature*, Vol. XXIX, PP., 573-591.

5. Spengler Joseph J (1971). *Indian Economic Thought.* Duke University Press, Durham, NC.
6. Sihag Balbir S (2014). Kautilya: *The True Founder of Economics.* Vitasta Publications, New Delhi.
7. Wolters O W (1999). History, *Culture, and Region in Southeast Asian Perspectives,* Revised Edition. Cornell Southeast Asia Programme, Ithaca, NY.
8. Strauss Leo (1987). Niccolo Machiavelli. In: Strauss, Leo and Joseph Cropsey Eds., *History of Political Philosophy,* University of Chicago Press, Chicago.
9. Machiavelli N (1994). *Selected Political Writings.* Edited and Translated by David Wootton, Hackett Publishing, Cambridge.
10. Barber William J (1967). *A History of Economic Thought.* Penguin Books, Baltimore, Maryland.
11. Grampp William D (2000). What Did Adam Smith Mean by the Invisible Hand? Journal of *Political Economy,* 108, 441-465.Rothbard M (1995. *Economic Thought before Adam Smith: An Austrian Perspective on the History of Economic Thought.* Volume 1 Edward Elgar, Aldershot.
12. Burnett Charles (2005). Leonard of Pisa (Fibonacci) and Arabic Arithmetic. www.muslimheritage.com Drekmeier Charles (1962., *Kingship And Community In Early India.* Stanford University Press, Stanford.
13. Smith Adam (1790/ 1982). *The Theory of Moral Sentiments.* Edited by DDRaphael and AL Macfie; Liberty Fund, Indianapolis.
14. Basham A L (1959. *The Wonder that was India.* Grove Press, New York.
15. Keynes John M (1936). *The General Theory of Employment, Interest, and Money.* Harcourt Bruce Jovanovich, New York, London.

Kautilya and Machiavelli on Justice, Prosperity and National Security

End Notes

[1][8] Boesche (2002, P 104) remarks: Paternalistic in an almost literal sense, Kautilya saw the people of the kingdom not as active citizens but as passive subjects cared for by the king and the state. Arguably the entire notion of a welfare state, in which the state was responsible for those in need either by providing jobs or by supporting those who could not survive without assistance, was first described in the history of political ideas by Kautilya.

Kautilya recommends that the government not only should help the old, sick, children and the helpless but also should provide insurance against natural disasters to everyone. Thus, the usual distinction between a residual and a universal welfare state may not be a very useful one in describing Kautilyan state (See [9] Barr (1992) for such a distinction).

[2]Let me provide a small sample of a very odd assertions made by Roger Boesche (2002):

(i) He (p 34) writes: But then, again, Alexander the Great, who must have been one of Kautilya's models, was happy to conquer and assimilate those whom earlier Greeks regarded as strangers or barbarians (barbarous).

Arthashastra literature started in India somewhere between 600-650 BCE. India was way ahead of Greeks so there was not much to learn from them. Well, Alexander cannot be a role model for anyone. He was a murderer of his good friends and most likely, he lost the battle to an Indian king and returned back.

(ii) Boesche (p 32) writes: As with Hobbes, the goal of science was power. 'Power' is (possession of) strength and 'strength changes the mind', which means that Kautilya' wish would be for power to control not only outward behavior, but also the thoughts of one's subjects and enemies.

He does not even come close to what Kautilya was concerned about. Kautilya is worried about a very important concept in economics known as: *Time Inconsistency or Credibility Problem* that a partner or an ally might not keep his promises. This concept re-emerged after more than two thousand years and Presscott and Kyland received Nobel Prize for rediscovering it.

(iii) Boesche (p 62) remarks: If detailed record-keeping is a sign of new despotism, as some such as Weber and Foucault have claimed, then indeed Kautilya's kingdom was despotic.

Kautilya first came up with the concept of taking Census. He was the founder of statistical economics ([10] Sihag,2013). United States and European Countries undertake census. Are these countries despotic?

Boesche (pp 61-62) notes: The king 'should conceal, as a tortoise does his limbs, any (limb) of his own that may have become exposed.' Boesche, thus, shows his ignorance of the concept of asymmetric information.

Kautilya strongly believes that the possession of private information provides advantages in bargaining and in preparation against potential adversaries. Akerlof won the Nobel Prize for rediscovering this concept.

(v) Boesche e (p 59) writes: Demanding that subjects work hard in their specialised functions of the division of labour also leaves no time for public life. 'For, men being of a nature similar to that of horses', wrote Kautilya, 'change when employed in works... They should carry out the works according to orders, without concerting together'.

Boesche misses the point and misinterprets this statement. Shirking, stealing is a serious problem all over the world. In USA, employees steal more than the customers, they write emails, talk on the phones and do other things unrelated to their jobs. Nobel laureate Joseph Stiglitz and others recommend paying efficiency wages (higher than the market wages), and supervision to reduce this moral hazard (shirking: not doing what they are supposed to do). Two thousand years ago, Kautilya takes notice of this problem and suggests efficiency wages, supervision along with moral persuasion to check it. This has nothing to do with the private lives of individuals at their homes.

[3][11] Huei Chun Su (2009) writes, 'In other words, emphasising the notion of negative liberty is to interpret Mill's principle more from the position of stronger members in a community. If we think about the liberty of the weaker members in the same community, Mill's principle is actually a protection of their positive liberties. In short, Mill's principle of liberty can be interpreted from the other angle: the purpose of limiting some people's liberty is to protect everyone's liberty of life and body'. Su is quite liberal in interpreting Mill's negative liberty as positive liberty. Mill was a strong supporter of slavery and could never think of empowering the weaker sections of society. Moreover, the powerful would not allow their power to be curatailed in any way. On the hand, Kautilya's rajarishi would empower the weaker sections of the society.

Division of Responsibilities	Factors Relevant to National Security	Desired Attributes	Appropriate incentives	Feasibility
Why to do, that is undertake cost-benefit analysis	King (Prime Minister/ President)	Ethical, Far-sighted, Foresighted	Moral Duty and Enlightened self-interest	Unlikely, no such requirement to become President or Prime Minister
	Advisers	Far-sighted, Foresighted	Moral and Material	Yes
How to do (implementation)	Chief of Defence	Knowledgeable about use of weapons, expertise in strategy and tactics	Moral and Material	Yes
	Military	Trained and Enthusiastic	Moral, Material and fairness in awards	Yes
	Scientists/ Engineers	Understanding of both Theoretical and Applied Knowledge	Moral and Performance-based compensation	Yes

Information	Intelligence	Knowledgeable, uncompromising	Special training, material and moral incentives	Yes
	Armament	Self-sufficiency in producing armaments that provide an edge over a potential adversary	Providing appropriate incentives to scientists, engineers and manufacturers	Yes
Support	Public	Unwavering	Prosperity and Fairness	Yes

Kautilya's goal is to have strength and an edge in every component of national security. Unless weapons aree (i) more advanced than that of a potential adversary (the edge) and (ii) are produced domestically (self- sufficiency), there is always a threat to national security. This is just as true of modern USA as well as modern India, as we know.

References

1. Machiavelli N (1994), *Selected Political Writings*, edited and Translated by David Wootton. Hackett Publishing, Cambridge.
2. Kautilya Vishnugupta (4th Century BC), *The Arthashastra,* Edited, Rearranged, Translated and Introduced by L N Rangarajan.
   Penguin Books, 1992, New Delhi, New York.
3. Kangle R (1965/2000), *The Kautilya Arthashastra,* Part III. Motilal Banarsidass, Delhi.

4. Kissinger Henry (2014), *World Order.* Penguin, New York.
5. Sihag Balbir S (2014a), *Kautilya: The True Founder of Economics.* Vitasta Publications, New Delhi.
6. Drekmeier Charles (1962), *Kingship and Community in Early India.* Stanford University Press, Stanford.
7. Smith Adam (1776/1976), *An Inquiry into the Nature and Causes of the Wealth of Nations.* Edited and with an Introduction, Notes, Marginal Summary, and Index by Edwin Cannan. The University of Chicago Press, Chicago.
8. Boesche Roger (2002). *The First Great Political Realist: Kautilya and his Arthashastra.* Lexington Books, New York.
9. Barr Nicholas (1992). Economic Theory and the Welfare State: A survey and Interpretation. *Journal of Economic Literature*, XXX,741-803.
10. Sihag Balbir S (2013). Kautilya's Arthashastra: The Origin of Statistical Economics during 4th CE. *Journal of Rajasthan Statistical Association*, Vol. 2: 1-14.
11. Su Huei Chun (2009). Is social justice for or against liberty? The philosophical foundations of Mill and Hayek's theory of liberty. *The Review of Austrian Economics*, 22 (4): 387-414.
12. Sihag Balbir S (2014b). Kautilya on Far-sight, Foresight and Freedom. Paper presented at the International Seminar on Kautilya on April 9, 2014, organised by Institute of Defense Studies and Analyses, New Delhi.

Kautilya, Fibonacci and Samuelson on Discounting

End Notes

[1]Mattessich (2000, p 203-204) remarks: Kautilya's *Arthashastra* is not merely significant for only for business accounting but also government accounting, with some stretch of imagination it may be regarded as a forerunner of national income accounting since the ultimate purpose of Kautilya's work was to strengthen the economy of the entire nation. Its significance lies in the attempt to

offer accounting concepts of fairly general validity…; This treatise may even be called in evidence for the close relationship between micro- and macro-accounting concepts.
Also see Balbir S Sihag (2014a, Chapter 5).

[2]See Balbir S Sihag (2014b) for details.

[3]*Fibonacci's Other Trial and Error Method to find the Solution*: He (P 460) explains the other method as: You indeed put it that he has 12 denari of which he made double in the first trip, and he thus had 24 denari from which he spent 12 denari and thus remained for him another 12 denari, of which he made double in the remaining two trips and he spent in each 12 denari: there remained for him at the end 12 denari. Therefore, in the position I erred in value by plus 12; therefore, you put it that he had 11 denari from which, as he made double in the three trips and spent in each 12, there remained for him at the end 4 denari, namely 8 fewer than in the first position. And therefore, this position is too large. When you say: for the 1 which I decreased in the capital I approximated more closely by 8; how many shall I decrease again so that the approximation is decreased 4 further? You therefore multiply the 4 by the 1, and you divide by the 8, the quotient will be ½ of one denari; this subtracted from the 11 denari leave (1/2)10 denari for the capital. Or from the multiplication of the first error by the second position, namely 132, you subtract the 48 that results from multiplying the second error by the first position, leaving 84 which divided by the difference in errors leaves (1/2)10.

[4]Barro (2006) defines probability of a disaster as: Actual and potential economic disasters could reflect economic events (the Great Depression, financial crises), wartime destruction (world

wars, nuclear conflicts), natural disasters (tsunamis, hurricanes, earthquakes, asteroid collisions), and epidemics of disease (Black Death, avian flu). I use the twentieth-century history of economic disasters to assess disaster probabilities, sizes of contractions, and default probabilities.

[5]Grampp (2000) proposes: A way to get things straight about Smith or anyone else. It is to begin by distinguishing between (a) what the author actually said, (b) what is implied by what he said, (c) what can reasonably be inferred from it, (d) what we may conjecture he meant, (e) what he conceivably could have meant, and (f) what it would be convenient to believe what he meant. The next step is to stay as close as possible to points (a) and (b), to know that about point (c), the operative word is 'reasonably', and to move as far as point (d) only when all else fails, or never at all. Distinctions (e) and (f) are left to those who, to paraphrase George Stigler, make the study of economic ideas a work of the imagination.

[6]Peter Bernstein (1996, p 18): Up to the time of the Renaissance, people perceived the future as little more than a matter of luck or the result of random variations, and most of their decisions were driven by instinct. When the conditions of life are so closely linked to nature, not much is left to human control. As long as the demands of survival limit people to the basic functions of bearing children, growing crops, hunting, fishing, and providing shelter, they are simply unable to conceive of circumstances in which they might be able to influence the outcomes of their decisions. A penny saved is not a penny earned unless the future is something more than a black hole.

Similarly, O'Connor JJ and E F Robertson (2001) remark:The first surviving example of the Indian numerals in a document in Europe was, however, long before the time of al-Banna. The numerals appear in the *Codex Vigilanus* copied by a monk in Spain in 976. However, the main part of Europe was not ready at this time to accept new ideas of any kind. Acceptance was slow, even as late as the fifteenth century when European mathematics began its rapid development which continues today.

References

1. Barro Robert J 2006. Rare disasters and asset markets in the twentieth century. *The Quarter Journal of Economics* 121 (3), 823-866.
2. Barro R J and Urs´ua, JF (2012). Rare Macroeconomic Disasters. *Annual.*
3. *Review of Economics,* 4(1). 83–109.
4. Bernstein Peter L (1996/1998). *Against the Gods*. New York: John Wiley & Sons.
5. Burnett Charles (2005). Leonard of Pisa (Fibonacci) and Arabic Arithmetic. www.muslimheritage.com
6. Ehrlich, Isaac and Becker Gary S (1972). Market Insurance, Self-Insurance and Self Protection. Journal *of Political Economy,* 80 (4), 623-648.
7. Fisher Irvine (1931). *The Theory of Interest.* New York: Macmillan. Available online at: http://www.econlib.org/library/YPDBooks/Fisher/fshToI.html.
8. Frederick Shane, George Loewenstein and Ted O'Donoghue (2002). Time Discounting and Time Preference: A Critical Review. *Journal of Economic Literature* XL (2), 351-401.
9. Goetzmann William N (2004). Fibonacci and the Financial Revolution. Working Paper 10352 National Bureau of Economic Research, http://www.nber.org/papers/w10352,March.
10. Grampp William D (2000). What Did Adam Smith Mean by the Invisible Hand? *Journal of Political Economy,* 108 (3), 441-465.
11. Jensen Michael C and Martin J Bailey (1972). Risk and the Discount Rate for Public Investment. Social Science Research Network (SSRN), Electronic Library at: http://papers.ssrn.com/ABSTRACT=390110

12. Kautilya Vishnugupta (4th Century BC. /1992). The Arthashastra,
Edited, Rearranged, Translated and Introduced by LN Rangarajan. New Delhi, New York: Penguin Books.
13. Kautilya Vishnugupta (4th Century B C /2000). *Maxims of*
14. *Chanakya,* by Subramanian, VK New Delhi: Shakti Malik, Abhinav Publications.
15. Mattessich R (2000). *The Beginnings of Accounting and Accounting History- Accounting Practice in the Middle East* (8000 BC to 2000 B. C.) and Accounting Thought in India (300 B. C. and the Middle Ages). New York: Garland Publishing.
16. O'Connor J J and E F Robertson (2001. History topic: The Arabic numeral System. http://www-history.mcs.st-and.ac.uk.
16. Raju Chandrakant (2013). Euclid and Jesus. Penang, Malaysia: Multiversity and Citizens International.
Sihag Balbir S (2014a). *Kautilya: The True Founder of Economics.* New Delhi: Vitasta Publishing.
17. Sihag Balbir S (2014b). Kautilya on Selection, Implementation and Evaluation of a Project. Sangeeta Sharma, Pankaj Nagar and Inderjeet Singh Sodhi (eds.) in Governometrics and Technological Innovation for Public Policy Design and Precision, IGI Global, Hershey, PA, USA.
18. Samuelson Paul A (1964). Principles of Efficiency: Discussion. *American Economic Review Proc.,* 54 (2), 93-96.

Arthashastra: The Origin of Statistical Economics

End Notes

[1]C K Raju (2011): I think the evidence for the Indian origin of probability is clear from the aksa sukta in the Rg Veda, the theory of Vedic metre and the Mahabharata. Statisticians now accept it.

[2]*Inferential Statistics:* Kautilya (p 198) states: Vishalaksha says 'never can a single person arrive at the right decision. –The work

of government is dependent on [complete] knowledge – that which the king personally knows, that which is reported to him and that which he has to infer. To find out what is not known, to clarify doubts when there are alternatives, to obtain more information when only a part is known – all these can be done only with the help of advisers. Hence a king shall conduct his deliberations with advisers of mature intelligence. (As the saying goes;) 'Despise no one, [but] listen to all views; for, wise man pays heed to all sensible advice, even those of a child' (1.15).

According to Marcello Basili and Carlo Zappia (2005, p 4): Keynes (1921, p 12) distinguished between direct and indirect knowledge. The former is 'that part of our rational belief which we know directly," the latter is "the part which we know by argument'. Keynes explained: our knowledge of propositions seems to be obtained in two ways: directly by contemplating the objects of acquaintance and indirectly, by argument, through perceiving the probability-relation of the proposition, about which we seek knowledge, to other propositions

Chandrakant Raju remarks: Regarding Keynes, the belief in direct and indirect knowledge is obviously nothing original. All Indian philosophies (Nyaya-Vaisesika, Samkhya-Yoga, Buddhist, Advata-Vedanta) have pratyaksa and anumana as the base of knowledge. The anumana in Indian tradition includes both logical and statistical (or probable) inference as is clear from the Lokayata criticism of it.

[3]Seidenberg (1962, p 515) observes: Hence we do not hesitate to place the Vedic altar rituals, or, more exactly, rituals exactly like them, far back of 1700BCE. To summarise the argument: the elements of ancient geometry found in Egypt and Babylonia stem from a ritual system of the kind observed in the Sulvasutras.

[4]Drekmeier (1962, 35) writes: 'From roughly the seventh to the fourth century BC, India was the scene of the formulation

and spread of a remarkable number of doctrines, pantheist and materialist, atheist and rationalist. Many asserted the complete freedom of the human mind from religious doctrine and were outspoken in their criticism of the Vedas and the Brahmanical system –going so far as to call the Vedic teachers imposters.' He (1962, 105) adds: 'It may have seemed to many in the sixth and fifth centuries that instead of yearning for a golden yesterday, men might confidently anticipate a bountiful age yet to come.'

[5]Clearly, Kautilya was two thousand years ahead of the estern thinkers. AMachina notes, both Pascal and Fermant were still dealing only with expected value. Machina (1987) remarks, 'During the development of modern probability theory in the 17th century, mathematicians such as Blaise Pascal and Pierre de Fermant assumed that the attractiveness of a gamble offering the payoffs (x_1, …, x_n) with probabilities (p_1, …, p_n) was given by its expected value $\bar{x} = \Sigma\ x_i\ p_i$.

[6]*Arrow (1971) defines an ideal system as*: Under such a system, productive activity and risk-bearing can be divorced, each being carried out by the one or ones best qualified.

Kautilya not only understands this principle but also appliesd it. Sternbach (1965, Vol. I, p 512) comments on Kautilya's suggestion on interest rates as: Therefore, in such enterprises where the capital appeared to be endangered it was not possible to advance loans ith a fixed rate of interests which amounted to one and a quarter percent per month because the lender realized that in such a contract he was running too great a risk. Therefore, the law harmonised with the requirements of economic conditions permitted in such cases to receive or to agree to higher rates of interests.

[7]*Kautilya (p 144) explains the role of education as*: The sole aim of all branches of knowledge is to inculcate restraint over the senses. He (p 636) labelsd some emotions as 'obstacles' to achieving the gain from campaigns. He listsd these as: Passion, anger, timidity, compassion

leading to aversion to fighting, recoiling from awarding deserved punishment, baseness, haughtiness, a forgiving nature, thinking of the next world, being too pious, meanness, abjectness, jealousy, contempt for what one has, wickedness, distrust, fear, negligence, inability to withstand harsh climate (cold, heat or rain) and faith in the auspiciousness of stars and days." He did not believe in fate or superstitions. He (p 621) wrote "A king who trusts in fate and does not believe in human effort will fail because such a king never begins a work and never achieves anything.

References

1 Arrow Kenneth J (1971). 'Insurance, Risk and Resource Allocation', Chapter 5 in Essays in the *Theory of Risk Bearing,* Elsevier Publishing, p. 134-143.

2. Basili Marcello and Carlo Zappia. 'Ambiguity and uncertainty in Ellsberg and Shackle', Department of *Economics,* University of Siena 460, 200.

3. Bernoulli, E. (1738). 'Exposition of a New Theory on the Measurement of Risk' English translation, Econometrica, 22 1954, pp. 23-36.

4. Bernstein, Peter L. (1996/1998). Against the Gods, John Wiley & Sons, New York.iddle, Jeff (1999), 'Statistical Economics, 1900-1950' *History of Political Economy,* Vol. 31, No 4: 607-651.

5. Camerer, C. & M. Weber (1992). Recent developments in modelling preferences: Uncertainty and ambiguity, *Journal of Risk and Uncertainty,* 5, 325-370.

6. Dequech, David (2000).'Fundamental Uncertainty and Ambiguity', *Eastern Economic Journal,* pp. 41-60

7. Emmett, Ross B. (1999). "The Economist and the Entrepreneur: Modernist Impulses in Risk, Uncertainty, and Profit", *History of Political Economy,* pp. 29-52.

8. Epstein Larry G (1999).'A Definition of Uncertainty Aversion'. RES, p. 579-608.

9. Friedman Milton and Savage Leonard J (1948).'The Utility Analysis of Choices Involving Risk'.JPE, August, p. 279-304.
10. Kautilya Vishnugupta (4th Century B C). *The Kautilya Arthashastra,* Part II, An English Translation with Critical and Explanatory Notes, R P Kangle, 2000, Motilal Banarsidass, Delhi.
11. Kautilya Vishnugupta (4th Century BC). *The Arthashastra,* Edited, Rearranged, Translated and Introduced by L N Rangarajan, Penguin Books, 1992, New Delhi, New York.
12. Knight Frank H (1921). *Risk, Uncertainty And Profit,* Reprinted 1967, Sentry Press, New York
13. Machina Mark J (1982). 'Expected Utility' Analysis Without The Independence Axiom, *Econometrica,* March, pp. 277-323.
14. (1987). '"Choice Under Uncertainty: Problems Solved and Unsolved'. *Journal of Economic Perspectives,* p. 121-154.
15. Mukerji Sujoy (1998). 'Ambiguity Aversion and Incompleteness of Contractual Form'. AER December, p. 1207-1231.
16. Munier, Bertrand R (1991.'Nobel Laureate: The many Other Allais Paradoxes', *JE Perspectives,* p179-199.
17. Von Neumann J and O Morgenstern (1944). *Theory of Games and Economic Behavior,* Princeton: Princeton University Press.
18. Pratt, John W. (1964). 'Risk-Aversion in the Small and in the Large', *Econometrica,* pp. 122-136.
19. Rabin Matthew (1998). 'Psychology and Economics'. *JE Lit.* p, 11-46.
20. Rajaram NS and Frawley, David (2001). Vedic Aryans and the Origins of Civilisation, Third Edition, *Voice of India,* New Delhi.
21. Raju Chandrakant (2011). 'Probability in Ancient India'. *Handbook of the Philosophy of Science,* vol 7. Philosophy of Statistics, ed. Prasanta S Bandyopadhyay and Malcolm R Forster. General Editors: Dov M Gabbay, Paul Thagard and John Woods. Elsevier, p. 1175–1196.

21. Schlesinger Harris and Doherty. Neil A (1985). Incomplete Markets for Insurance: An Overview, Journal of Risk and Insurance, p. 402-423.
22. Seidenberg A (1962).'The Ritual Origin of Geometry'. *Archive for History of Exact Sciences,* Vol. 1: 488-527.
23. SeidenbergA (1978). 'The Origin of Mathematics'. Archive for *History of Exact Sciences,* Vol. 18: 301-342.
24. Sihag, Balbir S (2014). *Kautilya: The True Founder of Economics,* Vitasta Publishing, New Delhi.
25. Starmer Chris (2000). 'Developments in Non-expected Utility Theory: The Hunt for a Descriptive Theory of Choice under Risk'. JEL, Vol. XXXVIII, June, p 332-382.
26. Sternbach Ludwik (1965). *Juridical Studies in Ancient Law,* Motilal Banarsidass, Delhi.

Arthashastra: The Origin of Mathematical Economics

End Notes

[1]Seidenberg (1962, p 515) observes: 'Hence we do not hesitate to place the Vedic altar rituals, or, more exactly, rituals exactly like them, far back of 1700 BCE. To summarise the argument: the elements of ancient geometry found in Egypt and Babylonia stem from a ritual system of the kind observed in the Sulvasutras.'

Baudhayana has been acknowledged as the author of *Sulbasutras.* Jagat Pati Joshi (2008, p 157) points out: The structures reveal that the Harappans had a good idea of geometry, particularly mensuration. They had a scale based on the decimal system. For measuring bigger areas, they perhaps used ropes. Surkotada had yielded a charred rope. Incidentally, the earliest Vedic geometrical treatises on geometry are called sulba sutras, deriving their name from sulba which means rope.

[19] Kazanas (2009, pp 132-133) remarks: Be it noted that *karpasa* is the only word for cotton in Sanskrit. It is found first in the sutra texts, in Gautama's (1,18) and in Baundhayana's (16.13.10) Dharmasutra. Cotton cultivation appears only in the mature SSC,

after 2600. Thus, these sutra-texts can be placed at this period at the earliest, i.e., 2600. SSC= Sarasvati-Sindhu Civilisation also known as Harappa Civilization.

[2][20] Mattessich (2000, p 203) remarks: Kautilya's *Arthashastra* is not merely significant for only for business accounting but also government accounting, with some stretch of imagination it may be regarded as a forerunner of national income accounting since the ultimate purpose of Kautilya's work was to strengthen the economy of the entire nation.

[3]Kautilya (p 544) states: Events, both human and providential, govern the world (and its affairs). Acts of God are those which are unforeseeable and whose origin is unknown. If the cause is knowable and, hence, foreseeable, its origin is human. If an act of God results in (helping) the achievement of one's objective, it is good fortune; otherwise, it is misfortune. (Likewise,) any human action which increases one's wealth is a good policy; otherwise, it is a bad policy.

Sihag (2014, Chap. 5): *Analysis of Variance*: The above statement amounts to the specification of a regression model and separating the total variation (in the dependent variable, wealth) into explained and unexplained (random) components. According to Kautilya, a policy should not get credit for positive changes in wealth if that is due to random factors (he calls them 'good fortune'). Similarly, a policy should not be blamed if there are negative changes in wealth due to unfavorable random variables. It implies that Kautilya's goal is to explain and predict the changes in the dependent variable. It may be noted that the evaluation of a policy depends on the ability to explain and predict. Indeed, according to Kautilya, explanation and prediction are the most important values of a discipline.

Thus, his implicit regression model may formally be specified as follows:

$W = X\beta + \varepsilon$ (12.3)

Where, W =wealth, the dependent variable, X= exogenous policy variables, which may be used to acquire wealth, ε = random error (the acts of God). Incidentally, the most important assumption of regression analysis that the error terms are independent of the right hand side variables, X, that is, Cov (X, ε) = 0, is clearly satisfied in the above statement. Additionally, the Covariance (ε_t, ε_t-1) = 0 since acts of God are likely to be independent of each other across different years. It is not claimed that he knew the implications of these assumptions.

Also see Chap. 10 for additional applications of statistical analysis.

[4]Philip Mirowski (1991fn 5, p 149) observes: However, the bare format of symbolic expression should not be confused with mathematical reasoning. A more satisfactory approach needs to take into account the subtleties of mathematical discourse: an article couched entirely in prose but concerned with an elaborate discussion of the use of mathematics in economics may make many profound mathematical points, whereas another article which includes an equation or two in a footnote as irrelevant window-dressing effectively has little or no mathematical content at all.

[5][21] Raju (2014, p 49) summarises his finding as: Euclid, the geometer and Claudius Ptolemy, the astronomer were pure fabrications, like the stories of the Copernican and Newtonian revolutions. And these are just examples of what was obviously a large-scale and systematic effort, spread over centuries.

Such fabrications are still continuing. For example, [22] David E Rowe (2001) remarks: Euclid was reputed to have told King Ptolemy that there were no royal roads' to mathematical knowledge (though many over the centuries seem to have thought that Euclid's Elements provided the path of least resistance).

[6]Not only mathematics originated in India, but its development continued until the 17th century. For example, [15] Raju points out: The calculus had developed in India, over a thousand year period, from the 5th to the 15th c. for accurate calculations with planetary models, needed for the calendar – the key technology for monsoon-driven agriculture. It was used to obtain very precise trigonometric values (eventually to the 9th decimal place). Precise trigonometric values were critical also for navigation."

Similarly, [23] Struik asserts: "Ancient India may still yield many more mathematical treasures. We now know for instance, that the Gregory-Leibniz series for $\pi/4$ can be found in a Sanskrit manuscript ascribed to Nilakantha (1500CE).

References

1. Ingrao B and G Israel (1990). *The Invisible Hand: Economic Theory in the History of Science*. MIT Press, Cambridge.
2. Mirowski P (1989). *More Heat than Light.* Cambridge University Press, New York.
3. Mirowski Philip (1991). The When, the How and Why of Mathematical Expression in the History of Economic Analysis. *Journal of Economic Perspectives*, Vol. 5, No. 1, 145-157.
4. Weintraub E Roy (2002). *How Economics Became a Mathematical Science*. Duke University Press, Durham and London.
5. Seidenberg A (1962). The Ritual Origin of Geometry. Archive for History of Exact Sciences, Vol. 1: 488-527.
6. Sihag Balbir S (2014). *Kautilya: The True Founder of Economics.* Vitasta Publishing, New Delhi.
7. Kautilya Vishnugupta (4th Century BC). *The Arthashastra*, Edited, Rearranged, Translated and Introduced by L N Rangarajan, Penguin Books, 1992, New Delhi, New York.
8. Raju Chandrakant (2013). Euclid and Jesus. Multiversity and Citizens International, Penang, Malaysia.
9. Ferriros, Jose (2005). Dogmas and the Changing Images of

Foundations. http://galileo.fcien.edu.uy/dogmas_and_changing_images.htm.

10. Mahavira (850/1912). The *Ganita-sara-sangraha of Mahaiviracarya* with English translation and notes, by M Ranga Chariyar. Government Press, Madras.
11. Millay Edna St Vincent (1892-1950). Euclid alone has looked on beauty bare. http://www.poemhunter.com/poem/euclid-alone Joshi Jagat Pati (2008). Harappan Architecture and Civil Engineering. Infinity Foundation and Rupa, Delhi.
12. Vahia Mayank and Srikumar M Menon (2013). A possible Harappan Astronomical Observatory at Dholavira. Journal of *Astronomical History and Heritage* 16 (3).
13. Hall Rachel (2007). Math for Poets and Drummers. http://www.sju.edu/"rhall RajuChandrakant (2011). Teaching Mathematics with a Different Philosophy –II, Calculus without Limits. Science and Culture, July-August, Vol. 77, NOS 7-8, 280-285.
14. Ebert Sebastian and Philipp Strack (2015). Until the Bitter End: On Prospect Theory in a Dynamic *Context. American Economic* Review, Vol 105 (4) 1618-1633.
15. Wolters O W (1999) History, Culture, and Region in Southeast Asian Perspectives, Revised Edition. Cornell Southeast Asia Program, Ithaca, NY.
16. Scherer F M (2001). An Early Application of the Average Total Cost. *Journal of Economic Literature* Vol. 39, No. 3 (Sep.), 897-901
17. Kazanas Nicoles (2009). The Rgveda Pre-dates the Sarasvati-Sindhu Culture. Aryan Invasion Theory, Fabrications and Fallouts, Vol. 1, *Vivekananda Kendra Patrika,* Vol. 40, 79th issue.
18. Mattessich Richard (1998). Review and Extension of Bhattacharya's Modern Accounting Concepts in Kautilya's Arthashastra. *Accounting, Business and Financial History,* Vol. 8, No. 2: 191-209.
19. Raju Chandrakant (2014) Is Science Western in Origin?

Multiversity, Medusa, Goa, India.

20. Rowe David E (2001). Looking back on a Bestseller: Dirk Struik's A Concise History of Mathematics, Notes on the AMS, Vol. 48, No. 6, 590-592.
21. Struik Dirk (1987). *A Concise History of Mathematics*, 4th edition. Dover Publications, Mineola, NY